CRITERIA
A JOURNAL OF FIRST-YEAR WRITING
2012–2013

Edited by
Mary K. Jackman and Lee Gibson

SMU.

Southern Methodist University
Department of English
Discernment and Discourse Program
P.O. Box 750435
Dallas, TX 75275-0435
smu.edu/english/firstyearwriting

Cover image: © Southern Methodist University
Design and production: Rebecca Horn, rhorngraphics, rlrchorn@verizon.net

Kendall Hunt
publishing company

www.kendallhunt.com
Send all inquiries to:
4050 Westmark Drive
Dubuque, IA 52004-1840

Copyright © 2012 by Southern Methodist University

ISBN 978-1-4652-0695-4

Kendall Hunt Publishing Company has the exclusive rights to reproduce this work, to prepare derivative works from this work, to publicly distribute this work, to publicly perform this work and to publicly display this work.

All rights reserved. No part of this publication may be reproduced, stored in a retrieval system, or transmitted, in any form or by any means, electronic, mechanical, photocopying, recording, or otherwise, without the prior written permission of the copyright owner.

Printed in the United State of America
10 9 8 7 6 5 4 3 2 1

"When I use a word," Humpty Dumpty said, in rather a scornful tone, "it means just what I choose it to mean—neither more nor less."

"The question is," said Alice, "whether you can make words mean so many different things."

"The question is," said Humpty Dumpty, "which is to be master—that's all."

Through the Looking-Glass
—Lewis Carroll

CONTENTS

vii To the Student
ix From the Editors

STUDENT WORK

3 The Immortal Thoughts
of a Higher Level Thinker
IAN HILL
5 Presentation Review:
"HeLa Cells, Human Research
Ethics, and Genetics"
HANAN HASSAN
7 Intrusive or Necessary?—An
analysis of Skloot's presence [draft]
TAYLOR CORRIGAN
10 Intrusive or Necessary?—An
Analysis of Skloot's Presence
[Final]
TAYLOR CORRIGAN
13 Ownership of Genetics
ASHLEY SHIN
16 Finding Your Definition
MICHELLE KO
20 Triumph with Sacrifice
CAMERON SMITH
22 The Validity of John Ciardi's
Arguments in Favor of the Study
of the Humanities
GABRIELA GARZA SAN MIGUEL
25 Beyond Education
ELISHAH RAMOS
30 Claiming My Education: Yesterday,
Today, and Tomorrow
DANIELLE KATZ
34 Community in Higher Education
MADDY DOCKERY-FUHRMANN
38 Somebody to Lean On
STEPHANIE NEWLAND
42 My Dream
HOLLY LABRY
44 A Tale of Two Worlds
Working Together
SKYLER BLOOM

48 Efficient Transportation
LAUREN FIELDS
51 A Burst to Be Diverse
MICHAELA ZOOK
56 Deciding Peace
TREVOR ANDERSON
59 A Doctrine of Life
ANDREW BLANCHARD
62 Chasing a Fantasy
VICTORIA GADSON
66 Beautiful Struggles
ASHLEY ROMO
69 Chasing Guinevere:
The Feminist Movement's Effect
on the Transformation of Guinevere
WILL MCNAMARA
73 Ethics in All Aspects of Life
ALEX MENZEL
78 Sweatshops: A Look at America's
Clothing Industry
ALEX MIRABILE
86 Race and Reality TV
MARQUELLE D.B. SMITH
91 Lady Gaga: Just a Thing
in Our Imaginations
JESSIE CRAFT

**A Tribute to Earlier SMU Writing Students
and to the Instructors Who Taught Them**

95 **1990–91** Arguments, not Facts,
Have Persuasive Power: A Theory
of Knowledge
XIAOFENG XU
98 **1991–92** Two Views on
Imperialism: Victim and Victimizer
CHRISTOPHER KENNIFF
102 **1992–93** The Death Penalty:
Revenge Disguised as Punishment
DIANE MILLER
105 **1993–94** SMU: Supporting Human
Rights or Human Debasement?
ROBIN RASNAKE

109 **1994–95** Banning Smoking: Our
    Only Hope
    JAMES BOX
115 **1995–96** Homosexuality
    and Baptist Ideals
    KATHERINE ECHOLS
121 **1995–96** *La Vida Loca*
    (The Crazy Life)
    EDDIE FRAZER
125 **1996–97** How King Changed Time
    BRUCE A. LYNCH
128 **1998–99** Analysis of the Present
    Day University
    CARRYE RUDOLPH

ON EDUCATION, DISCERNMENT, AND DISCOURSE

133 From *What's College For?*
    ZACHARY KARABELL
134 Letter from Thomas Jefferson to
    Nathaniel Burwell on the Education
    of Women
136 Claiming an Education
    ADRIENNE RICH
140 keeping close to home: class and
    education
    BELL HOOKS
151 The Quest for Community
    in Higher Education
    PARKER J. PALMER
161 Abraham Lincoln
    Second Inaugural Address
163 John F. Kennedy
    Inaugural Address

APPENDIX
The Revision and Editing Process, Revision Worksheet, Editing Worksheet, and Correct Writing Basics

169 Discernment and Discourse:
    Course Descriptions
170 Class Attendance and Office Visits
171 Awards and Honors
    The Writing Center
172 The Altshuler Learning
    Enhancement Center
174 Central University Libraries:
    Ask a Librarian
    Research Resources
175 Researching Like a College Student
176 Computers on Campus
    Blackboard
177 On Grading
178 Standards for Evaluation
179 Avoiding Bias
180 On Plagiarism
181 Statement on Academic Honesty
182 Revising and Editing Process
184 Revision Worksheet
185 Editing Worksheet
186 Basics: Some Conventions of
    Correct Writing

TO THE STUDENT

Over thirty years ago, two writing instructors were sitting around in the common room of the Department of English in Dallas Hall, talking about ways to help their students become better writers. They knew that reading polished essays by professional writers helped students see how these writers developed a thesis, employed transitions effectively, and incorporated quotations gracefully. Still, the instructors felt, there were problems using essays in the average college anthology as models for student writing. In the first place, these pieces were written by professional writers. Many first-year students at SMU were just beginning to engage in the arduous task of learning to write well; they had little hope of approximating the work of professional writers. In fact, the writing instructors had found, the best models for student writing were essays written by other students.

On that spring afternoon, the idea for *Criteria* was born. *Criteria* would be a collection of the best essays written by first-year students at SMU. These would not be perfect essays, the instructors knew, but they would be good essays that could serve as models for the next year's writing students. Before the semester was over, the two instructors had gathered outstanding essays from all the other teachers of first-year writing at SMU and had begun the task of selecting the best of these essays and editing them for publication. In those pre-computer days, this meant retyping the essays and then reducing them to fit a 5.5" x 8.5" page format. The editors even had to design and lay out the first issue themselves.

Fortunately, *Criteria* was well-received by students and faculty members, and it has continued to play a vital part in the teaching of writing at SMU ever since. Now professionally designed and typeset, *Criteria* has more than doubled in size from its first issue. What has not changed, however, is the belief of the founding editors that student essays provide the best model for other students learning to write.

—*Pam Lange*

FROM THE EDITORS

Here it comes again: a new semester. And this year, the new semester, in addition to bringing new students into our classrooms, will bring new courses and curricula in our new first-year writing program, Discernment and Discourse. Anything new always challenges us, bringing both confusion and opportunity, threatening to daunt as well as to enlighten—ask any of your students; they know this all too well.

Along with the new semester, comes *Criteria* with a new publisher and perhaps some new pieces in our Education section; at this stage of preparing copy for publication, we are unsure what will remain and what will be lost. Newness, change is always exciting, but hardly ever easy.

In the midst of the new, however, we have found in our review of prior issues of *Criteria*, something old but timeless; and we have resurrected it in the Appendix: revision and editing worksheets with a section on basic conventions of correct writing. These pages disappeared from *Criteria* about twenty years ago. Sometimes in navigating through the new and untried, we look to something familiar as we would to an old friend. As in last year's *Criteria*, we have included a tribute section to past writing instructors and their students, these from the 1990s. The works, including headnotes, are exactly as they originally appeared. Some of you who for several years have been teaching first-year students how to write may recognize some of your assignments or texts or even students. Again, we come back to our theme of the new with the old. And isn't it remarkable that our profession, teaching, allows us to reinvent ourselves, to become new, with each new semester?

We want to thank writing teachers—new and old—who submitted student work for this year's issue: Stephanie Amsel, Joan Arbury, Carolyn Channell, Alane Hall, Marta Harvell, Carrie Johnston, Samantha Mabry, Pauline Newton, Nancy Srebro Park, Kristen Polster, Ona Seaney, Ross Sloan, Lori Ann Stephens, Megan Mary Tinning, Vicki Tongate, and Angela Wood. Remember, the journal depends on participation from *all* first-year writing faculty to represent fully the work we and our students are doing. The first-year writing journal is a collaborative effort from start to finish. With your continuing contribution and classroom use, as it was initially envisioned, *Criteria* will persist in reflecting and enhancing the reading and writing lessons we teach and learn.

Thank you, everyone who has contributed to the production of *Criteria 2012-2013*. In addition to the DISC faculty listed above and to the students who have trusted us with their work, we particularly thank Rebecca Horn of rhorngraphics for her always excellent assistance with manuscript production; Vicki Hill for permitting us to use her article, "Avoiding Bias"; Nina Schwartz for her continued support; Pam Lange for her always good advice; Carolyn Channell, David Doyle, Pat Feldman, Rebecca Graff, Diana Grumbles, Marta Harvell, Vicki Hill, and Diana Howard for their assistance in up-dating the Appendix; Susie Duarte, Leslie Reid, and Brooke Guelker for their dependability and good humor in times smooth and rough, old and new.

—*M.K.J.*
—*L.G.*

The editors of *Criteria* offer these essays as examples of original expression by the students for the first-year writing classes of Southern Methodist University. The ideas contained in them are those of the individual writers and do not necessarily reflect the opinions of the editors, the faculty, or the university.

Acknowledgments

"Claiming an Education," from *On Lies, Secrets, and Silence: Selected Prose 1966-1978* by Adrienne Rich. Copyright © 1979 by W.W. Norton & Company, Inc. Used by permission of W.W. Norton & Company, Inc.

Inaugural Address. John F. Kennedy. Friday, January 20, 1961. Inaugural Addresses of the Presidents of the United States. Bartleby. 1989. Web. Mar. 2012. http://www.bartleby.com/124/pres56.html

"keeping close to home: class and education," by bell hooks from *Talking Back: Thinking Feminist, Thinking Black*, 1989. Reprinted by permission of South End Press. Copyright © 1989 by Gloria Watkins.

Letter to Nathanial Burwell by Thomas Jefferson. March 14, 1818. *Encyclopedia Britannica:* eb.com. Web. 24 May 2011. http://www.britannica.com/bps/additionalcontent/8/116914/Document-Thomas-Jefferson-The-Education-of-Women

"The Quest for Community in Higher Education," by Parker J. Palmer from *Creating Campus Community: In Search of Ernest Boyer's Legacy*, Wm. M. McDonald, Ed., by permission of John Wiley & Sons, Inc. Copyright © 2002 by John Wiley & Sons, Inc.

Second Inaugural Address. Abraham Lincoln. Saturday, March 4, 1865. Inaugural Addresses of the Presidents of the United States. Bartleby. 1989. Web. Mar 2012. http://www.bartleby.com/124/pres32.html

Excerpt from pages 12-14, *What's College For? The Struggle to Define American Higher Education*, by Zachary Karabell. Copyright © 1999 Zachary Karabell. Reprinted by permission of Basic Books, a member of the Perseus Books Group. Pg. 136.

Quotation from *A Writer Teaches Writing*, 2nd ed., by Donald Murray, reprinted by permission of Houghton Mifflin. Copyright © 1985.

Student Work

The work in this section represents a variety of responses to a range of assignments that students encounter in their writing classes: assignments that allow them to explore their own lives; to observe and make sense of the SMU community; to consider the value and purpose of education; to analyze texts of all sorts; and to research issues that hold meaning for them, evaluating and synthesizing sources as they discover and articulate the point they want to make to their readers. We hope that these examples of first-year writers' work will stimulate thought and class discussion while also providing models of effective writing.

During their second meeting, Ian Hill's 1301 class wrote a diagnostic essay on the common reading, The Immortal Life of Henrietta Lacks, *answering the question, "Why should we read about "the woman in the photograph"? This timed writing, written in about forty-five minutes, did not require in-text citations or a works cited page. What elements of this essay stand out?*

The Immortal Thoughts of a Higher Level Thinker
Ian Hill

1   Henrietta Lacks, whose "[immortal cells] launched a medical revolution," was a poor black woman from Virginia who didn't know that her cells were being taken from her, or that they would prove to be world changing. She died before the effects of her cells were even realized. Henrietta is the main topic of the book *The Immortal Life of Henrietta Lacks*, a book by Rebecca Skloot that tells the stories of Henrietta, her family, the doctors that took her cells, and Rebecca herself, on the journey for truth. But why should this matter to me? I'm a college freshman, majoring in Theatre. I have more important things on my mind than cell culturing. But Henrietta's story is more than a scientific information book about the polio vaccine. In its pages lies a question of ethics that remains unanswered by Skloot, because it is left up to the reader. The whole point of college is to move students out of the mindset of a high school student and give us the tools to be a higher level thinker, and Skloot's book requires just that. To be able to bounce around opposing views on one idea is the very definition of a higher level thinker, and the ideas *The Immortal Life of Henrietta Lacks* puts forth certainly have opposing views. In this way, this book should be very important to a college freshman, as it serves as an introduction into higher level thinking.
2   Should the doctors have taken Henrietta's cells without her permission or knowledge? Was it ethical to use a woman's biological property for financial gain, and then not share any of the profits with her? These are the questions Skloot raises at the beginning of the book, or at least the most pivotal ones. As a student and a higher level thinker, looking at the questions objectively is what I'm meant to do, but I have to admit, when I first read what happened, I leaned toward the sides of the scientists. After all, what are the "rights" of one woman compared to the discoveries and advancements made in science for the whole world? In the grand scope of things, the world benefitted in far greater a way than it would have if Dr. Gey (the doctor who originally took her cells for research) had not taken her cells. But upon entering college, I was encouraged to look at the opposing view: Henrietta's basic rights as a human were violated in the name of science, and if that were fair for her, it should be fair for all. We are all

created equal, so logically, we should all be victim to biological robbery from doctors in the name of "science." Obviously, this is not the case, so Henrietta was treated unfairly, her family was put into a poor circumstance, and her cells became associated with corruption. I kept this thought in my mind as I went over the book, and there were times when I noticed that I had been closed off. Reading about the family life, Deborah's hardships with Galen, Elsie being committed, Henrietta herself suffering with cancer and not being able to see her children, I would shut off my empathetic side and just read those passages coldly. But going through them again I opened up to them so that I could feel for the family, which is what Skloot intended. But that counteracted my excitement towards the scientific advancements being made; the fact that medicine was moving so far ahead thanks to the violation of this woman's rights, a woman who I now felt empathy towards. I now had opposing views in my head, which is the exact thing a college student should always be able to do.

3   Henrietta herself, her story, her life, Rebecca's journey, Deborah's hardships, and all the details of science in the book don't matter to me. I care about them, but when I think about things that *matter*, they are all very far down the list, if not just off the list. What matters to me is the advanced thinking level that this book requires. Skloot offers facts and stories about "the woman in the photograph" and leaves it up to us to make a decision, but a college student will be able to look at multiple views, and see both their points and fallacies. This book serves as an excellent introduction to higher level thinking, and is important for college freshman as a beginning to their educational journey.

During fall of 2011, SMU hosted three lectures from experts in various fields to address the scientific, medical, and ethical issues raised in the common reading, The Immortal Life of Henrietta Lacks. *Hanan Hassan attended one of these lectures and offers a review. Is her review successful? Why?*

Presentation Review: "HeLa Cells, Human Research Ethics, and Genetics"

Hanan Hassan

1   The final presentation in SMU's Gartner Honors Lecture series on the common reading, *The Immortal Life of Henrietta Lacks*, took place on Wednesday, September 21, 2011, in the Hughes-Trigg Forum. Students eagerly filled the empty seats and soon the floor, too. The speaker was Dr. Fred Grinnell, a professor of Cell Biology at the University of Texas Southwestern Medical Center. He appeared relaxed and approachable as he came on stage, a tall, thin man in khaki pants and a button-down shirt, his glasses poised near the tip of his nose. He let the curious faces watching know that "if anyone has any questions you can just . . . yell out." This set the tone for the lecture to follow. In a concise, straightforward manner, Grinnell effectively used Rebecca Skloot's book as a platform to introduce first-year students to current research in genetics and the evolution of science.

2   Dr. Grinnell presented a coherent argument addressing issues in the common reading, such as whether taking residuals during a medical treatment and using them in research is unethical if the patient is not told, as Skloot implies in her book. He also traced historical and ethical challenges in bioethics such as consent, research, and the use of African-Americans as test subjects during segregated times in America. Rather than simply listing a series of dates and experiments, Dr. Grinnell made the cases more real by projecting actual pages from sources such as the *New England Journal of Medicine*, the *New York Times*, and the *Belmont Report*. These visuals served to make the cases in Skloot's book more real.

3   Dr. Grinnell also differentiated between research and treatment, so students could classify Henrietta Lacks's procedure as distinct from the new procedures that have developed as a result of genetic research. He defined *treatment* as a procedure that continues as long as the patient gets better, and *research* as the procedure that continues until the research is over, even if the patient, or testing subject, as in this case, gets worse. Furthermore, Dr. Grinnell referred to the *Ethical Principles for Medical Research Involving Human Subjects*, which states, "the well being of the human subjects should take precedence over the interest of science and society." Doctors who do not abide by this principle believe that

conducting uninformed research is justified because in this way, a small number of people can benefit many and so help the common good.

4   Finally, Dr. Grinnell explained genetic medicine, which allowed students to see how the advancements Skloot describes continue in cell research today. Getting down to basics, he explained the evolution of the words *disease, patient,* and *cure*. Disease used to refer to symptoms and the feelings of an actual patient, but now diseases can be predicted before a person is even born. Patients were once people who were feeling less than their best, but now patients can even include embryos—those unborn, and utterly dependent, forms of life. Third, a cure was a treatment for a disease, whereas now cures can prevent a person from having a disease or having a child who is likely to have a disease. I found this topic to be the most interesting. Although I lack expertise in genetics, I was still able to follow Dr. Grinnell's compelling argument about how everyday life is changing as a result of discoveries in far-away labs.

5   Dr. Grinnell had a great delivery as he moved from different sides of the room, making everyone feel included. He also had a well-prepared PowerPoint that featured more visuals than words. Aural learners had his articulate words to guide them, while visual learners could focus on his reader-friendly PowerPoint. Although it was obvious that Dr. Grinnell is a well-informed researcher and lecturer accustomed to speaking to advanced students in the medical field, he was able to explain complex ideas to first-year college students who may have little or no knowledge of biology and ethics. Dr. Grinnell was also very approachable and stayed after the lecture to answer any questions students may have had.

6   Some students later criticized Dr. Grinnell for not mentioning his views on the ethical issues Skloot raises. The key issue was whether it was ethical to take Henrietta Lacks's tissue samples for research without her knowledge. However, he clearly stated that the "doctors really should have asked her when they shaved two pieces of her cervix." Some students felt he strayed off topic when he entered the area of genetic research. However, I felt it served his purpose of bringing issues from the 1950s forward to the present day. Genetics research is his field of expertise. He defined genetics as the future of science. Covering it in the presentation made the talk relevant to today, not just a rehash of Lacks's story.

7   Seeing how the issues Skloot raises relate to scientific discoveries today makes the common reading relevant to *our* lives. Attending this lecture certainly enhanced my understanding why Skloot's book provided a thought-provoking common reading for the Class of 2015.

Taylor Corrigan's class examined Rebecca Skloot's role in writing The Immortal Life of Henrietta Lacks *and the differences her narrative "presence" may have made. Corrigan worked through several drafts to improve her ideation and to polish her style. Here is an early draft followed by her final revision. Do these revisions improve her essay? In what ways?*

Intrusive or Necessary?—An analysis of Skloot's presence [draft]

Taylor Corrigan

1   Rebecca Skloot, the author of *The Immortal Life of Henrietta Lacks,* serves as an important link throughout the book's progression of Henrietta's tie to science and the medical world, and how it would forever change the course of her and her family's life. Skloot's presence is necessary for the personal quality of the book and enables the reader to connect with the Lacks family as opposed to just reading about their lives from an outsider's point of view. The emotional bond that evolves amid the Lacks family and the reader is made possible by Skloot's involvement during times of their family turmoil, religious experiences, personal conflicts, as well as in other aspects of their life—watching Skloot's own personal evolution through the process also leads the reader to have a more open-mind set towards issues of race, ethics, and religion. Rebecca Skloot's presence in *The Immortal Life of Henrietta Lacks* is vital to the book because she develops a personal connection between the reader and the Lacks family; therefore, she develops into a more open person, allowing the reader to accompany her on her own journey of self discovery and encouraging the reader to follow her lead.

2   By making herself such a key part of the book, Skloot makes it possible for readers to understand something that they are so far removed from. However, in order to do this, Skloot had to first form her own connection with the family while earning their trust to accept her into their lives. Getting to know the Lacks family was not an easy task as Skloot tried to convince them for years she only wanted to help—that she was not just another journalist there to exploit them. Although this was a long, and at times, a futile undertaking, Skloot was not only able to talk to the family but also able to develop a deep relationship with them that helped the Lacks' in countless ways. This personal involvement is evident throughout many scenarios in the book. The first time the reader gets a true look into what Henrietta's family has had to go through is depicted when Skloot describes her many attempts to get in touch with them. The family has been sought after so frequently and bombarded by reporters so extensively that it has come to a point where the family has ultimately turned its back on anything having to do with Hela. After finally getting her hands on the phone number of

Henrietta's daughter, Deborah, all Skloot was left with were the phone numbers of Deborah's father and her two brothers, leaving Skloot to say, "I wouldn't hear her voice again for nearly a year" (54). The realization that it was that difficult for Skloot to come in to contact with the family demonstrates how guarded the Lacks family has become. In seeing their attitudes toward anything related to Hela or their late mother, the reader is able to understand just how much damage and strife these cells have caused for the Lacks'. If Skloot had not been part of the narrative, the reader would not have been able to see first hand the lasting impacts of an event that occurred more than 60 years ago.

3   Skloot's involvement is also key later in the book when she meets other members of the Lacks family. The reader is able to see how this event has affected their everyday lives and has left the family with nothing to show for it—despite the fact that without Henrietta's cells, none of the medical advances would have been possible. Without Skloot's presence and her shared experiences, the reader would have no inside connection in to what the Lacks' life is like now, or be able to grasp a true understanding of the hardships that Henrietta and her family faced. One instance where it is possible to see into their lives through Skloot is seen when she meets Cootie, Henrietta's first cousin. Skloot takes a drive to visit Lacks Town, a single road about a mile long where Henrietta grew up. Skloot's journey to this seemingly 'other world' really takes the reader into what Henrietta's life was like and helps the reader to understand one of the reasons why Henrietta received such poor medical attention. The low standard of living in Lacks Town is made evident when Skloot drives up to Cootie's house, a run down shack that he had built himself. Skloot describes the house as virtually empty, saying that "there was no couch, just a few metal folding chairs and a barber's chair anchored to the linoleum floor, its cushions covered entirely with duct tape" (80). As the reader, it is hard not to develop some sort of compassion for this family—here they are, the descendants of a woman who possibly made the biggest contribution to both the scientific and medical worlds, and yet they live in poverty with no recognition—least of all no health insurance. Given the ability to see into the lives of family members like Cootie allows the reader to form emotional ties with these people and develop a sense of compassion for a family they do not even know. The fact that Skloot is able to include herself in the narrative and be a part of these events brings a certain authenticity to the text that would be impossible to convey without telling it from firsthand experience.

4   Another advantage of Skloot's presence is that the reader is able to follow her as if she was guiding them along a path—helping them to draw their own conclusions about the events that unfold. As a result, readers can make personal discoveries and experience their own journeys of realization. Her personal involvement in the book allows the reader to see Skloot's own reactions to certain events, as well as her personal growth and development as the story progresses. At the very end of the book, in one of the last scenes, Gary, Deborah's cousin,

visits Deborah and Skloot. He arrives just after they have returned from the mental hospital where Elsie, Henrietta's daughter, was sent to live. Deborah becomes so worked up after everything she has been through that day that she and Gary start to pray. Their praying becomes so intense and emotional that Skloot stood watching in amazement, "dumbfounded, terrified to move or make noise, frantically scribbling notes" (292). This moment, shared between Gary and Deborah, so vibrantly conveys the toll this has taken on the family and shows that they have come to take comfort in religion as a way to deal with the medical issues that they cannot understand. While they are praying to God, Gary asks Jesus to "give [the cells] to her" (293), begging him to take the burden off of Deborah and place it on someone else, namely, Skloot. After all of this happens and Gary and Deborah have calmed down, Skloot makes an important realization and says "in that moment, reading those passages, I understood completely how some of the Lackses could believe, without a doubt, that Henrietta had been chosen by the Lord to become an immortal being. . . . Angels are like that. The Bible tells us so" (296). It is here that Skloot's whole mindset changes and she now understands where the Lacks' have been coming from. Whereas at the start of her story she was a scientific journalist who was skeptical of religion and lived her life from a scientific standpoint, she was now able to step back and accept the religious dimension of the Lacks' life. It took Skloot the whole story to have this open-mindset towards religion, life, and people. Seeing how these people changed her attitude is inspiring and contagious—leaving the reader wanting to make their own personal revelation just as Skloot made her own. By watching Skloot's mindset change throughout the course of the book, the reader is encouraged to reflect on their own views and hopefully open their mind set as well.

5   In *The Immortal Life of Henrietta Lacks,* Rebecca Skloot's involvement is not only beneficial, but also necessary. Her developing relationship with the family, illustrated over the course of the book, works to personalize the story and allows the reader to develop a bond with the family—feeling as if they are right there in the room with Deborah and Gary, praying to God to lift the burden of Henrietta's cells from their shoulders. Skloot's ability to act as a bridge for readers to see into the lives of the Lacks family makes it possible for them to form their own connections with the family and to develop a sense of remorse and understanding for what the family has been through. The personal quality given by Skloot's narration also leads the reader to make a connection with Skloot, in turn leaving them with a more open-mindset than they had prior to reading the book. Ultimately, Skloot not only leads the readers on a journey of self-discovery, but also shows them into the worlds of medicine and science—exposing the truth of the Hela cells and the course of events that led scientists to make advances in the areas of tissue culture and human genetics, as well as progress into the issue of medical ethics.

Intrusive or Necessary? —An Analysis of Skloot's Presence [Final]
Taylor Corrigan

1   As the author of *The Immortal Life of Henrietta Lacks,* Rebecca Skloot serves as an important link between her readers and the Lacks family by bridging their different worlds. Her presence is vital to achieving the personal quality of her book and enabling her readers to connect with the Lacks family as opposed to simply reading about their lives. Skloot's own evolvement also leads readers to a more open attitude toward issues of race, ethics, and religion. Rebecca Skloot's presence in *The Immortal Life of Henrietta Lacks* is vital because she develops a personal connection between readers and the Lacks family. Consequently, Skloot emerges as a more open person, allowing readers to accompany her on a journey of self-discovery.

2   Skloot's involvement makes it possible for readers to grasp the lasting effects of the Lacks family's struggle with the medical and scientific worlds. However, to convey their hardships, Skloot first had to form her own connection with the family. Getting to know this family was not an easy task, and although at times her efforts were futile, Skloot was eventually able to develop a deep relationship with them. The first time readers glimpse the impact of the research on the Lackses comes when Skloot describes her many attempts to contact the family. Reporters had been bombarding the Lacks family for so long that the family ultimately turned its back on anything pertaining to HeLa cells. After Skloot finally reached Deborah, Henrietta's daughter, the only information Skloot received from her was the telephone numbers of Deborah's two brothers and her father, leaving Skloot to say, "I wouldn't hear her voice again for nearly a year" (54). The constant attack of reporters was so overwhelming that the family tried to cut their ties with their mother's cells altogether, and anyone interested in information would need to convince the Lacks men to change their minds. When Skloot eventually got through to the Lacks residence, a young boy answered and at the sound of Skloot's voice yelled to Day, Henrietta's husband, "Get Pop, lady's on the phone about his wife cells" (54). Skloot later learns that the boy knew the reason for Skloot's call because white people only called his father about HeLa cells. Seeing how difficult it was for Skloot to contact the family demonstrates how guarded the Lacks family has become. Their attitudes toward anything related to HeLa or their late mother convey the damage these cells caused the family. Without Skloot's presence, the lasting impacts of an event that occurred more than sixty years ago would not have been apparent.

3   Skloot's presence is also important later when she meets other members of the family and takes her readers more deeply into the Lackses' lives, leading them to form even stronger emotional ties to the family. Without Skloot's presence and her shared experiences, readers would be unaware of the family's current lifestyle and would be unable to form a true understanding of the hardships that the HeLa cells have caused Henrietta and her family. One instance when readers see into the Lackses' lives occurs when Skloot takes a drive down a mile-long road, the place where Henrietta grew up, to meet Henrietta's first cousin, Cootie. The low standard of living is obvious when she arrives at Cootie's house, a dilapidated shack that he had built himself. Skloot describes the house as virtually empty: "There was no couch, just a few metal folding chairs and a barber's chair anchored to the linoleum floor, its cushions covered entirely with duct tape" (80). Skloot's journey to this run-down area helps explain one of the reasons behind Henrietta's poor medical attention. Readers cannot help but develop some compassion for a family living in poverty while their mother's cells are making researchers wealthy. Seeing into the lives of family members like Cootie allows readers to form emotional ties with them and develop a sense of compassion for a family they have never met.

4   Another advantage of Skloot's involvement is that she can help readers draw their own conclusions from the events she describes, while seeing her reactions to events as well as her personal growth as the Lackses' story progresses. At the very end of the book, Deborah's cousin, Gary, visits Deborah and Skloot after they return from touring the mental hospital where Henrietta's daughter had been sent. After their long day, Deborah and Gary begin to pray together, and Skloot can only stare, "dumbfounded, terrified to move or make noise, frantically scribbling notes," while their praying intensifies (292). This shared moment between family members portrays the emotional toll this event has taken on the family and shows that they take comfort in religion when dealing with medical issues they cannot understand. When they finish praying, Gary points to a passage in the Bible and instructs Skloot to read it: "There is, of course, a physical body, so there has to be a spiritual body" (295). Skloot now realizes that the family views HeLa as Henrietta's spiritual body, saying, "In that moment, reading those passages, I understood completely how some of the Lackses could believe, without a doubt, that Henrietta had been chosen by the Lord to become an immortal being . . . Angels are like that. The Bible tells us so" (296).Here, Skloot abandons her scientific attitude and understands where the Lackses have been coming from. While Skloot starts as a scientific journalist who is skeptical about religion, she finishes by accepting the religious dimensions of the Lackses' lives and by acknowledging that faith is sometimes the right answer. Seeing the way that this family is able to change Skloot's attitude is inspiring and contagious—leaving readers eager to experience their own revelations just as Skloot experiences hers.

5   Rebecca Skloot's involvement in *The Immortal Life of Henrietta Lacks* personalizes her story and helps readers develop a bond with the family. The personal quality of Skloot's narration leads readers to connect with Skloot as well, and she then leads them on a journey of self-discovery and greater insight into both the medical and the scientific worlds. Without her presence, readers would be unable to understand the Lackses' complex relationship with religion and the erratic actions they take to avoid anything pertaining to Henrietta's cells. Skloot urges readers to value the lives of those patients who are subjects of this research and to question the validity of the treatment they receive. Therefore, without her, readers might have been unwilling to broaden their views on religion and the ethics behind medical research.

Work Cited

Skloot, Rebecca. *The Immortal Life of Henrietta Lacks*. New York: Broadway Paperbacks, 2010. Print.

For their final essay in Ashley Shin's English 1300 class, students took a position on an issue raised in the common reading, Rebecca Skloot's The Immortal Life of Henrietta Lacks. *Shin argues strongly against the extraction of tissue from individuals without their consent. Does she develop her argument clearly? Is her argument easy to follow? Do any of her segments need clarification?*

Ownership of Genetics
Ashley Shin

1   Human beings are created with unique features and endless character traits that mold them. The different eye color, hair texture, height, and many other descriptive observations define the individual. The DNA from each cell's nucleus contains secret codes that form the physical appearance and regulate the physical body. DNA can be manipulated in laboratory by enzymes being cut to specific sequence genes. Since genes can be patented, extracting tissues without prior knowledge to patients should not be authorized. Individuals should be able to deny use of their tissues for scientific research because tissue cells carry traceable genetic identity.

2   This traceable identity is not protected by any privacy acts regarding research on tissue cells. The Health Insurance Portability and Accountability Act limits privacy violation; however, scientific research annuls the act by exposing identification. As Rebecca Skloot explains in *The Immortal Life of Henrietta Lacks,* Lacks and her family had no knowledge that doctors and scientists were stripping cells out of her body. Permission and consent had not been given. The doctors simply assumed that the compensation for medical treatment would be the removal of several cell particles. The press finally revealed the ownership of the immortal cells as the HeLa cells when these cells started to contaminate other cultivations. Society began blaming Henrietta Lacks for the widespread death of other cells. The family was not only furious over not having prior knowledge of these hidden cells, but also enraged over the accusations. The doctors and scientists exploited a negative perspective on the HeLa cells and on Lacks herself, despite their intention to advance medical research. Some doctors, especially Hsu, even asked Lacks's children "to test everybody's blood to see if [they] all got that cancer [their] mother had" (Skloot 184). The genetics from Lacks provided a glimpse of the genes of her children as well. The world would know some information about the Lacks children from the HeLa cells. Hsu mentions, "she could learn much more from testing the family's blood today" (Skloot 190). The Lacks family's health information was neither protected nor kept confidential. The "implied act" of privacy was disregarded.

3   When information from their tissue cells is released to strangers, including researchers and doctors, individuals start to feel insecure. For example, during

the summer of my sophomore year, I was hospitalized. At the emergency clinic, the nurses and technicians came to my ward and took some blood out of my body. They figured that the abnormal liver counts caused extreme pains to my abdomen. The hospital was not only testing for my liver counts daily, but also testing for sexually transmitted diseases, chances of pregnancy, and traces of drugs. Even though it was standard procedure, I did not feel comfortable about the doctors taking extra amounts of blood without my permission. I assumed that they were observing my digestive system. Every year, the same doctor recommends that I have my liver regulated. He performs several biopsies and gastroscopies while I am under anesthetics. I would never be able to know what the doctors do with my body while I am sleeping. The doctors may have surgically taken some tissue particles illegally and stored them somewhere. Knowing parts of me are in the hands of an outsider stirs up anxiety and uncertainty. The tissue cells contain personal information that even I do not yet know.

4   Some people may believe that it is unnecessary to request consent with regard to medical advancement. Experimenting and analyzing the tissue cells can perhaps create vaccines and medical procedures. However, the fourth amendment of the Bill of Rights expresses the "right of the people to be secure in their persons, houses, papers, and effects, against unreasonable searches and seizures." Materialistic things are considered personal property; and without a search warrant with probable cause, nobody can be subject to examination. In other words, people have the right to choose to allow or deny the usage of their tissue cells because these cells belong to and compose an individual. Therefore, patients may deny use of their tissue cells unless certain law permits surrender of them. The Nuremberg Code, the Declaration of Helsinki, and the Universal Declaration of Human Rights provide only limited guidelines in obtaining optimum protection and well-being of patients. If laws or acts were established and regulated with respect to these declarations, then patients would have security over their tissue cells.

5   Individuals should be granted the freedom to deny the use of tissue cells for scientific research. Not only do these cells contain facts about personal identity, but they also contain personal details. This data may provide the general descriptions of the assembly of the person. This information can be used to clone an individual or genetically change the individual. If this revelation occurs, human beings will be subject to science forever. The priority of scientific analysis will become far more significant than the morals and ethics of humans. Also, the personal details encompass personal experiences. Every part of the individual's life history is engraved into these cell particles. Thus, patients should have the power to prevent scientists and researchers from using their cell particles without their consent.

Works Cited

The Bill of Rights to the United States Constitution. The Charters of Freedom. Web. 15 Nov 2011. <http:/www.archivdes.gov>.

Declaration of Helsinki—Ethical Principles for Medical Research Involving Human Subjects. World Medical Association, Inc. Web. 15 Nov 2011. <http:/www.wma.net>.

The Health Insurance Portability and Accountability Act of 1996 (HIPAA). U. S. Department of Health and Human Services. Office for Civil Rights. Web. 15 Nov 2011. <http:/www.hhs.gov>.

The Nuremberg Code. Rpt. from *Trials of War Criminals before the Nuremberg Military Tribunals under Control Council Law.* No. 10, Vol. 2, pp. 181-182. Washington, D.C.: U. S. Government Printing Office, 1949. Print.

Skloot, Rebecca. *The Immortal Life of Henrietta Lacks.* New York: Broadway Paperbacks, 2010. Print.

The Universal Declaration of Human Rights: A Living Document. Web. 15 Nov 2011. <http:/www.un.org>.

Michelle Ko writes a letter to this year's incoming class urging them to find their own answer to the "educated person question." Is this good advice?

Finding Your Definition
Michelle Ko

Dear Future SMU Students,

1 As a current student of this required seminar course, I write this letter to give you an insight into what is to come during your first semester at SMU and to challenge you to do better than I on this assignment. By doing so, you will hopefully have much greater and more rewarding experiences during your years at SMU.

2 Sometime during your first semester, you will be assigned to read Thomas B. Jones's "The Educated Person" in *Criteria*. In this essay, Jones describes a flashback to his college graduation, when his commencement speaker emphasized that the educated person question should be asked early in people's careers and serve as the "center of [their] lives" (11). The speaker's comment leads Jones to look back at his four years of college and to realize that he has never asked the educated person question before and his studies have never gone beyond the required courses for his major. He has merely "drifted from one classroom to another, followed the required paths toward graduation, and never [taken] responsibility for making [his] own academic decisions" (12). In his concluding paragraph, Jones lists all the differences in his college years that could have occurred and describes the characteristics of an "educated person." According to Jones, an educated person is someone who engages in "a lifelong process of learning, study, reflection, experience, and action—not just four years of classes" (12).

3 Jones's essay will be the first of many you will read based on the educated person question. From reading most, if not all, of these essays, you will first learn the opinions of well-established writers, such as Norman Cousins's claim that the ratio of humanities and sciences taught in colleges should be increased, Zachary Karabell's theory that education is being "dumbed down," and Adrienne Rich's argument that women should "claim" their education. You will then proceed to gain insight from SMU's own writers, such as Amy Kopycinski's definition of an educated person, Grace Lin's reason why people should be educated and Maggie Hart's categorization of the broad concept of knowledge. When you are reading these essays, some of you will develop an eerie, uneasy feeling that sometime during this course you will also have to write a what-is-your-definition-of-an-educated-person essay. Unfortunately, you are correct. After reading all of these essays, you may think to yourself, "How on earth am I supposed to come up

with another definition or expand on Kopycinski's already exhaustive definitionor talk about something that seems to have been already thoroughly talked about?" Well, I am now going to complicate the matter further and add my own perspective on this issue of defining an educated person: there is *no* definition.

4   As you can see from the variety of answers to the educated person question by the various *Criteria* authors, the term is very difficult to define. It may seem simple at first, similar to how Amy Kopycinski initially thought of the term as "someone who knows a lot of information about a lot of different areas" (13). However, like Kopycinski, you quickly realize no one is capable of achieving the unlimited amount of knowledge available, and "a lot of information" is too vague to be considered a definition. Also, people who know a respectable amount of information regarding their field of study or anything in general exist all around the world, and no one can say that an engineer is "more educated" than a lawyer or vice versa, because their expertise lies in different areas. As a result, a concrete definition is hard to create without that definition becoming either too broad or too specific.

5   Another reason why defining an educated person is so difficult is that everyone has his own opinion about who or what an educated person is. People have different religions, family backgrounds, cultures, ethnicities, political views, surrounding environments, and other influences that shape them and allow them to develop their own set of moral values. Differences in thoughts and beliefs are inevitable, and as a result, everyone's definition is bound to vary. It is impossible for anyone, even with the greatest depth in knowledge, to come up with an umbrella definition that encompasses the thoughts of every religion, culture, and political view, and satisfies everyone. So here, I add an explanation to my previous claim of a lack of a definition: There is no definition because *it is different for everyone.*

6   How do you come up with your own definition? I came to a realization about my own during our class discussions in English. We were assigned one or two essays in *Criteria* for homework each day, and we would discuss them during class. In every eloquent and flawless essay I read, I generally agreed with everything the authors said and assumed it was the same for everybody else in my class, thinking, "How could anybody ever disagree with any of these people? Everything they're saying seems so right." Well, I was dumbfounded every single class. Whether it was a single sentence in the writing, the tone of the author, or the overall idea the author was suggesting, at least one person in the class always found something to disagree with in each essay. It was almost a culture shock for me, as I sat listening to my classmates, unable to understand how anyone could see a flaw in such perfect essays. During the first few classes in which we debated the essays, I was frustrated and angry. Everything my classmates said sounded dumb and pointless, and it seemed to me as if they

were just unhappy that whatever the author wrote did not match their political views or beliefs. I could not understand why my classmates could not see that everything the authors wrote was right.

7   As we discussed more essays, however, I began to be more open-minded. I put my frustrations aside and listened more closely to what my classmates were saying, and I began to embrace the differences in political views, religions, and moral standards my class represented. I neither agreed nor disagreed with my peers' thoughts, but simply reemphasized the idea that everyone is different and that it is okay to agree to disagree with others. It is not that I didn't know this before; in the increasingly open and diversifying world that we have today, most parents and teachers teach their children about diversity and to accept one another, and the idea is engraved in our brains since early childhood. However, from these classroom discussions I experienced firsthand this idea in a real-life situation. From this experience, I relearned the idea that everyone is different, and I was able to take a step closer to discovering my own definition—or the lack of one—of an educated person.

8   The key to finding your own definition is experience. Your experience could be one incident that leads to your groundbreaking epiphany or a steady series of lessons learned through several events. Everyone probably has a different way of finding her own definition of an educated person, just as everyone is different with different ways of learning. Your experience could be inside or outside of the classroom; you may learn in class the step-by-step process on how to drive a car, but only when you actually start driving a car on the streets will you get used to the feel of driving. Kopycinski finally arrives at her definition of an educated person after discussing the issue during class, deliberating about it for several days, watching a movie in class, then deliberating about it some more. Hart has a model figure, her brother who is a Yale student, who she knows is an educated person even though she does not exactly know what that means, and she also has her experiences in her CTV class and dorm room to explain her categorization of intelligence. All individuals have their own experiences, from which they discover their own versions of the definition of an educated person.

9   So here is my challenge to you all: Try to experience everything SMU and the world have to offer and learn from it. After every experience, you will be one step—no matter how big or small—closer to finding your very own definition of an educated person. Even if you start with a broad, basic meaning or struggle to find one, every event will help you carve it into perfection that you personalize for yourself. Put yourself out there, experience it all, and learn from it. Whether it is meeting new people everywhere you go, reading all the possible books you can put your hands on, trying new sports, studying like there is no tomorrow, taking the most random class on the course list, skydiving, falling in love, or going to all the parties every weekend, try it all. You will either find

a new passion or interest or realize that you absolutely hate it. Whether you stick with the sport and continue it forever or reconfirm that you were never meant to be a skydiver and were destined to be a doctor, you will have learned something. After all the experiences, I hope you find a definition that can guide you through the rest of your life and your journey to becoming the educated person you want to be.

Best of luck,
Michelle

Works Cited

Cousins, Norman. "How to make People Smaller Than They Are." *Criteria 2011-2012: A Journal of First-Year Writing*. Ed. Mary K. Jackman and Lee Gibson. Dallas: SMU Department of English, 2011. 23-25. Print.

Hart, Maggie. "What Is an Educated person?" *Criteria 2011-2012: A Journal of First-Year Writing*. Ed. Mary K. Jackman and Lee Gibson. Dallas: SMU Department of English, 2011. 89-92. Print.

Jones, Thomas. "The Educated Person." *Criteria 2011-2012: A Journal of First-Year Writing*. Ed. Mary K. Jackman and Lee Gibson. Dallas: SMU Department of English, 2011. 11-12. Print.

Kopycinski, Amy. "My Discovery of the Educated Person." *Criteria 2011-2012: A Journal of First-Year Writing*. Ed. Mary K. Jackman and Lee Gibson. Dallas: SMU Department of English, 2011. 13-16. Print.

In his summer writing course, entering first-year student Cameron Smith read Hugh Kenner's controversial 1960s article "Don't Send Johnny to College" and determined that Johnnies are still arriving fifty-plus years later. Smith doesn't want to be one. Should anyone?

Triumph With Sacrifice
Cameron Smith

1   Abilities, talents, and opportunities make a difference in how we attain our life goals, as does our willingness to take risks. People who have not taken risks cannot succeed in their future endeavors because they will never see the value of an education. Hugh Kenner, author of "Don't Send Johnny to College," writes about a new wave of students and educators who are entering the college atmosphere. These incoming people he calls "Johnnies," people who go through the motions of life without taking risks, without grasping knowledge given to them in effective ways. In comparison, Kenner describes the "Real Students," who when mixed with their opposites, the "Johnnies," create chaos between them. Reflecting on the risks I have taken, I believe I should not be included on Kenner's Johnny list because of my hunger for learning—I am willing to take risks to achieve goals that follow from educational success.

2   A hunger thrives through me. When I was younger, many educators told my parents that I would have difficulties learning for the rest of my life. Luckily, my parents didn't take their advice and treat me like I have a mental deficiency. Ever since, I have worked to do more than people expected from me, staying up until three or four in the morning grasping key information or finding more information that wasn't in my textbooks or notes. Kenner asserts, "A student has a vocation for study. But there's really nothing that Johnny comes to campus burning to learn about" (128). He explains how "Johnnies" have no *burning* desire to learn, unlike me; this hunger runs like a gene in my family, always driving me to achieve bigger and better things through hard work and sacrifice.

3   I've always taken risks and chances, which have consistently been beneficial to me. If I refuse to venture "outside-the-box" or out of my "comfort zone," I'll never see what's on the other side waiting for me; the taste of finishing what I start will forever elude me. Kenner observes, "What [Johnnies] illustrate isn't primarily the 'inability to express oneself,' i.e., technical difficulties with the English language. What they illustrate is something deeper, probably irremediable: a happy willingness to emulate the motions of thought" (129). Kenner says that expressing ourselves in our own ways, thinking "outside-the-box," conveys emotions, which invests in our education. For instance, when I did science projects in class during high school, I departed from what was planned and did operations differently, just to see other outcomes. These outcomes may

not have always been correct, but they taught me something that I otherwise would have never learned. Back in high school and now in college, I was and am still terribly frightened to take some courses that promise to be challenging. Yet, I have always wandered into the unknown, lost but not *lost*, knowing that by living with faith in God I can attain anything I set my mind to.

4   Kenner's essay makes people wonder about what group they might belong to: the Johnnies or the Real Students. It did for me, and I soaked in all the information he offered. After being in college for less than a month, my mind has expanded with information, changing my life in ways that never seemed possible to me before. Higher education should be enjoyable. We should not think in terms of "black and white," but think "outside-the-box" and see what we can do with our higher education—because it may take us higher than we have ever imagined.

Work Cited

Kenner, Hugh. "Don't Send Johnny to College." S*aturday Evening Post* (Nov 14, 1964). 12-16. Rpt. In *Criteria 1987-88*. 127-132. Print.

Gabriela Garza San Miguel's 1301 class debated whether John Ciardi's argument for studying the liberal arts, written over fifty years ago, remains relevant and persuasive today. She believes it does. Is her argument convincing?

The Validity of John Ciardi's Arguments in Favor of the Study of the Humanities
Gabriela Garza San Miguel

1 Universities have become more competitive with each other as they strive to provide their students with a superior college experience. To do this, they not only focus on the technical academic aspects, but also on other factors that compose the life of a university student. Colleges want to graduate well-rounded people who are able to contribute effectively to society, and the liberal arts, or humanities, play a fundamental role in achieving this goal. John Ciardi, a former college professor, discusses the importance of studying humanities in his article "Another School Year—What for?" This article, despite having been written over fifty years ago, still illustrates and convinces students of the importance of the humanities in their college education through arguments that have not lost their validity with time.

2 Ciardi's essay continues to be relevant to today's university students because they can directly relate to his encounter with his pupil. The student Ciardi describes has enrolled in a humanities course, just as current college students have to do. It does not come as a surprise that, similarly, a number of students today question the importance of liberal arts in their college education. However, Ciardi's response to this "beanpole with hair on top" (17) is still an excellent way to represent the intrinsic value of the humanities in a student's life. He succeeds in showing that an individual's life is divided into time periods and that some of these periods will undoubtedly end up as wasted hours if a person lacks knowledge beyond technical matters. Ciardi portrays people that have this deficiency as being "badly stuck for something to do when [they are] not writing checks" (18). Ambitious students do not want to see themselves in this situation because, as Ciardi writes, a successful life includes more than just a stable job. Students want to have significant discussions and be able to stand by their points of view through well-structured arguments. Ciardi succeeds in making them value the possibility of doing so through the knowledge they can gain by studying the liberal arts.

3 Not only does Ciardi's characterization of solely technical people continue to be accurate in present times, but his description of a civilized person is still comparable with the way an educated person is perceived today. People are considered to be educated if they possess knowledge of a wide range of

themes, not merely as people who have technical comprehension in a single area, as complete as that knowledge may be. So, saying that educated people are simply people with a degree would be an inaccurate assumption. On the contrary, educated people understand that they always have something new they can learn and that, in some cases, they can learn this knowledge only through others' experiences. Students today are more aware of this than ever because they are constantly bombarded with an enormous amount of information by the media. However, all this information, as it comes from different backgrounds, tends to contradict itself in different ways. Consequently, students have had to become more selective with the information they absorb. The outcome of this selective process will nevertheless be solid and valid if, as Ciardi explains, it is based on a number of perspectives from differing contexts. As these points of view can best be obtained through studying the liberal arts, students can be easily persuaded to participate actively in them.

4   In addition, regardless of how many years have passed, universities continue to teach the liberal arts and to emphasize their importance in forming students' perspectives in countless areas. On that account, these institutions express in their mission statements the importance, as well as the means, of graduating polished human beings who are able to form valid opinions over a broad spectrum of topics. Southern Methodist University, for example, states, "[SMU] seeks to enhance the intellectual, cultural, technical, ethical and social development of a diverse student body. SMU offers undergraduate programs centered on the liberal arts" (*Description*). Mission statements such as this, which highlight the importance of the liberal arts, welcome thousands of students every year. They do not, however, welcome just any type of student. They welcome students who choose to go to university over going to a technical school because they are eager to evolve, not only into people who have technical knowledge, but also into well-rounded human beings capable of actively contributing to the welfare of society. Ciardi points out that "college is not only to train you, but to put you in touch with what the best human minds have thought" (18). Ciardi's essay about college education portrays in a concise manner the current mission of universities. Hence, by reading his article students will be able to confirm their decision to go college and simultaneously remember that the liberal arts and college go hand-in- hand.

5   Ciardi's arguments in favor of the study of the humanities may be disputed, but so may every other statement anyone has ever made. Ciardi excels in illustrating the importance of the humanities in college education by providing his readers with situations and points of view to which they can easily relate. So, it would show an utter lack of judgment to say that Ciardi's arguments are not relevant to today's student body. Preparation to face any situation that can arise without previous warning is, at the end of the day, the outcome students expect from college. Ciardi shows that they can begin to build the foundation they need

to do so through the study of the liberal arts because these subjects offer general knowledge and intellectual skills from hundreds of generations. Therefore, it is not an overstatement to affirm that Ciardi easily persuades students to engage in the humanities and helps them to understand they need to do so to make the most out of their college experience and out of their lives when college is over.

Works Cited

Ciardi, John. "Another School Year – What for?" *Criteria 2011-2012*. Ed. Mary K. Jackman, and Lee Gibson. Dallas, Texas: SMU Department of English. 17-19. Print.

Description of the University. Southern Methodist University. Web. 20 Sep. 2011.

Elishah Ramos uses texts both ancient and modern to assert the validity of a humanities-based education. Can ancient wisdom retain its relevance to the modern world? Does Ramos successfully establish this relevance?

Beyond Education
Elishah Ramos

1   In "The Allegory of the Cave" Plato explains to his student, Glaucon, an interaction between someone who has become enlightened and someone who is ignorant. Plato explains to Glaucon that the ignorant man is not ignorant because he chooses to be so, but rather, it is just how he was raised and, sadly, his ignorance is all he knows. Plato argues that by nature, people are ignorant due to the restrictions of their mundane lives. People who want to learn, however, can emerge from this ignorance and can take off the veil of blindness. He exemplifies the new vision through an analogy in which he states that if a man were to leave a cave and then suddenly emerge into the light, he would note the difference between the objects he now sees and the shadows he once knew. According to Plato, an educated person is one who emerges from his ignorance and explores philosophy. Although I generally agree with Plato, he neglects that education is not just an observation to be made upon learning of a brighter and bigger world. Education also means getting involved and interacting with the existing world, which goes beyond just observation and theory. Furthermore, education is merely a gateway to what is truly valuable: wisdom. Wisdom is obtained through experience, whereas an education is solely the beginning of a greater understanding of wisdom.
2   In his conversation with Glaucon, Plato describes a hypothetical situation in which prisoners are held captive in a cave and the only truth they know is the shadows that authoritative figures present them. Plato makes a good analogy and correctly states that if someone has been in a certain environment then that is all that he is accustomed to. For instance, if a child is raised in a household in the countryside with no connection to the media and away from pop culture or the influence of society, then the child will have a very different reality and way of life than one who was raised in a big city. Both of these children are raised in completely different realities, and as they grow, they will see the world through different lenses. I understand the extreme polarities of two people who were raised in different environments because I have witnessed a variation of Plato's hypothetical example myself.
3   When I went into high school, I noted the polarities of someone born and raised in one world in comparison to someone who was born and raised in a completely different one. I came from a middle school for academically talented but economically disadvantaged kids throughout all five boroughs of New York

City. As a child, I was raised in a Latin household, where I was expected to speak solely Spanish and to live the culture, which meant knowing all aspects of it, and expecting *arroz con pollo* with *tortillas* on the side for dinner. In my middle school were kids from all over the city with similar experiences, where we all were brought up by immigrant parents and expected to continue our heritage, as well as to receive a proper education to become intelligent and successful people someday. Here I could relate to people because we were taught to challenge ourselves, and always seek the highest academic possibilities. Upon entering high school, however, I was introduced to a new approach to education, one that not only educated a student, but a whole person. In essence, that is what Plato argues is needed. Plato makes the claim that education is about enlightenment, and my high school leaned toward enlightenment, which requires interaction with the surrounding world.

4   In a Waldorf school a student is not merely an academic sponge, expected to learn concepts for the sake of grades, but rather a whole person who needs to grow academically, emotionally, and spiritually. A student is not drilled with concepts through a textbook or lectures, but through physical, emotional, and spiritual methods that integrate the disciplines of movement, fine arts, and practical arts into the study of humanities, science, math, and technology. Coming from a school where grades were emphasized and academics were the primary reason for school, this whole notion was absurd to me. Rudolf Steiner, the man who started this type of education in Stuttgart, and his Waldorf way of thinking, at first was nothing but a joke to me, because I did not understand what real education is. I could not see how the teachers expected me to learn to be a healthy and balanced human being through all these bizarre classes such as basket weaving, book binding, and perspective drawing. To me, education was solely the academic aspect of life, and I could not understand the concept of educating an entire person through school. But through my high school years, I learned that education surpasses the mere classroom experience and the lecture an instructor may give, and that we need a more rounded education to truly learn.

5   Education means not only the memorization of facts, theories, and formulas, but also the continual interaction that involves the progress of mankind, which is something that not many people understand. When choosing which high school I wanted to attend, I had several qualities in mind as an ideal. I was used to a small school environment, and that interested me, the feeling of community. I had looked into several small schools in the City, all of which seemed quite promising. While some schools did promise community, the Rudolf Steiner School felt genuine in its claim to being a family. When school began, I had a hard time adjusting to this new family because it all seemed foreign to me. My experience relates to how Plato describes a prisoner ascending into the light and how uncomfortable, and possibly in pain, he may be. As I observed my

classmates flourish in everything they did, I was uncomfortable and looking for a way out from this lunacy they called Eurythmy. What did prancing around the room to the words of a poem or the melody of one of Chopin's works have to do with getting me into college? However, now as I look back, I see that the prancing was an initiation to wisdom.

6   Wisdom does not entail knowledge gained while sitting at a desk, but while making observations of our environment. Waldorf education means the embodiment of interaction with the surrounding world. Every morning we would recite a poem, which began, "I look into the world" and was followed by observations on the world, God, and ourselves, and collectively joining them together as one. Most other schools promised to get me ready for college, but only Steiner made the promise of getting me ready for the world. I could have gone to a school practicing the "early college" type of education, but something was special about educating the whole person, and that is what captivated me. Through Waldorf education, I have learned to respect and to love bigger things than just the superficially concerning topics in life. I have learned about the arts, cultures, humanities, history, human development, sciences, sculpting, mathematics, music, and how to make felted gnomes, all of which have broadened me as a person. This broadening has helped me realize that this type of education and early steps of wisdom mean freedom.

7   Education is what enables freedom in a thinking world, but it does not end there. Goethe once said, "None are more hopelessly enslaved than those who falsely believe they are free," and he is right (Goethe). Although most academic institutions lead their students to believe that they are being prepared for the real world, they in fact are not, because they lack vital aspects of the working world, such as culture. Martha Nussbaum, a Professor of Law and Ethics at the University of Chicago, argues that culture stems from the humanities and that "the humanities supply essential ingredients for a healthy business culture" (Nussbaum). An educated person could know culture, due to the education that he received, but the wise person knows how to apply it, and does so efficiently in the thinking world. Because of the education I have received, I understand that education does not end in the classroom, but not many people know how to apply what they have learned to real experiences. After having experimented with a very diverse education, I am inclined to learn more, from as many resources as possible, and, according to Thomas B. Jones, that is what an educated person does.

8   In his essay, Jones confesses that had he thought of what education really means, he would have sought it out more. He claims that if he could have remade his undergraduate experience, he would have focused on a broader education, as opposed to a primary focus on a diploma stressing one specific area of study. He too agrees that an education is not merely learning certain specialties for a potential career, but rather it is learning how to be a whole person. To him

an educated person is he who can pose a legitimate question and seek its true answer. The true answers to life are not behind a simple formula, but they are to be answered by a thinking man, one who earnestly attempts to understand life.

9   Likewise, Norman Cousins has a similar opinion about the qualities of an educated person, and he expresses this in his essay "How To Make People Smaller Than They Are." In this essay, Cousins states that the humanities might not necessarily contribute directly to a career, but nonetheless, they are essential to life, and that is what makes an educated person. Cousins writes, "but even if it could be demonstrated that the humanities contribute nothing directly to a job, they would still be an essential part of the educational equipment of any person who wants to come to terms with life" (Cousins 24). His acknowledgement that the humanities are not only applicable in the work field, but also directly applicable and influential to life is crucial. Education is not only an internal thought, but also a manifestation of mankind. What good is it to have a diploma from an institution if we cannot interact with the world around us? Education must be applied to the physical world and the people and objects within it. The ability to interact with an ever-changing world and with people who have diverse opinions and ideas is priceless, and that is a quality that no institution can teach. No one can be taught how to behave or react in every circumstance of life, nor can one be told how everything in life is going to occur, which is why wisdom is far more essential in the thinking world than an education from any institution.

10   Although Plato and other scholars stress the importance of an education that enables individuals to emerge from ignorance, they only briefly mention, if at all, the importance to live life in a constant thinking state. I have known some people who lack a college education, and despite their situation, are true thinkers because they are on a constant journey to find the answers to the most pressing matters in their lives. Reflecting Jones's definition of an educated person, each of these individuals embodies the concept of an education. Going even further, these people offer something that no institution can provide: wisdom.

11   An education can offer but so much suggestion to life, even through the humanities; however, education alone lacks the experience that true wisdom requires. An individual who receives a degree from an institution is not automatically as well-suited for a job or task as someone who has years of experience at performing the same task. If a married couple is going through a tough time in their marriage and seek marriage counseling, they are more likely to seek help from the professional with years of experience, and if possible, personal experience through several years in a marriage. They seek the elder counselor because he or she offers wisdom that a textbook cannot.

12   In the thinking world, as much as an educated person is valued, wisdom comes with a much higher price. Wisdom is attained through experience, and through experience one learns what does and does not work. That is what is truly important to learn. Plato and the other scholars are correct in their argu-

ments, but they neglect to mention that what is most important in all sorts of education is the attained wisdom. An educated person might be able to write a well-thought-out essay, but a wise person goes beyond that. The wise person has learned that it is not enough to write and convince oneself that the essay was well done; rather, he will use all the resources available to make sure that it is realistic and applicable to life. The wise person has learned that going to the Professor and the LEC and asking one last person to review the essay is crucial to his success; therefore, he will make sure he does to succeed. A wise person does this not solely to achieve a high grade, but to advance and learn through the process. As he has several people review his essay, he learns from his mistakes and gains a broad perspective from them. Thus, he will absorb their wisdom as he builds his own. Even though in a small scenario, this wisdom will prove valuable because the student uses it to continue to grow and learn.

Works Cited

Ciardi, John. "How to Make People Smaller Than They Are." *Criteria, a Journal of First-year Writing*. Eds. Mary K. Jackman and Lee Gibson. Dallas: SMU Department of English. 2010. 11-12. Print.

Goethe's Opinions on the World, Mankind, Literature, Science and Art, translated by Otto Wenckstern. London 1853. Web. p. 3 books.google.de. http://en.wikiquote.org/wiki/Johann_Wolfgang_von_Goethe. 10 Nov. 2011.

Jones, Thomas E. "The Educated Person." *Criteria, a Journal of First-year Writing*. Eds. Mary K. Jackman and Lee Gibson. Dallas: SMU Department of English. 2010. 28-30. Print.

Nussbaum, Martha. "Cultivating the Imagination." Room for Debate. *The New York Times*. 17 Oct. 2010. Web. http://www.nytimes.com/roomfordebate/2010/10/17/do-colleges-need-french-departments/cultivating-the-imagination. 10 Nov. 2011.

Plato. "The Allegory of the Cave." *Criteria, a Journal of First-year Writing*. Eds. Mary K. Jackman and Lee Gibson. Dallas: SMU Department of English. 2010. 17-23. Print.

Overcoming obstacles and meeting new challenges are tasks that all students face as they struggle to claim their educations. Danielle Katz shares her experience and finds connections with that experience in her class readings. Can readings they encounter in class help students manage their daily lives? How does Katz's essay show these connections?

Claiming My Education: Yesterday, Today, and Tomorrow

Danielle Katz

1   As my dad walked me into school, like he had done every morning of first grade, I could feel the anxiety rising inside my little body. My dad came into my classroom every morning to help me solve the morning "brainteaser" on the white board. Unlike most of my peers in first grade who had already begun their journey to read, I struggled with reading and writing. As a result, the classroom was a confusing, terrifying place for me. I went to the nurse every day because "my stomach hurt"; I didn't like to learn, and I lacked confidence in the classroom. I was a discouraged, undiagnosed dyslexic student attempting to learn in a learning environment that was not suited for me. The following year, I went to a school called Jemicy, which is a renowned school for dyslexic students. There, learning became fun because I was taught in multi-sensory ways that helped me learn. I gained new confidence in the classroom and learned that I am capable of achieving anything so long as I persist and tell myself I can.

2   My need, struggle, and ability to compensate for my dyslexia have resulted in a "can do" attitude and a determination to be successful in all aspects of my life. This determination motivates me to claim my education rather than to receive it. In "Claiming an Education," Adrienne Rich discusses the difference between the verb "to claim" and the verb "to receive." Rich defines "to claim" as "to take as the rightful owner; to assert in the face of possible contradiction" (33). She defines "to receive" as "to come into possession of; to act as a receptacle or container for; to accept as authoritative or true" (33). To Rich, the difference between the two verbs is "between acting and being acted-upon" (33). One who claims her education lives her life actively by taking responsibility for her actions, and does not just "drift" through life (Jones 12).

3   As a dyslexic student, *receiving* my education is not an option. Some "students" may have the luxury of going to class and understanding the material just well enough to get "satisfactory grades," high Cs and Bs. But these students fail to realize that they are selling themselves short and ignoring so much potential knowledge. Rich describes this group of students as "bluffing at school and life instead of doing solid work" (35). By overcoming my struggle to read, I have proved to myself that I can do anything. What may be satisfactory grades for some students are the grades that ignite my determination to work harder, to

achieve grades I'm proud of, and to become educated. Rich writes that "clear thinking, active discussion, and excellent writing are all necessary for intellectual freedom, and that these require *hard work*" (36). Since I know I'm capable, I do the hard work I need to do to claim my education.

4   As I begin my seventh week at SMU, I've already taken many actions to claim my education, from meeting with my professors to attending math help sessions to getting feedback on my essays in the Writing Center. But one of the most meaningful actions I've taken to claim my education was to attend the first lecture of the Tate Lecture Series. This lecture featured James A. Baker III, senior statesman and former Secretary of State, and Fareed Zakaria, who is Editor-at-large of *TIME* and host of CNN's "Fareed Zakaria GPS." David Gergen, a Senior Political Analyst for CNN, moderated the discussion. The current economic situation and the US presence in Afghanistan and the Middle East were the main issues discussed. Attending this lecture was a significant step in claiming my education because I've never been drawn to the political or economic situations before. However, I knew this was a great opportunity to take advantage of what SMU has to offer and to gain education outside of my major and normal areas of interest.

5   I was pleasantly surprised by the lecture. Although the speakers told jokes that I did not have the background to understand and sometimes used vocabulary that was beyond my comprehension, I found myself continually thinking about what each speaker said. I enjoyed listening to the opposing views of each speaker and sorting through the issues in my own mind. Not only did I find the speakers engaging, but I learned about current national issues—issues that are now especially relevant to me, since I can legally vote.

6   Before the lecture, while I was waiting in line with my voucher to receive my ticket, a man asked me if I was interested in sitting on the stage instead of in the audience. After being assured that I wouldn't have to participate if I sat on the stage, I followed him to my seat in front of the entire audience. I sat so close to the speakers that if I had wanted to touch them, I could have extended my arm and brushed the sleeves of their suits as they walked past me to take their seats. This made the experience even more exciting and educational, because sitting close to the speakers made it easier to focus on what they were saying and to stay engaged.

7   Attending the lecture forced me to leave my comfort zone and to try something new, like sitting on the stage in front of the entire audience, without knowing what to expect. In this way, I claimed my education by "acting" and expanding my knowledge of the current national political and economical situations (Rich 33). I was not a "receptacle or container" waiting to "come into possession of" these national issues that are relevant to my life, but rather I acted "as the rightful owner" of my education by pursuing knowledge outside of the classroom (33).

8   Just as I claimed my education by attending a Tate Lecture, Elle Woods in the movie *Legally Blonde* claims her education as well. Woods, a blonde and beautiful senior at UCLA, applies to Harvard Law School to be with her ex-boyfriend, Warner. While students around Elle view her only as a beautiful but unintelligent blonde and doubt her ability to be accepted into law school, Elle dedicates herself to assuring her admission. As Rich would say, Elle "took responsibility toward [herself]" and "resist[ed] the forces in society that say women should be nice, play safe, have low professional expectations, drown in love and forget about work" (35). Elle defies those around her by claiming her education, getting accepted to Harvard, and eventually graduating first in her class.

9   Elle and I both value our educations as belonging to us, and therefore we will not let anyone interfere. As SMU graduate Anna Lee proclaims in her essay "Claiming My Education," she wants "an education that is [hers] and [hers] alone" (14) and she asserts, like Rich, that we are the "rightful owners" of our educations (33). Lee discusses how in her hometown of Alma, Georgia, "women pride themselves most of all on their appearance" and young girls "are taught to keep the same 'passive silence'" (35) that Rich describes" (13). Lee originally agreed with this "Southern Belle" belief that intelligence "hind[ers] [females] because it threatens the male population with whom [southern] women are destined to bond themselves in the holy sanctity of marriage" (13). However, when Lee read Rich's essay a second time "with a more open mind," she began to understand and even agree with Rich's ideas (13). This second reading of Rich's essay gave Lee "the courage to be 'different,'" (35) and actually claim her education in college, unlike most of her friends back home who were indeed "diligently seeking their MRS degrees" (13). Lee, like Elle, has made the decision to prove to herself and to those around her that she has the power, the courage, and the determination to claim her education.

10   Elle Woods, Anna Lee, and I are all alike in that we will all take the necessary actions to claim our educations. We dedicate our time outside of class to hard work and to achieving our goals. In her essay "The Confidence to Claim an Education," SMU student Emma Richardson writes, "But it is what students do outside the classroom that determines who will benefit most from their education based on who claimed their education as their own" (72). Students who put forth minimum effort will receive the minimum information necessary to pass a course and will only be "passive recipients" of their educations. On the other hand, the three of us "claim [our] education[s] by knowing that everything [we] do is an opportunity to learn, and [we] will seize those opportunities and know that what [we are] doing is worth extra time," because these opportunities are what ultimately let us find success and learn the most in life (Richardson 73).

11   As a confused and struggling first grader, I learned that academically I have to spend more time and exert more effort than most of my peers. But my

dyslexia has positively influenced me by teaching me that to succeed, I must claim my education. I always seek help from a professor or tutor if I'm confused in a class. I view all subject material and new experiences as opportunities to gain knowledge. And, most importantly, I never take my education for granted. I know that the actions, choices, and decisions I make now will ultimately create the person I will become. I intend to choose my classes carefully with specific goals in mind and to strive to do the best work that I can do. I also plan to learn as much as I can about the world around me outside my major and to try to see that world through every lens available. I am claiming my education.

Works Cited

Lee, Anna. "Claiming My Education." *Criteria Archive*. Eds. Lee Gibson *et al.* Dallas: SMU Department of English, 2011. *Passim.* Print.

Legally Blonde. Dir. Robert Luketic. Metro-Goldwyn-Mayer, 2001. Film.

Rich, Adrienne. "Claiming an Education." *Criteria 2011-2012, A Journal of First-Year Writing.* Eds. Mary K. Jackman and Lee Gibson. Dallas: SMU Department of English, 2011. 33-36. Print.

Richardson, Emma. "The Confidence to Claim an Education." *Criteria Archive.* Eds. Lee Gibson *et al.* Dallas: SMU Department of English, 2011. *Passim.* Print.

A university, like a small city, offers students many communities they can join. Yet finding one where they fit can often be daunting. Maddy Dockery-Fuhrmann finds her community in an elite academic program, while Stephanie Newland locates hers in her residence hall. How important is a sense of community? How do these essays convey that importance?

Community in Higher Education
Maddy Dockery-Fuhrmann

1   A community is like a coal burning fire. When all the coals are in the fire, they stay hot. If one coal is removed, it will stay hot for a little while, but it will cool down quickly. This is a perfect description of a community of learners and how I best relate the importance of community in higher education. In "The Quest for Community in Higher Education," Parker Palmer states that "Community in higher education is not optional but essential if we wish to pursue our mission with full integrity" (Palmer 46). I agree one hundred percent with this statement. I believe that building a stronger sense of community across the entire student population of Southern Methodist University needs to be a top priority for the school. I also believe that building up a stronger sense of a "community of scholars" needs to be a top priority for the Hilltop Scholars Program.

2   In his essay, Palmer describes a community of scholars as "colleagues with common roots in the depths of the intellectual tradition working together to seek new insights into the world's wonders" (46). This means that as colleagues, students and faculty push one another and stimulate each other's thinking. This description accurately portrays an ideal community, but Palmer also discusses the big obstacle to achieving such a community: the tendency for people to lean toward competitive individualism and leave the idea of community by the wayside. Palmer says that the mission of higher education is "knowing, teaching, and learning" (46). These three concepts are best executed within a community, but easily distorted into individualism.

3   Knowing, Palmer explains, is easily thought of as the result of individual genius and the amount of knowledge one person can gain with hard work. Then the idea of teaching and learning becomes a "one-on-one exchange" from a very educated teacher to a less educated student. These perceptions of education simply will not do. Like Palmer says, "we fail to develop genuine intellectual capacity in the next generation" (Palmer 46). The teaching dynamic must shift into a collaborative experience of growth and learning where the students and teachers bring their full knowledge and intellectual capacity to the classroom so that they may experience the highest level of thinking possible with all of their potential combined. The less we realize the importance of community and

make it a priority to form one, the less we will grow as an intellectual body and the more we will hinder future generations' progress.

4   In "Community," Travis Talaric explains his frustration coming to SMU after growing up in the college town of Boulder, Colorado. The University of Colorado has an intense sense of school spirit and school pride that can be found all over Colorado. I grew up in Denver, and even I was constantly aware of the rivalry between the University of Colorado at Boulder and Colorado State University. Coming to SMU, Talaric was completely unsatisfied with the lack of school pride and sense of community. He witnessed this lack of pride the most in the poor attendance at school football games. However, I have noticed this trend more so within my classes so far at SMU. I see an incredible lack of an academic community. I do not see students striving for greatness. I see many students who fear having opinions or trying to learn in class. I have noticed a general norm in the classroom: students experience a stifling fear of judgment by their peers to the point that they will not speak up, have the courage to state their beliefs, or take intellectual risks by asking questions or discussing big ideas. Seemingly, everyone wants to get out of class so they can get on to the more important part of their lives—the parts where they achieve what they want in the isolation of their individualism, completing assignments and projects successfully, but never using other students or the setting of a classroom to really push them to think more deeply and to gain new perspectives to enhance their own learning. I believe that a sense of school pride is demonstrated when it comes to supporting the football team and showing school spirit. However, I also believe that first, students must come together as a community of learners because that is why we are here at this highly esteemed university. With this ideal in mind, the experiences of "knowing, teaching, and learning" become more collaborative processes that enrich all parties involved.

5   In "The SMU Community According to Etzioni," SMU graduate Christiano Gallo states that "Southern Methodist University's mission statement decrees that the university must maintain 'traditional values of academic freedom and open inquiry' and 'must develop an increasingly diverse and able faculty and student body'" (Gallo 81). To be quite honest, I do not see this mission being pursued with much effort. Compared to the high school I attended, I have been overwhelmed by the lack of diversity that I have seen at this school. It seems to me that SMU focuses on the surface of diversity, seeking students of different races and hometowns. However, they seem to make no effort to bring diversity to this school in the types of students with different beliefs, backgrounds, and non-academic interests. I don't feel that the school encourages students to bring to the school their full and unique selves. Students are encouraged to fit a mold socially and this trend is perpetuated because it is not challenged in the classroom. SMU has a unique personality that subtly discourages diversity in

the way students think, the way they behave, and the way they dress. What we need to do from this point is to make creating a scholarly community a priority for the school and trust that the rest will follow.

6   In my first semester here at SMU, I have been immensely grateful to be a part of the Hilltop Scholars Program, but it has not entirely fulfilled my expectations. I was under the impression that it was an honor to be invited into the program and that I would be treated accordingly. I expected the caliber of class participation to be pushed to be the best it could be and that I would be treated with respect because I would be expected to be a leader in the SMU community. Most of these expectations remain largely unfulfilled

7   In the Meadows School of the Arts, on the other hand, I have found exactly what the Hilltop program is lacking. The theatre department is selective and very small. Because the program is of such a high standard and so small, each individual is treated with respect and with the expectation that they will do their very best, succeed while in school as well as after graduation, and stay in the program all four years. There is a strong give-and-take relationship between students and faculty. Because acceptance into the program is such an honor, students are expected and pushed to work hard and hold one another to high expectations to create the best work possible. At the same time, because the program is small, students expect respect and attention from the faculty to help them grow to their fullest potential.

8   The aspects of community I find in the theatre department are all reasons why I joined the Hilltop Scholars Program. However, since being here, I do not feel that I am expected to be more of a leader at SMU than if I were living in any other residence hall. This feeling could be due to the large number of students or the lack of academic programs. Either way, the most important thing for students and faculty of HSP and all of SMU is to hold each other to higher expectations. This university is known for having a majority of students involved in Greek life. This social dynamic influences students to edit their personalities, their beliefs, and their appearances to be accepted into these social communities. Despite this dynamic, each individual, student or teacher, must recognize that we are at this school to learn for four years, not just to network for our future careers.

9   We need one another to maintain our intellectual curiosity and growth. We need to share ideas and to push each other's thinking to create an academic community that will then transfer to all other aspects of the school. Once this happens, I would be willing to bet that we see the Gerald J. Ford Stadium entirely filled at home games. We need to stay a part of a community of scholars because without that fire, our individual coal will cool quickly, and we will waste our intellectual capacity.

Works Cited

Gallo, Christiano. "The SMU Community According to Etzioni." *Criteria Archive*. Eds. Lee Gibson *et al*. Dallas: SMU Department of English, 2011. *Passim*. Print.

Parker J. Palmer. "The Quest for Community in Higher Education." *Criteria 2011-2012, A Journal of First-Year Writing*. Ed. Mary K. Jackman and Lee Gibson. Dallas: SMU Department of English, 2011. 46-55.

Talaric, Travis. "Community." *Criteria Archive*. Eds. Lee Gibson *et al*. Dallas: SMU Department of English, 2011. *Passim*. Print.

Somebody to Lean On
Stephanie Newland

1   The primary trait that I lack is confidence. In my mind, other people are always smarter, prettier, more driven, and just better than I am. Because of this attitude, I do not usually voice my opinions, state my ideas, or take control of anything; I automatically assume that anything I say or do is without merit or value. Although I still need to work on strengthening my confidence, SMU's community atmosphere, specifically the Hilltop Scholars Program, has given me the enormous confidence boost I need to step out of my comfort zone and make my ideas a reality. The films *Legally Blonde, Renaissance Man,* and *Higher Learning* each portray individuals who need greater self-confidence, which comes from the support of their communities. In "The Quest for Community in Higher Education," Parker Palmer outlines specifically how community can build up confidence. Additionally, in "The SMU Community According to Etzioni," Christiano Gallo illustrates how confidence promotes involvement, and involvement promotes confidence. The support I feel from various members of the SMU community has provided me with experiences that have helped me to understand how Palmer's ideas foster confidence. Also, encouragement from others has opened my eyes to how involvement can instill confidence. Community gives us somebody to lean on. Somebody to lean on gives us confidence.

2   Lack of support from a surrounding community can strip someone of her confidence. In *Legally Blonde,* Elle Woods begins Harvard Law School with little support from her family, ex-boyfriend, and most other students because "all people see when they look at [her] is blonde hair and big boobs" (*Legally Blonde*). Because of this lack of encouragement, she is unprepared for her first day of class and becomes embarrassed, which places her in a state of self-doubt. In addition to being academically ill-equipped, Elle soon learns that her ex-boyfriend is now engaged to someone else, which diminishes her confidence even more. She almost gives up on law school until she meets Paulette and Emmett. Both individuals give Elle helpful advice for moving beyond her ex-boyfriend and succeeding in law school. Soon, Elle regains her confidence and begins to thrive in her classes. She even gets the opportunity to serve as an intern on a murder case. As Elle blossoms through law school, she is able to apply what she learns to help her win this murder case as a first-year law student. Her accomplishment shows how she takes back her confidence and uses it to put her skills to work, trusting that she can take control of an actual case. Elle embraces her confidence vowing, "No more trying to be somebody I'm not" (*Legally Blonde*). She is

able to develop this attitude because support from her community revitalizes her confidence. This community gives Elle somebody to lean on.

3   Elle recaptures her confidence with the community support of her friends while Bill Rago, in the film *Renaissance Man,* recovers his confidence through the positive effect he has on his students. Rago ends up teaching a group of misfit soldiers on an army base after he loses his job and has to file unemployment (*Renaissance Man*). Through this unfortunate experience, Rago loses his confidence and is unenthusiastic about teaching students who have "never thought before" (*Renaissance Man*). His hesitation about teaching continues until he starts to see his students taking an interest in *Hamlet*. The community of students gives Rago back his confidence through their interest in *Hamlet* and through their support of his teaching style. Nathan Hobbs, one of Rago's students who later ends up in prison, even writes Rago a letter saying he would only sign up for classes "if they had a few teachers like you [Mr. Rago]" (*Renaissance Man*). With his newfound courage, Rago fearlessly teaches the soldiers, which makes them more confident in their abilities to learn. As this relationship displays, community support provides confidence, which subsequently produces more confident individuals who are not afraid to speak their minds and accomplish their goals. This back and forth confidence adds to the overall dynamic of their communities. Therefore, just as community sparks confidence, confidence sparks community.

4   Another instance of a student discovering confidence through community support appears in the film *Higher Learning*. Malik Williams, a student at fictional Columbus University, acquires his confidence from Mr. Phipps, a professor in the university community. Even though Malik at first seems extremely confident, even arrogant, this is a façade because he is too embarrassed to reveal his true self. Because of his lack of confidence, Malik does poorly on his schoolwork and this pattern continues until Mr. Phipps steps in to offer his support. Phipps quotes Frederick Douglass saying, "Without struggle, there is no progress," suggesting that hard work is necessary to earn good grades (*Higher Learning*). Eventually, Malik takes this advice to heart, produces an extremely well-written final paper, and finds the confidence he needs to continue his success. Malik does not initially possess confidence; however, through the support of his community, he eventually becomes confident and succeeds.

5   Parker J. Palmer illustrates the importance of this sense of community in providing students with the confidence they need to be successful in college. I often feel like Palmer when he states, "I feel in community when I have a chance to voice my opinion" (Palmer 48). Having the support to openly share my ideas while receiving "meaningful responses to what I have to say" increases my confidence. When people accept my ideas, I feel more appreciated and certain that what I say matters (Palmer 49). For example, in a recent Oracle class, my teacher asked us to give suggestions for improving her class. Usually, I would

just keep my mouth shut. Nonetheless, because of the confidence I have gained throughout the semester, I raised my hand and told Ms. Feldman that I thought adding another BBC documentary on brain function would be a positive addition to the Oracle curriculum. Once I made this suggestion, many other students made statements in agreement, assuring me that my idea was a good one. So, the more I use my newfound confidence, the more confidence I gain. Nevertheless, if it had not been for the support I received from my fellow students, I would never make suggestions in class again. Because of the classroom community's support, I am now not so timid about sharing my thoughts and getting involved in class.

6   Getting involved and becoming a part of something new requires confidence. In fact, Christiano Gallo describes how many SMU students become involved in a number of campus organizations. Such involvement can only be the product of courage reinforced by the community. Even though some organizations on campus promote cliques, they "can all be considered communities" because of the "common interests, kinship, and loyalty" shared among the individuals (Gallo 82). In high school I was minimally involved because I was afraid to take responsibility or control of anything. In contrast, I decided to start college by getting very involved, even though my confidence was not as developed as it is now. My decision to jump in and make the most of my experience here at SMU has proven to be the right one as my teachers and friends constantly encourage me in the organizations I chose to join. Because of my improved confidence, I have become a part of Mustang Heroes, Program Council, the Pre-Medical Society, the Pre-Dental Society, and One 28. Moreover, I am a distinguished Hilltop Scholar as well. These organizations "provide a type of bond, a foundation [I] can rely on" (Gallo 82). These organizations give me something and somebody to lean on.

7   The most rewarding program I have been a part of so far is the Hilltop Scholars Program because it is the community that has given me the most confidence. The friendships I have developed throughout the semester are special, and I have never felt so loved and supported by my peers. Most of my new friends can quickly realize when I am worried or stressed about what I want to do. For instance, to demonstrate her support, one of my friends recently decorated a card with inspirational verses from the Bible. She told me to tape it on my desk so I could look at it when I needed reassurance. I did what she said and her card helps me every day. Even though we have been friends only a short time, her touching demonstration showed me that my fellow Hilltop Scholars are special, community-oriented people. Because of the tenderness and encouragement I receive from the Hilltop community, I know I can "fail—and still be supported" (Palmer 48). Thanks to the Hilltop Scholars program, I am more confident and more willing to break out of my comfort zone.

8   We all need somebody to lean on, especially those of us with low self-esteem. I know that I have never taken full advantage of my education because my lack

of confidence inhibits me from fully participating. I hate to think that I am not making the most of what I am learning or of what life has to offer just because I am too scared to speak up. When I started college, I made the decision to start fresh, get involved, explore what SMU has to offer, and be who I want to be. Trying all these new things with a low-self esteem has been intimidating. Yet, the encouragement I have received from my friends and teachers in the SMU community has increased my confidence. Now that my self-assurance is much stronger, maybe people will start to look to me as a source of confidence. Maybe, just maybe, people will finally see me as somebody they can lean on, too.

Works Cited

Gallo, Christiano. "The SMU Community According to Etzioni."*Criteria Archive.* Eds. Lee Gibson *et al.* Dallas: SMU Department of English, 2011. *Passim.* Print.

Higher Learning. Dir. John Singleton. Columbia (New Deal), 1995. DVD.

Legally Blonde. Dir. Robert Luketic. MGM Home Entertainment, 2001. DVD.

Palmer, Parker J. "The Quest for Community in Higher Education." *Criteria 2011-2012: A Journal of First-Year Writing.* Eds. Mary K. Jackman and Lee Gibson. Dallas: SMU Dept. of English, 2011. 46-55. Print.

Renaissance Man. Dir. Penny Marshall. Touchstone Pictures, 1994. DVD.

After watching, reading, and analyzing Martin Luther King, Jr.'s "I Have a Dream" speech from August 1963, students in Holly Labry's English 1300 class set out their own dreams, imitating Dr. King's style and cadences. Where do these echoes occur?

My Dream
Holly Labry

1   I am honored to be at Second Presbyterian Church with Youth Visions, declaring what is necessary to improve our great city of Memphis.
2   I stand here today to declare my plea to help our great city. Memphis is a city shaped by many historic events. Together we have survived the yellow fever epidemic, created a historic music district, and founded St. Jude Children's Research Hospital, all of which allow us to offer so much to the world around us.
3   So why do we let such a great city suffer? Why do we allow the people in the institutions to cripple our public school systems? Why do we not stop all the gang violence in our streets? Why, after all this time, do we still feel the racial division throughout our city? We will not be the city that we desire if we do not answer these questions.
4   Let us not be hindered by our past, but from that past create a better future. Go back to your neighborhoods; go back to your schools; go back to your churches, and preach to them what we say here today. Every change starts within an individual; and without you, we cannot transform our city of Memphis.
5   We cannot do this alone. We, the citizens of Memphis, must unite and plow through the fields of disparity. We can never go back to these terrible and unfair ways.
6   I have a dream today.
7   I have a dream that I will be able to stand in front of Memphis and help resolve these unanswered questions.
8   I have a dream that one day the citizens of Memphis will not have to move their homes to other districts to send their children to better public schools. That one day, students of the public institutions will be able to learn the necessities to attend a university, which will allow them to create a better future for themselves. That one day, the teachers will actively teach, and not let these children continue uneducated. And on this day, the students of the Memphis public schools will be able to make a change in the world.
9   I have a dream today.
10   I have a dream that the people will live by the Golden Rule: "Do unto others as you would have them do unto you." And not be scared to help a person in need because you are too afraid of what others will think.

11 I have a dream that the violence and gang activity will stop and the people of this great city will walk in public and feel no fear.
12 I have a dream that the racial divisions of this city will transform and the upper class will help the ones stricken with poverty.
13 Let us not sit in our nice homes and look across the street to see a family living in terrible conditions and do nothing about it.
14 We must take action.
15 Let us come together to resolve these issues in our public school systems, in gang violence, and in the racial clashes that divide our city.
16 Let us create better school institutions.
17 Let us stop gang violence in our streets.
18 Let us eliminate the large gap that separates the rich and poor.
19 Let us create an atmosphere in which the students can go to school knowing that what they learn will prepare them for the world that lies ahead: a world where families can go out at night and not be afraid; a world where such a large division between the upper class and those who are less fortunate no longer exists.
20 Through this dream, we can and will recreate Memphis and transform it into the city it deserves to be.

For their final paper in Skyler Bloom's English 1301 class, students proposed changes to specific problems or solutions to troubling conditions in a community they know well. Would Bloom's proposal succeed? Should community service be required of all SMU undergraduates? Why? Why not?

A Tale of Two Worlds Working Together
Skyler Bloom

1   With their heavy workload, students often find it hard to see past their ten-page papers and their upcoming Economics tests. On top of those concerns, it's nearly impossible to recognize any problems outside of Southern Methodist University when they walk to class down the perfectly manicured lawn, lined by live oak trees and blooming flowers. It is a beautiful campus without a doubt; however, a brief drive outside of the extravagant Highland Park area paints an entirely different picture—an urban, impoverished, and needy picture. The City of Dallas needs volunteers, and SMU and its students would be greatly affected by working alongside the city. The university has an obligation to produce students with empathy and an understanding of these polarizing levels of society. Community service encourages this socioeconomic class interaction and also teaches students to consider others' circumstances altruistically. As Parker J. Palmer suggests, a sense of community between the academy and those outside it seems to be lacking. If SMU implements an undergraduate requirement of fifty hours of community service, then students would acquire a better appreciation for their own circumstances, develop an improved work ethic and time-management skills, and enhance the bond between the larger community and the university.
2   A community service requirement would also allow students to better appreciate their own circumstances and privileges. In my experience, I have found a very weak correlation, if any, between material possessions and happiness. For instance, I spent my four high school summers volunteering in a "soup kitchen" near our house. During my time serving food to the homeless, I found that the homeless people receiving the food were generally nicer, and appeared to be happier, than many of the wealthy families I knew. From a selfish standpoint, volunteering at the soup kitchen was one of the most rewarding things I have ever done. Completing my civic duty made me feel like a member of society rather than a solitary individual. It is no secret that SMU has a reputation for having an inordinate number of upper-class students. That being said, it is the obligation of these fortunate SMU students to work with those who are not so fortunate. It is similarly the university's job to produce quality members of society, which requires attributes such as humility. In the same way that Warren Buffet, one of the world's richest men, is a top supporter of higher taxation among the wealthy, SMU students need to participate in community service.

By doing so, they would realize that often the things we do for others are the most rewarding.

3   Not only would a community service requirement teach students humility, it would also allow students to develop a work ethic and effectively employ the time-management strategies that many college students lack. Long past are the days when the majority of college students worked their way through college with a full-time job while trying to maintain a high GPA. At least in my experience at SMU, I have come across very few students who are employed full-time. Additionally, most of those students who played sports or who were involved in their high school organizations are unlikely to continue their involvement in college. In fact, according to Dr. Carol Clyde, the Director of SMU's Community Engagement and Leadership Department, ninety percent of SMU freshman reported completing some sort of community service as a part of their high school graduation prerequisites. Yet, only thirty percent planned to continue their service in college. Thus, students are left with a copious amount of unstructured time. Some students wisely use their free time—studying in the library, maintaining their health, or joining a group or club; however, a significant number of students do not use their non-study time wisely. While free time is and should be highly valued on a college campus, spending fifty hours over the course of four years serving the larger community is not an unreasonable requirement. And some SMU students agree: according to my survey of New Century Scholars, completing 5 hours of community service a month was both rewarding and enjoyable—17 out of the 24 students surveyed (71%) supported a community service requirement. Additionally, community service would serve the purpose of the job that many of the modern day college students have never had. Even better, community service would teach students a work ethic on behalf of personal reward, which would ultimately help produce diligent, hard-working employees for our country's businesses.

4   Implementing a fifty-hour community service requirement spanning four years for SMU undergraduates would allow students to learn humility and a work ethic while also building a sense of community between Dallas and the university. Dallas, one of the largest cities in the country, is not often considered a college town. Unlike smaller towns in which a university or college becomes central to commerce and social interaction between students and citizens, Dallas and SMU have developed without a close relationship. Thus, community service would allow Dallas and the university to be more involved with and invested in each other. Palmer refers to the Princeton 55 project as a way Princeton graduates give back to their alma mater to help its graduates get jobs upon graduation. This is a reverse scenario of society repaying the university, but serves the same purpose of strengthening ties between the outside world and the academy. While SMU is obligated to produce academically qualified students, its mission should not end there. It should include producing students aware of their civic

duty by requiring community service, thus fostering and sustaining a sense of community between the university and Dallas.

5   SMU's Community Engagement and Leadership Department provides a number of exciting options for students looking to get involved in community service, both locally and abroad. Dr. Clyde has been instrumental in accommodating students' interests. Community service projects range from alternative spring break in the Caribbean to full-time volunteering jobs in underprivileged areas of Dallas. Additionally, SMU provides a service house for those that want to live with people who are also highly involved with community service. As mentioned previously, the New Century Scholars complete a minimum of five hours of community service each month, and all live on the same floor in McElvaney. Even if students have no desire to adapt their living arrangements on behalf of community service, plenty of community service projects exist. For instance, Dr. Clyde discussed students playing BINGO and setting up a "Senior Prom" for residents of a retirement home. Therefore, once the undergraduate requirement is in place, students would have nearly unlimited options to choose an interesting project.

6   The debate surrounding community service in the curriculum has been ongoing in SMU's history. One of SMU's founding mission statements has been to work more closely with the surrounding city of Dallas. Efforts such as the Bridge program, which gives Dallas Independent School District students favorable admissions consideration, have proved that SMU is committed to work with the city. However, the community service participation among undergraduate students is still lagging. After interviewing Oregon Senator Chip Shields (1989 SMU graduate), I found that restrictions on increasing community service participation have hardly improved over the past thirty years. Senator Shields discussed his thwarted efforts for increased funds for community service programs. He said that funding for community service was one of his top priorities, but was nowhere near the top of the Student Senate's agenda.

7   Dr. Clyde currently plays a similar role in the advocacy of increased student involvement that Senator Shields played twenty years ago. Implementing mandatory campus-wide community service requires a number of inputs such as effort, funding, and time, all of which have a common denominator of additional (and in the eyes of some, unobligated) work. Many professors question the benefits of working community service into their teachings because of the lack of funding. For instance, Dr. Clyde and a professor who included community service in a course a few years back both discussed the difficulties of transporting groups of students to and from service projects. Granted, their concerns and their resistance are valid; however, I think too often they overlook the advantages of the practical applications that community service can serve in what Palmer calls "the hidden curriculum."

8   Facing these limitations, I also propose an alternative for consideration:

requiring professors to incorporate community service into their individual class curriculum. If student-operated community service is not viable, then professors should implement service projects in their own curriculums and classrooms. These projects can take the form of field trips, or simply a class food-drive; in any case, the professor can design projects to fit his or her curriculum. For instance, an Economics professor can assign a field trip to a fundraising campaign to raise money for a community park. In this scenario, students would be completing community service while practically applying the (sometimes abstract) undergraduate curriculum.

9   Although this proposal will meet resistance, implementing a community service requirement will have an advantageous impact on students and the community. Dr. Clyde noted that SMU "is big on philanthropy but dedicates less time and effort to individual community service." Philanthropy and community should go hand-in-hand to serve and partner with the larger community of Dallas. In addition to the benefits of community service on SMU students, the city of Dallas will have roughly 8,000 undergraduate students working to serve the areas and people who most need their help. Dr. Clyde mentioned that Community Engagement and Global Engagement Competencies are being discussed for the new curriculum of 2012. It is important that the new curriculum of 2012 have a community service requirement to allow students to appreciate their own circumstances, to learn commitment and a work ethic, and to build a rapport with city of Dallas. Community service will allow students to get away from their ten-page English papers and Economics tests to help those who are in need, while contemplating what matters to them as college students and helping to shape who they are going to become.

Works Cited

Clyde, Carol. Director of Community Engagement and Leadership. Telephone Interview. 26 November, 2011.

Palmer, Parker J. "The Quest for Community in Higher Education." Afterword. *Creating Campus Community: In search of Ernest Boyer's legacy.* Wm. M. McDonald, Ed. Rpt. In *Criteria: A Journal of First-Year Writing 2011-2012.* Eds. Mary K. Jackman and Lee Gibson Dallas: SMU Department of English, 2011. 46-55. Print.

Shields, Chip. Oregon State Senator. Personal Interview. 26 November, 2011.

Lauren Fields's final 1301 paper explores the SMU campus and its facilities to determine what more the university could do to enhance its efforts toward sustainability. Would her proposal work at SMU?

Efficient Transportation
Lauren Fields

1   When one looks through the parking garages at Southern Methodist University, one cannot ignore the assortment of luxury vehicles. Statistics show that 69 percent of students who attend SMU and 95 percent of SMU employees commute by the use of single occupancy vehicles, many of which are not energy efficient ("Green Report Card"). Although SMU makes an effort to encourage students to drive electric or low emission cars by offering them preferential parking, the majority of students' vehicles run solely on gasoline, which increases the pollution level around campus. As a result, SMU was given a "B" by the transportation department when it comes to the ratings of the Green Report Card in 2011. SMU, however, could improve its evaluation in several ways. One such way would be to establish a car-sharing program on campus. A company that has now spread its domain to over 230 colleges in the United States and that would be a great addition to SMU is called Zipcar.

2   Zipcar is a membership-based car-sharing company that was established in the early 2000s in Cambridge, Massachusetts. The services of Zipcar enable customers to rent energy efficient cars twenty-four hours a day, seven days a week. The minimum rental time is one hour, while the maximum rental duration is four days. The vehicles must be reserved before needed, either online or by telephone. Renters must also satisfy a few requirements to become an eligible Zipcar motorist. First, a renter must be a Zipcar member, which includes an annual fee of sixty dollars. Second, a renter must possess a valid United States driver's license. Third, if the renter is under twenty-one, his or her university must have a signed contract with the company, which states that students age eighteen or above are able to rent Zipcars. While most college students are unable to rent cars due to a minimum age requirement of twenty-five, they are able to rent from Zipcar. Fourth, a renter must have a clean driving record, which contains no major traffic, drug, or alcohol violations ("Membership Requirements"). Any student who can fulfill all of these requirements would be able to rent a Zipcar and jump onto the fast track to an easier transportation method as well as to helping sustain the environment.

3   Zipcar's assembly of vehicles provides a transportation solution that reduces the carbon footprint and thereby minimizes greenhouse gas emissions, which would provide SMU with a healthier environment. The goal of the university would be to reduce the number of personally owned cars and to create more

room for this type of system. If fewer students were to bring their cars to college, more parking would be available for Zipcars. Studies show that for every Zipcar used, twenty personally owned cars are taken off of the road ("Green Benefits"). This emphasizes the idea that establishing a car-sharing system would in turn lead to less congestion on the roads, on and around campus.

4   Not only is Zipcar beneficial for the environment, but it is also easy on the pocketbook. Inexpensive rental rates make renting a Zipcar a cost-efficient solution because it would be much less expensive than each individual purchasing his or her own car and having to pay for gas and campus parking. Standard Zipcar student fees include a registration fee of twenty-five dollars with an hourly rate of seven dollars or a daily rate of sixty-six dollars. These fees may seem expensive, but when the cost is split among four or five passengers, seven dollars an hour sounds quite reasonable. This is especially true when gasoline, insurance, and 180 free miles are all included within the Zipcar rental fare. Zipcar will provide our campus with both easier and more efficient ways of getting from destination A to destination B. Students will no longer have outrageous cab fees and no more waiting in lines to take the bus.

5   It would not be a difficult task for SMU to develop this type of program. Because it is a private university and is supported by funds from endowment and tuition, it has the leeway to make its own choices. Even more helpful, Zipcar already has locations in Texas. Within the past two years, public universities in Texas such as the University of Texas, Austin; Baylor University; Rice University; and UT Dallas have established this car-sharing program as a method to improve their campus sustainability. Each of these campuses has anywhere from two to eight Zipcars. Since these universities are still in the initial stage of using Zipcar, they have yet to determine whether or not they need more vehicles. If public universities were able to get the approval to bring Zipcars to their schools, it should be no problem for SMU to join the team as well.

6   Although Zipcar has many positive aspects, it is also important to look at the possible negatives of bringing this car-sharing system to campus. First of all, most students would prefer to have their own car versus having to rent a car whenever they need to go somewhere. Just because the university has a car-sharing program doesn't mean that it is going to stop a good amount of students from bringing their cars to campus. SMU would have to start small to see if students would actually use the program so that it wouldn't just be a waste of space. Secondly, Zipcar depends on its members to keep the cars clean and to return them on time, full of gas. If a member did not follow through on these responsibilities, those actions could affect all subsequent users. Third, a Zipcar member's account that becomes inactive due to failure of use is charged twenty dollars per month. However, a responsible member who calls the company to cancel the account before it becomes inactive can avoid this monthly penalty. Lastly, a renter could be falsely accused of damaging a vehicle. Since there are

numerous users per day, it would be hard for the company to determine which customer did the damage. A Zipcar employee would need to check the vehicles upon return to ensure that this situation does not occur. All of these conditions should be evaluated before establishing Zipcar at SMU.

7   Bringing Zipcar to our campus would be very simple, considering that it wouldn't take up much room. If Southern Methodist University were to sign a contract with Zipcar, its parking allocation could begin with five spots on the top floor of the Binkley parking garage. The company's portable office could be located in the corner of the garage, next to all of the cars. Users could have easy access to Zipcars by using their SMU identification cards as a method of signing in, unlocking/locking their cars, as well as tracking their usage. Once SMU evaluates how many people use the program, the University will be able to determine whether or not it should expand its fleet.

8   After evaluating this proposal, I can see no reason why any university wouldn't want to experiment with such a system. If SMU were to bring Zipcar to campus, I believe that it would have a favorable impact on the students, faculty, staff, campus, and most importantly, on the environment, by providing a straightforward solution to improving energy efficiency in the world around us.

Works Cited

"Green Benefits." *Green Benefits, See Why Car Sharing Is Sustainable—Zipcar.* 2012. Web. 01 May 2012. <http://www.zipcar.com/is-it/greenbenefits>.

"Green Report Card 2011: Southern Methodist University." *The College Sustainability Report Card.* 13 Aug. 2010. Web. 30 Oct. 2011.<http://www.greenreportcard.org/report-card-2011/schools/southern-methodist-university/surveys/campus-survey#transportation>.

"Membership Requirements." *Membership Requirements—Zipcar.* 2012. Web. 30 Oct. 2011. <http://www.zipcar.com/utdallas/apply/membership-requirements>.

While discussions about ethnic and gender diversity are common in a university setting, discussions about socio-economic diversity based on social class are less so. Michaela Zook uses her own class origin as a starting point for a consideration of diversity programs at SMU and asks if these programs accomplish their goals. Can personal experience combine with research to produce new understanding? Does Zook succeed in doing so?

A Burst to Be Diverse
Michaela Zook

1   It was a crisp April day—the type unique to the Midwest when the snow begins to melt and the grass to emerge from its dormant state. The sun was bright as I toured the huge University of Illinois campus, holding the neon orange pamphlet that outlined all of the reasons why I should attend the University. My peppy tour guide, clad in a polo of the same neon orange color, walked backwards facing the tour group and asked us collectively where we were from. As we "oohed" and "ahhed" at the rich green-and-ice quad and the new athletic facility, a few people muttered the names of their hometowns. Since most of my fellow tour goers lived in the state of Illinois, I piped up and said "Winnetka" instead of my standard "Chicago" response, which I say when I doubt my inquirers are familiar with my small suburban town just north of Chicago. Following my response, a dad accompanying his child on the tour remarked from the back of the pack of visitors, "You must come from a wealthy family." His statement hung awkwardly in the air as the throng of tourists continued walking and the words finally faded when our tour guide pointed out the newly built dorms so we could avert our attention to "ooh" and "ahh" them. I did not feel offended by his comment, but I felt singled out by the stranger's implied criticism. Sure, Winnetka bears the brunt of some criticism by people who consider us snobs, and my high school supposedly inspired the movie *Mean Girls,* but I consider my family and myself very humble. I know how lucky we are to call such a safe and prosperous town home, and that man had no right to make such a public and tasteless comment.

2   This instance with the stranger demonstrates that socioeconomic status represents one type of diversity. Our society puts much effort into encouraging racial tolerance, and this country's history comprises an epic push towards gender equality. Yet socioeconomically we have decided that there are winners and losers. If the circumstances had been altered and someone had asked what ethnicity I identify with, a condescending remark about my being white would have been blatantly wrong. But a snide comment about my hometown sat awkwardly while nobody reacted to it. If this man had been better prepared to deal with all types of diversity, each person on that tour would have benefitted to

some degree by sharing the company of a tolerant individual. For this as well as other reasons, universities should prepare students to engage with all types of diversity because these universities would then produce more accepting, informed, and fulfilled young adults.

3   Many universities understand the benefits that ensue from promoting diversity, but struggle to implement such programs. Former Harvard president Derek Bok concurs with the notion that universities should prepare students to engage with diversity. In addition to encouraging tolerance for those who differ from us, Bok's findings state that encountering diversity "Not only broadens experience but also helps students improve the powers of critical thinking by challenging them to respond to different values and perspectives" (Bok 195). Bok posits some additional gains that students glean from engaging with diversity, including becoming "More civically active, more inclined to help others, and more committed to improving their communities" (Bok 195). Promoting diversity, however, is not without its problems; namely, the means by which a university encourages its students to engage with diversity can present issues. Bok demonstrates the difficulty in this task by noting that

> If courses and workshops are voluntary, they tend to "preach to the choir" by attracting mostly undergraduates who are already interested in other cultures. If college tries instead to make the courses and workshops mandatory, it runs the risk of making blacks feel uncomfortable at being singled out for special attention and white students feel unjustly suspected of bigotry and intolerance. (Bok 206)

Universities face a dilemma in promoting diversity because to open every student's mind, one group will inevitably feel socially singled out or threatened.

4   Not only would university-implemented preparation for encounters with diversity yield more well rounded students, but these students would also profit by preparing for these inevitable encounters—unless students live in a bubble. At first, this simplification may sound humorous, yet my life thus far has resembled a bubble. At my large public high school, white students make up the overwhelming majority. Now I attend Southern Methodist University, a notoriously homogenous university in terms of race and socioeconomic status. I have engaged with little diversity in my life, yet I know that after graduation, I will enter the real world where many of my peers will not have the same background as mine. I confidently consider myself a tolerant person, and I foresee myself entering the real and diverse world with relative ease. However, one cannot simply predict that he or she will be an excellent journalist before ever opening a notebook.

5   A silly example of how sheltered universities like SMU are appears in the viral YouTube video called "Sh*t Sorority Girls Say" in which a college-age male dons a blonde wig and a girl's clothing and mocks a stereotypical sorority

girl. This satirical video trivializes sorority girls and confines the scope of their lives to drinking, shopping, and boys. The final scene of this four-minute video shows the cross-dressed star drunkenly stumbling down a dorm hallway as he remarks, "Becca, there's a black guy!" The video clearly mocks a school with little racial diversity, like SMU, so when my friends and I watch it we nervously chuckle at the sad reality it portrays. We live in a sort of fantasy bubble where racism does not affect us, but as I observed on my tour of the University of Illinois, people can victimize others for all types of diversity, not just racial diversity. A little push from SMU can help us pop that bubble and increase the tolerance we have for people who do not share our background, preparing us for the real and diverse world ahead, and that is why SMU should offer more diversity programs.

6   Integration among people who do not share our same experiences or heritage cannot be forced, however, and even after that barrier has been broken down, students may still abstain from mingling with their dissimilar peers. Take the SMU dining hall, for instance. The tables appear segregated by very obvious factors such as race, yet further inspection reveals that students just like to sit with their friends. The same phenomenon occurs on a typical Friday night when tennis players hang out with tennis players and fraternity members fraternize. Bok concurs with the notion that universities can appear less racially integrated than they actually are because "Black students stand out and their tables are instantly noticed" (Bok 203). Critics of such self-segregation might reference the circulating rumors that certain fraternities on campus denied students membership because of their ethnicity or sexual orientation, but the majority of students would admit that they willingly chose whom they hung out with last Friday night.

7   Although universities cannot force integration, our society is ever integrating, as evidenced by the fact that in 2003 minorities made up only 19.9 percent of the student body at this university, and today they make up roughly 25 percent (Miller). Whether segregation is voluntary or involuntary, the diversity at play is inevitable, and universities like SMU should embrace the opportunity to produce more tolerant students.

8   But universities must not confine their diversity-promoting efforts to the student body. These efforts should also encompass the faculty and staff. Every day, an African American service worker cleans the Perkins third floor bathrooms while I brush my teeth. I do not have an issue with her presence, but I have seen some of my contemporaries close the door that the woman has propped open for easy access to her mop or complain to each other about how slowly she works. Likewise, former Stanford student bell hooks recalls "the contempt shown the brown-skinned Filipina maids who cleaned" the students' rooms (hooks 44). A disdainful attitude towards the minority service workers is apparent at both Stanford University and Southern Methodist University.

9 The lack of diversity we students have experienced may well contribute to intolerance for those whose racial identity differs from ours and lead to the contempt some students show the cleaning staff. Bok references a study, which supports the claim that students who identify with the racial majority interact mainly with one another, while minority students interact more readily with the entire ethnic mosaic of their peers. The study of 60,000 students who had enrolled in 26 selective colleges in 1976 and 1989 revealed that "88 percent of blacks claimed to know at least two white students well, while 55 percent of whites knew at least two black students well" (Bok 202). Members of the racial majority do not associate as readily with minorities, and since most SMU students belong to the white majority, the segregation can result in a condescending attitude towards minorities, including the service workers. Universities need to graduate students who can tolerate all varieties of people, including workers whose service we take for granted.

10 Study abroad programs are one way in which universities can prepare students to engage with diversity. I fully intend to study abroad at some point during my college experience. Through studying abroad, I will remove myself from the confines of Southern Methodist University's homogenous bubble. As Derek Bok points out, educating students about diversity can become unpleasant, lest one group feels attacked. However, universities can make engaging with diversity accessible and appealing to students by allowing them to gain academic credit in a foreign country. As former SMU student Huanlu Chen points out, in addition to broadening their education, "College students can experience different kinds of lifestyles and views of the world" (Chen 91). To breed more tolerant, informed, and fulfilled students, universities should prepare students to engage with all types of diversity, and studying abroad just might do the trick.

11 Last year when I finished touring the University of Illinois campus, I reflected on what little socioeconomic diversity I had experienced in my life. Southern Methodist University is not the easiest campus to begin my endeavors to learn from students who differ from me. But study abroad programs and classes on other cultures can educate students like me who yearn to know what lies outside the SMU bubble. This solution may not be perfect, but university programs in diversity can give us a taste of what waits for us in the real world.

Works Cited

Bok, Derek. *Our Underachieving Colleges*. Princeton, New Jersey: Princeton University Press, 2006. 195-206. Print.

Chen, Huanlu. "Necessity for College Students to Study Abroad." *Criteria Archive*. Eds. Lee Gibson *et al.* Dallas: SMU Department of English, 2012. *Passim*. 91. Print.

hooks, bell. "keeping close to home: class and education." *Criteria Archive.* Eds. Lee Gibson *et al.* Dallas: SMU Department of English, 2012. *Passim.* 44. Print.

Miller, Charity. "Bake Sale Blues." *Criteria Archive.* Eds. Lee Gibson *et al.* Dallas: SMU Department of English, 2012. *Passim.* 26. Print.

After reading and discussing President George W. Bush's 2002 speech to the United Nations, Trevor Anderson and his classmates were asked to "dissect the persuasive structure of [his] speech" and to analyze the way he uses the classic rhetorical appeals of logos, pathos, and ethos. Do rhetorical analyses such as Anderson's help us comprehend the motive as well as the meaning of a text? How are we better informed as a result of this analysis?

Deciding Peace
Trevor Anderson

1   The endeavor of maintaining peace on earth is similar to corking old faithful. After WWII, the United Nations was created to maintain peace between nations. However, differing opinions exist regarding the ways in which the United Nations can accomplish peace. Some people believe the U.N. is limited to enforcing mandates voted on by members of the U.N., and others believe that the U.N. is responsible for preserving peace even if it means war. The responsibilities of the U.N. were called into question when President Bush asked the council to act in Iraq beyond merely enforcing previously established mandates. Bush was unsuccessful in getting the U.N. to act outside of enforcing mandates because of a difference of opinion regarding the duties of the United Nations, but not because of the effectiveness of his argument in his speech to the U.N. Bush's speech is an effective argument in favor of U.N. action because he uses powerful emotions to provoke action, establishes his credibility early in the speech to give his argument more authority, and makes logically sound conclusions about real-world evidence to provide a logical basis for action in Iraq.

2   Through subtle word choice, images of horrible cruelty, and an ultimatum, Bush evokes the powerful emotions of fear and anger in the members of the U.N. council. He chooses specific words to evoke the fear of death in his audience; for example, in the beginning of his speech to the U.N, Bush uses words like "terrorist," "mad ambitions," and "massive scale" to instill in the delegates the fear of terrorists killing on a massive scale: "Our greatest fear is that terrorists will find a shortcut to their mad ambitions when an outlaw regime supplies them with the technologies to kill on a massive scale" (Bush 224). This statement alerts the members of the council that they should fear that their countries could be victims of a rogue regime, namely Iraq. Later, Bush combines anger with the feeling of fear through his description of the cruelties committed by the Iraqi regime on its own people when he says, "Ordinary citizens have been subjected to arbitrary arrest and imprisonment, summary execution, and torture by beating and burning, electric shock, starvation, mutilation and rape" (225). The President uses this statement to make the council angry at the Iraqi regime for the injustices against its own people. Additionally, Bush evokes fear and a

sense of urgency in the council when he cautions that if the U.N. doesn't act, it will become powerless, and the world will live in fear as a result: "Will the United Nations serve the purpose of its founding, or will it be irrelevant. . . . If we fail to act in the face of danger the people of Iraq will continue to live in brutal submission. . . . We must choose between a world of fear and a world of progress" (228- 230). Bush evokes fear, anger and a sense of urgency in the members of the council to make the council intervene in Iraq in a prompt and forceful manner. Early in his speech, Bush uses September 11th, his success in Afghanistan, and his position as leader of a powerful nation to establish credibility as an expert in terrorism and in dealing with issues in the Middle East. President Bush mentions the attack of September 11th as an emotional appeal, but also to remind the council that he knows, from first-hand experience, what killing on a massive scale is like: "We meet one year and one day after a terrorist attack brought grief to my country" (Bush 223). In the next paragraph, Bush establishes his credibility regarding the Middle East through his success in Afghanistan, "We've accomplished much in the last year—in Afghanistan and beyond" (223). This experience in Afghanistan is an effective credential because it makes Bush appear knowledgeable in dealing with the Middle East and with nations that foster terrorism. Throughout the rest of the speech, Bush uses "we" to align himself with the members of the United Nations and give himself credibility as a leader of a nation: "We have been more than patient. . . . Our common challenge. . . . If we meet our responsibilities, if we overcome this danger" (228-230). Because Bush presents himself as a credible source on the Middle East and terrorism, the delegates are more likely to believe his argument in favor of intervention in Iraq.

3   President Bush also uses inductive reasoning and syllogism to prove that Iraq is dangerous and requires immediate outside intervention. Bush uses inductive reasoning to show a high probability that Iraq has the intent to continue or to increase the production of chemical weapons. Bush says "the Iraqi regime said it had no biological weapons. . . . [Later] the regime admitted to producing tens of thousands of liters of anthrax and other deadly biological agents for use with Scud warheads, aerial bombs, and aircraft spray tanks. . . . Right now, Iraq is expanding and improving facilities that were used for the production of biological weapons" (Bush 226). In this example, Bush's logic is effective because it includes specific factual observations that suggest Iraq is dangerous because it has produced biological weapons. Later, Bush uses a syllogism supported by sound evidence to prove that Iraq is not only dangerous because of the weapons it produces, but also because Saddam Hussein is a liar who despises the U.N. Bush states that the U.N. gave Saddam an opportunity to show a commitment to peace when he says, "To suspend hostilities, to spare himself, Iraq's dictator accepted a series of commitments" (Bush 225). Bush then takes this major premise and applies it to a specific example when he states, "In 1991 Security

Council Resolution 688 demanded that the Iraqi regime cease at once the repression of its own people . . . this demand goes ignored" (Bush 225). As a result of Saddam's actions, Bush concludes that Saddam, and by extension Iraq, "has proven instead only contempt for the United Nations, and for all his pledges" (225). This syllogism further strengthens Bush's argument that Iraq is dangerous because it proves that Saddam, Iraq's leader, cannot be trusted by the world. Through deductive reasoning, Bush proves that Iraq intends to build a nuclear bomb: "Iraq has made several attempts to buy highstrength aluminum tubes used to enrich uranium for a nuclear weapon . . . Iraq's state-controlled media has reported numerous meetings between Saddam Hussein and his nuclear scientists, leaving little doubt about his continued appetite for these weapons"(227). In this statement, President Bush effectively supports his claim that Hussein intends to build weapons of mass destruction; as a result, Iraq presents an even greater threat to the world because of the nature of these weapons. Bush proves that Iraq is dangerous through sound logic supported by facts in an effort to convince the delegates of the U.N. to intervene in Iraq and prevent the death of innocent people.

4 Despite Bush's effective argument, the U.N. responded in Iraq by merely enforcing previously established mandates. Bush's argument may seem like it failed because the U.N. didn't declare war on Iraq; however, the argument set out to accomplish an unattainable goal. In the war in Iraq, as in all wars, many young men and women died; therefore, it is important to analyze our leaders' calls to war because, especially in our democracy, we, the people, have the right to determine if the cause is worth dying for. Bush helped to make a country believe in the need for a war on terror, and that is why Bush was so successful in his call to war.

Works Cited

Bush, President George W. "Remarks at the United Nations General Assembly, September 12, 2002." *Just War: A Wadsworth Casebook in Argument*. Eds. Sharon K. Walsh, Evelyn D. Asch. Boston, Massachusetts: 2004. 223-230. Print.

One way students can engage with historical events, which can sometimes seem remote, comes through a personal narrative by someone who witnessed these events. Andrew Blanchard examines one such narrative by a young Vietnamese woman who lived through the war in her country and later came to America. Does Blanchard's review show the relevance of this woman's experience to contemporary life? Can that experience bring her history closer to our own? What influence might a parent's words be on shaping a child's history?

A Doctrine of Life
Andrew Blanchard

1   In her book *When Heaven and Earth Changed Places,* Le Ly Hayslip tells the incredible story of her life and her journey from war to peace, both her own as well as her country's. She reveals the horrors she survived and the glory she has witnessed, and she puts it all in perspective by telling the story of those who are still trapped in a long-ago war. The book is filled with experiences that changed how Hayslip looks at life. Brutal images of war and barbaric actions fill the pages, and yet it is a peaceful moment in a rice paddy, alone with her father, that forever defines Hayslip's world. Here, her father tells her that she is a warrior, not of the sword, but rather of peace (31-33). This ideology becomes the lens through which she sees the world, the filter through which she judges her course of action, and the goal toward which she strives for the rest of her life—this ideology shapes her space.

2   Le Ly's father bestows his wisdom on her when she is very young, and she spends the rest of her life learning what exactly he meant. As the youngest daughter in her family, it is unorthodox for her to be placed in the role of warrior. But when she is merely nine years old, that is exactly what her father calls her to be. Because her older siblings are absent from the house, Le Ly's father chooses to pass on responsibility and duty to her by saying, "Your job is to stay alive. . . . Most of all, it is to live in peace and tend the shrine of our ancestors. Do these things well, Bay Ly, and you will be worth more than any soldier who ever took up a sword" (32-33). These words create the lens through which she views the world—sometimes in the wrong way. For many years, Le Ly thinks that to live in peace, she must first win it, and she spends many hours and days serving the Viet Cong with the noble intention of bringing peace to her people. Later, while living in the city, she believes that she will fill the void peace has left with the love and companionship of men. It is not until she is able to see past the war and latch onto the hope of a better life that she begins to truly understand what it is her father wants for her. Her father's words directly shape Le Ly's perspective on the world and reverberate through every action she takes for the rest of her life.

3   These words shape not only how Le Ly sees the world, but how she acts in it as well. Consistently throughout her narrative, Le Ly ponders what the wise warrior that her father spoke of would do, and she does her best to follow that course of action. In one such situation, Le Ly becomes a 'Black Marketer' in the hopes of being able to provide for her family. This decision goes against her childhood lessons in pleasing others. In serving the needs of Americans and by turning a profit, she becomes despised by her own people. After one guard talks to her "like [she] was *one of them*—a corrupt official, a running dog—the very people the Viet Cong had trained [her] to fight against: the ultimate traitors to [her] people," Le Ly felt "dirtier than ever before" (188-189). Despite this, she continues to follow her father's charge. Le Ly puts the needs of her family first and does everything within her power to provide for them, even to the extent of providing her own countrymen reason to despise her. The decision to become a Black Marketer and other decisions like it become truly life altering because each of them helps Le Ly to further understand the words of her father.

4   These lessons culminate in the death of her father. At that time, she is no longer "confused about where her [duties] lay" (214). His final lesson shows her that her duty is with her son "and with nurturing life, period" (214). By her father's death, she becomes thoroughly infused with a "determination to live, no matter what" (214-215). His words of encouragement are renewed in her mind and they blossom into their full meaning. His charge to be a warrior and his proclamation of peace becomes, for Le Ly, the freedom to choose a better life for her family. Up to this point, her actions have helped her to learn the true meaning of her father's words; finally, she is able to fully apply the lessons he shared so long ago to improve her world now. This shift from a doctrine of survival to a doctrine of life empowers Le Ly to leave Vietnam.

5   Even before she understands the full meaning of her father's words, Le Ly's goal is to become the woman he envisioned. Le Ly longs to fulfill this goal because she sees the ideal "warrior of peace" as right and good. Every action she takes—and every pain she endures—is for the purpose of becoming a warrior so that she might someday share her story and promote peace. In a sense, this goal gives her a cause. Having a cause does not make any painful experience more pleasant, but it does make that experience more bearable. It is a comfort to know that there is something greater—something beyond a trial to be faced: a good to prevail over the evil. Le Ly takes this comfort with her through war, torture, and even rape. Although this comfort cannot alter the awful circumstances repeatedly faced, it does shape her understanding of each experience. In a world turned upside-down, Le Ly finds her peace in the challenge her father has set before her.

6   Even the title of the narrative points towards the importance of her father's lessons. *When Heaven and Earth Changed Places* is Le Ly's personal story of

victory over of fear, oppression, and pain. From the beginning of the book, the world is portrayed as backwards, as if Heaven has changed places with Earth. This shows most clearly in the stages of Hayslip's life; as a prepubescent girl she is charged with becoming a warrior, as a young teenager she gives birth to a son and is quite literally thrown into the life of a grown-up, and as an adult woman she must return to her childhood to reconcile her past. Her perspective on the world—the eyes of a warrior, a high standard to judge her actions, and the goals she strives to achieve—allows her to see just how corrupt and inside out her world really is. Her father's lessons help her to see beyond her immediate situation to the hope his wise words set forth.

7   Throughout her book, Le Ly's understanding of what kind of a warrior she needs to be grows and changes. Initially, she imagines herself growing to be a warrior wielding a sword. As her understanding progresses, this sword develops into an olive branch. As a child she works for the Viet Cong. As a young woman she does what she can to survive—opposing all, but supporting none. And finally, as an American adult, she sees how wrong her world was and realizes that her father's intent was for her to change it. She then returns to Vietnam to set right what she had left unfinished, and in doing so, to fulfill her father's wishes. In this way, Le Ly's life progresses from a thirst for vengeance to a quest to secure peace. Hayslip ends her narrative with a parable of vengeance and forgiveness that shows vengeance to be a perpetual tumble towards hatred and death that can be cured only by forgiveness. This parable becomes an analog of the rest of the book and a direct personification of the lessons Le Ly's father taught her. But more than that, it is a reminder that what our "space" really needs, and what we deeply desire, is not found in a context of war, but in the healing power of forgiveness and reconciliation.

Work Cited

Hayslip, Le Ly with Jay Wurts. 1989. *When Heaven and Earth Changed Places.* New York: Plume. 2003. Print

Many students often have unrealistic expectations for what their lives after college will be like. Victoria Gadson's review of a novel that later became a popular film shows how these expectations can sometimes lead to tragedy. Can fictional representations such as these help students keep their expectations grounded in reality? Does Gadson's review convince her readers that they can?

Chasing a Fantasy
Victoria Gadson

1   Since its founding, the United States has been home to countless Americans who all want the same thing: prosperous and successful lives for themselves and their families. For many of them, the dream of living such a charmed life has seemed attainable through hard work and perseverance. Richard Yates's novel *Revolutionary Road* contradicts this widely accepted view of this American pursuit of happiness and presents a much grimmer view of the much sought after American dream. The dysfunctional marriage of Frank and April Wheeler, a young couple that on the surface lives a seemingly idyllic life in the suburbs of western Connecticut, serves as a backdrop for the novel's message. Yates renders a portrait of a world in which the Wheelers' deepest insecurities and unrealistic expectations of how things should be put them on a path to self-destruction. Through the life of the Wheelers, *Revolutionary Road* declares the American dream to be an unattainable fantasy of a perfect life that leads to disillusionment and tragedy for those who try to attain it.

2   In *Revolutionary Road,* the Wheelers show that the American dream is unattainable largely because people think of it as offering a perfect, ideal life. When combined with the unrealistic expectations that many people have regarding what they want their lives to be like, chasing after this popular cultural ideal can have severe consequences. The Wheelers find themselves caught up in a destructive desire for their own dream. Frank and April enter into their marriage with preconceived notions about what the model life is supposed to entail. In a discussion with Shep Campbell, a family friend, April talks about the expectations she had for her life long before she married Frank, saying, "I still had this idea that there was a whole world of marvelous golden people somewhere, as far ahead of me as the seniors at Rye when I was in the sixth grade; people who knew everything instinctively, who made their lives work out the way they wanted without even trying" (Yates 272). This is April's mentality when she marries Frank, a mentality that leads her to believe that like the golden people, she too can have an ideal life. Unfortunately, April's definition of an ideal life is one in which nothing ever goes wrong and little effort is required to maintain a flawless lifestyle, regardless of the circumstances. In essence, she strives for the American dream, reflecting the common belief that achieving it is synonymous

with living a perfect life. Like so many others, April finds out that this type of thinking can take one's longing for a prosperous, happy life and twist it into an impractical standard of living that makes it difficult for people to cope with anything less than perfection.

3   Driven by their desire for the American dream, the Wheelers' overwhelming need for perfection causes their life, starting with their marriage, to unravel. In the beginning of the novel, it becomes clear that their attempts to maintain the illusion that their life together is as flawless as they had hoped it would be from the start are not working when Frank's expectations for the opening night of April's play, *The Petrified Forest,* are countered by reality. As he makes his way through the crowd after watching the performance, he realizes that:

> [N]owhere in these plans had he foreseen the weight and shock of reality; nothing had warned him that he might be overwhelmed by the swaying, shining vision of a girl he hadn't seen in years, a girl whose every glance and gesture could make his throat fill up with longing, and that then before his very eyes she would dissolve and change into the graceless, suffering creature whose existence he tried every day of his life to deny but whom he knew as well and as painfully as he knew himself. (13)

While watching the play, Frank briefly sees in April the graceful young woman she was when he married her, but as the play progresses and her acting skills worsen, the vision is shattered, and he sees her as the woman she has become: a woman whose existence he barely tolerates because it forces him to accept that their life is not perfect. What Frank and April do not realize is that they have achieved the "true" American dream in the sense that while they are living a relatively prosperous life in the suburbs with two children and a stable income, their inability to see that the dream they are chasing is just a fantasy makes them intolerant of anything less than perfection. This intolerance causes them both to ignore many of the problems in their marriage and to pretend that everything is fine. As a result, they are often left with unresolved issues that continuously re-emerge in the form of explosive arguments and destructive behaviors that contribute significantly to the deterioration of their already failing marriage.

4   In addition to the unrealistic expectations that people often have, insecurities play a large part in causing the downfall of those who actively pursue the perfect American dream and refuse to accept the natural imperfections of life. After a disastrous visit from the Givings, Frank argues with April about her sanity and her claims that she does not love him. As their argument intensifies, Frank loses his temper and shouts, "What the hell are you living in my *house* for, if you hate me so much? *Huh?* Will you answer me that? What the hell are you carrying my *child* for?" (307). His harsh words are a result of his insecurities about being a man. He sees the ideal man as having it all: a good job, a happy family, and the love and affection of his wife. April's behavior towards him and

the instability of their marriage contradict that idea, leading him to feel insecure. Frank's definition of a man corresponds to the ideal of perfection in his and April's definition of the American dream. As such, when Frank is confronted with his deepest insecurity, his manhood, he is forced to recognize once again that his life is not perfect.

5   It is the Wheelers' unrealistic expectations for their life and Frank's insecurities about his manhood that intensify their desire for perfection and cause them to continue to chase after a fantasy version of the American dream that they refuse to recognize as unattainable, because the acknowledgement of its falsity would shatter the illusions that they have created in their minds about their life. Eventually, their denial of reality proves fatal, as Frank fails to realize that something is wrong when April is uncharacteristically nice to him on the morning of the day that she self-aborts their child and causes her own death. Had Frank accepted their marriage as it was, he would have realized that her niceness that morning was a result of her not wanting him to suspect that she had changed her mind about keeping the baby. Frank is so caught up in the idea of having the perfect life that he interprets her behavior as a sign that their marriage is improving. When he is confronted with April's uncharacteristically nice behavior, he thinks, "Could it be that they'd fought themselves out at last? Maybe this was what happened when there was really and truly nothing more to say, either in acrimony or forgiveness. Life did, after all, have to go on" (312). Here, he ignores his initial instincts that something is wrong and decides that they have exhausted their ability to fight, thinking that things can only get better regardless of what happened in the past between them. The consequences of this delusional way of thinking illustrate that the American dream is an unattainable and potentially dangerous fantasy because it is characterized by perfection in the minds of so many Americans.

6   The American dream often leads to the ruination of those who seek it largely because it has become distorted in the minds of so many people who overestimate its worth and idealize it to the point that it becomes an unattainable fantasy. The pursuit of this impossible dream takes its pursuers down a road that often ends in great sorrow. While there are many explanations as to why the American dream can become distorted in the minds of those who try to obtain it, Frank and April Wheeler illustrate that people have a fundamental need for stability in their lives, a need that causes many of them to set unrealistic goals. As it was with the Wheelers, this basic human need can easily turn into an unhealthy desire for perfection. It is natural for people to want to escape the imperfections of their lives, but when this desire begins to consume them to the point that nothing else matters but escaping reality and attempting to achieve a false dream, disillusionment and adversity will inevitably follow.

Works Cited

Yates, Richard. *Revolutionary Road*. 3rd ed. New York: Vintage Books, 2008. Print.

Ashley Romo's essay synthesizes aspects of the American Dream from James Truslow Adams's description in The Epic of America *and the behavior of the dysfunctional Walls family from* The Glass Castle *to determine how closely this family corresponds to Adams's ideal. Does her synthesis reveal a connection between these two texts? Can autobiography help to explain concepts in the way Romo proposes?*

Beautiful Struggles
Ashley Romo

1   The American Dream, interpreted by James Truslow Adams in *The Epic of America,* consists of two elements: moving forward while remaining grounded. That is to say, for people to achieve the American Dream, they must pursue a hot-blooded, passionate "vision of something nobler" while retaining a rooted foundation in agricultural, communal, and spiritual values (Adams 403). Roaming aimlessly through the country, the Walls family from *The Glass Castle* does not express the American go-getter attitude necessary to achieve their goal of a better life. However, from the various stages of poverty they experience on their journey, the family learns how to remain connected by the values of a "frontier mindset," community, and individuality. This family becomes like the Joshua tree they find in the Mojave Desert, appearing "ready to topple" yet with its roots firmly in place and made more beautiful by the struggles through which it perseveres (38). In this way, although the Walls family never completes the goal of building the Glass Castle, they do succeed in constructing a more firmly established family.

2   As Jeannette Walls reveals at the start of *The Glass Castle,* her family appears happy enough in their nomadic lifestyle, but this lifestyle has conditioned them to adopt a cycle of perpetual poverty that never prompts the Walls parents to act on their goals. The family routine begins every time they drive into a new town: they initially plan to find temporary housing and employment until they can build their permanent home of the Glass Castle. "All we had to do," Rex assures his daughter, is to "find gold . . . [and we'd] start work on our Glass Castle" (Walls 25). However, Rex begins to bring home suspicious amounts of money or supplies, resulting in the family's inevitable "checking out Rex-Walls style" from the town and moving to another one. This lifestyle gives no indication that Rex and Rose Mary Walls plan to work progressively toward their dreams of gaining wealth or building their ideal home, the Glass Castle. Even though the mother has a teaching degree that could bring a steady income into their home, Jeannette laments, "Mom hated teaching" (73). Rather, the family continually relies on the one-hit bonuses that Rex earns. The parents then quickly squander their small income on impractical luxuries such as Hershey bars and beer without regard for a budget. Even when thirteen-year-old Jeannette takes

charge of their household in Welch, she cannot stay committed to the budget she plans because her father uses her affection for him to coerce her into giving him extra cash for his alcoholic necessities (209). Thus, the Walls family shows no ability to rise above "the poverty, ignorance, lack of ambition, [and] shiftlessness of character [. . .] which kept so many thousands in the huts where they were born" (Adams 411). The family, in other words, wants to achieve success but "lack[s] the gumption to get the work done" (Walls 158).

3   When the Walls children, and later their parents, give up their isolated life in Welch for a new home in New York, they gain newfound confidence through the community they had previously neglected on the road. The Walls children gain support from each other, and their parents find strength by uniting with other squatters like themselves. Jeannette, Lori, and Brian began combining their efforts as a team toward their collective goal of a fresh city life even before arriving there. The three of them work all hours of the day earning money to add to their New York fund until they arrive, one by one. The trio even brings Maureen out of the dysfunctional Walls household to New York, where all the kids have a family dinner together and laugh "about the craziness" of Welch (251). Once Rex and Rose Mary Walls finally follow their children to the big city, they transition over time from being homeless to becoming squatters in an abandoned building. Jeannette comments that their new squat "looked pretty much like the house on Little Hobart Street." However, Mom and Dad do not behave as they did in Welch; much of their excitement about their new home is due to their bonding with a community of unruly people battling authority just like they do. Even after her husband's death, Rose Mary Walls remains grounded with her fellow squatters, even becoming part of a "board of the squatters," where she finds fulfillment and joy without her family living with her (288). As Jeannette reflects, "After all those years of roaming, they'd found home" (267).

4   Despite the vicious cycle of drifting that mars her childhood, Jeannette carries her childhood wonder and appreciation for the American countryside into her adult years, providing her a way of devaluing material goods. Growing up largely in the desert, Jeannette develops a deep admiration of the dry, open landscape. As the family rests outside one night, Jeannette tells Lori "how lucky [they] are to be sleeping out under the sky like Indians" (Walls 18). The following Christmas, the children are thrilled with the everlasting stars their father gives them, making fun of other kids that receive dinky plastic toys instead (41). As an adult, Jeannette continues to have a heart for the countryside, saving her from a complete conversion to the industrial mindset she has been shielded from as a child. At the close of her story, she trades her lavish apartment in New York for a country home with her new husband. She continues to work in the city, but also balances her industrial line of work with a self-sufficient lifestyle at home: gardening, repairing ceiling beams, and rejecting luxurious furniture for flea market couches purposefully in bad taste (287). Although Jeannette's older

sister and younger brother do not choose a country home as adults, they still carry their frontier values with them in the form of self-sustenance.

5   Away from the "home" in which they grew up, Jeannette, Lori, and Brian's self-sustenance flourishes due to their strong sense of individualism; this saving virtue helps the Walls children do what their parents could not: gain independence in their adult lives, achieve their dreams, and break free from their previous cycle. As Adams describes in *The Epic of America*, "The old life 'roaming through the frontier' was lonely and hard, but it bred a strong individualism" (409). An important lesson Jeannette learns in her "old life" is, "If you don't want to sink, you better figure out how to swim" (66). She applies this advice by strengthening her work ethic in school and later in her workplace at *The Phoenix*, working ninety-hour weeks and staying up until four in the morning. Her diligent nature earns her an apartment on Park Avenue and a sought-after job writing a weekly column, about which even her Mom approvingly comments, "You never had much going for you except that you always worked hard" (270). Additionally, Brian and Lori develop their own individual gifts through the self-dependent lifestyle in which they grow up. In her school years, Lori utilizes her creative talent to earn money to move to New York by selling posters she had made; as an adult, she incorporates her inventiveness into her new profession as a freelance artist in New York. Brave little Brian always protects his sisters growing up, and later uses his bravery to advance in the criminal justice field. By including the successful futures of her two closest siblings in her memoir, Jeannette emphasizes the significance of using talents to overcome struggles. Though their rugged childhoods tried the gifts they were born with, these three Walls children succeed in the end by "developing their greatness" (Adams 415).

6   The story of the Walls family, blemished and beaten though it is, stands as a symbol of hope to those with broken pasts themselves. People, carrying burdens of their previous troubles, often make mistakes that hurt others and themselves. Because of past restrictions on freedom, they may abandon all responsibility to the family they need the most, as Rose Mary does. Others may turn to addictive substances for happiness, like Rex, to glaze over the void of financial failure. Still more individuals may be born into impoverished lives that jeopardize their dreams of success. Those people, like the Joshua trees in Walls's memoir, may be tested by environments that test their foundation and values. However, the few people who use their turbulent circumstances to solidify their characters can withstand the situations that threaten to knock them down.

Works Cited

Adams, James Truslow. *The Epic of America*. Boston: Little, Brown, 1931.
    401-417. Print.
Walls, Jeannette. *The Glass Castle*. New York: Scribner, 2005. Print.

Will McNamara finds parallels in the evolution of a familiar mythological figure to the evolution of women's roles in modern society and offers a prediction about this evolution's next phase. Does he present these parallels convincingly? Does his prediction seem likely?

Chasing Guinevere: The Feminist Movement's Effect on the Transformation of Guinevere

Will McNamara

1   In the many versions of Arthurian legend, Guinevere is the creation and inheritor of each author's cultural background. As women change, so does Guinevere. Beginning as a delicate, silent trophy passed from king to king in *The History of Britain* and ending as a fierce, beautiful, and outspoken warrior in the film *King Arthur,* Guinevere's transformations parallel the feminist movement in Europe and, later, in the United States. The character of Guinevere acts as a glass through which we can perceive the degree of censorship of feminine qualities and the sheer weight of male oppression on the shoulders of women during each author's lifetime. Ultimately Guinevere's transformation tells a tale of women breaking the mold of societal customs and snatching the reigns of destiny away from those who would steer their lives for them.

2   Geoffrey of Monmouth's *The History of the Kings of Britain* portrays Guinevere as an oppressed and enfeebled noblewoman. After being abducted by Mordred and subsequently raped, she is considered to be Mordred's Queen (Wilhelm 61). Unlike in *Morte d'Arthur,* where Guinevere actively plans her adultery and deceives Arthur, Monmouth's Guinevere is thrown about like a rag-doll and passed from man to man as a spoil of war. During this time, women were expected to take care of the home and produce male heirs and nothing else. Women were greatly suppressed and had few or no rights. Marriages of noblewomen were not for love, but rather for the purpose of diplomacy and creating alliances between kingdoms. Monmouth, who lived in the 12th century, would have witnessed the silencing of women by the tyrannical rule of the Catholic Church. In Guinevere's instance, the Church would have blamed Guinevere for filling Mordred's head with lustful thoughts and thus the entire abduction and subsequent rape would have been almost entirely her fault. Vivian Hobbs describes the horrible circumstances the doctrine of the Catholic Church placed on such women in her essay "Guinevere: Unchristian, Invisible, Unvictorian." Hobbs explains:

> Since woman was blamed and punished for filling man's mind with lustful appetites that caused him to deviate from . . . moral and divine law, canon

law [decreed] woman could not enter church [showing] her hair [because it] was her glory and . . . attracted male attention. (165)

Women were considered direct descendants of Eve, and thus were unfairly and universally treated like temptresses. If they did not conform to the moral standards this male-dominated society imposed on all women, they were punished and forced into submission through imprisonment and even torture. Events during the course of Monmouth's life shaped his portrayal of Guinevere; thus, Guinevere's demeanor and actions were a direct reflection of the way women were forced to act during the 12th century. It is in Guinevere's subsequent transformations that we can view the advancement of women towards equality and rebellion against this oppression.

4   In centuries following the 12th, Guinevere became more and more mutinous and devious in her actions as women began to strain against the mold that had been forced upon them. Authors no longer told the tale of her seducing an enemy, but rather the King's best knight—Lancelot. In comparison to Geoffrey of Monmouth's account of a submissive Guinevere, Sir Thomas Malory's *Morte d'Arthur*, written in the late 15th century, portrays Guinevere as an active agent of corruption and seduction. Guinevere initiates the adulterous relationship with Lancelot and even goes so far as to convince him to kill Sir Mellyagaunce: "So Sir Lancelot looked upon the queen, if he might espy by any sign or countenance what she would have done. And anon the queen wagged her head upon Sir Lancelot, as who saith, 'Slay him!'"(Malory 68). *Morte d'Arthur* makes clear that Guinevere is much more rebellious and cunning than her previous incarnation. Yet again, events in the author's lifetime helped to shape his portrait of Guinevere. Though they were still heavily oppressed and overly censored, Malory witnessed women gain the right to own land and wealth, which brought them one step closer to equality with men. Thus, Malory inadvertently uses Guinevere as a mirror to reflect the contemporary conditions of women and their growing frustration with suppression.

5   As women slowly gained more rights and began to rebel against the tyrannical rule of men, portrayals of Guinevere became more insurgent and cunning. As the Protestant Reformation, the Enlightenment, and the woman's suffrage movement further increased the rights of women and inched them ever closer to equality and to breaking the unrealistic and oppressive mold forced upon them, so did Guinevere transform and become extremely cunning and deep in her reflections towards the chains of society that bound her. In 1856 Alfred, Lord Tennyson wrote *Idylls of the King,* a retelling of Arthurian legend that portrays Guinevere as a societal outcast—one who rejected the mold men, especially King Arthur, expected her to fit. Bell hooks, in her essay "The Significance of the Feminist Movement," notes that the need to struggle against oppression, in Guinevere's case, masculine oppression, is a vital stage in any battle for liberation. Hooks explains, "An important stage in the development

of political consciousness is reached when individuals recognize the need to struggle against all forms of oppression. Fighting sexist oppression is of grave political significance—it is not for women only" (831).Guinevere's adultery is more of a message to Arthur, and to all men, that women will no longer be silent or censored; rather, they will grab authority and equality of rule any way they can. Stephen Ahern views Guinevere as a character who, when denied control, reaches over and grabs the metaphorical steering wheel and yanks it. Her actions send Camelot careening into a ditch of destruction, but all the while sending the powerful message that there is nothing but death without women: equality between sexes is an absolute necessity. According to Ahern:

> Guinevere . . . chooses . . . to rebel against the constraints of her social position by affirming her right to live . . . as she desires. Her freedom of choice is limited by [her] world, but she . . . [asserts] her agency in the one arena in which she . . . can exert control—the arena of love. (97)

It is evident through Tennyson's portrayal of Guinevere that women are breaking out of and rejecting the mold, and thus the destiny a masculine society has created for them. In *Idylls of the King,* Guinevere becomes aware of her position in her society and rejects it outright. In comparison to the Guinevere of earlier Arthurian legends, Tennyson's Guinevere has a purpose for her adultery beyond simple lust or rebellion. The Guinevere of *Idylls of the King* transcends lust with her act of adultery that is instead a cry for revolt, and a harbinger of feminine revolution.

6   In the 21st Century, just as women have broken free from their societal mold and taken hold of their destinies, so has the depiction of Guinevere changed dramatically to represent the female gender newly freed from oppression. In the 2004 film *King Arthur,* Guinevere appears as a female warrior who wears hardly any clothing and exudes sex and danger with her every movement. When compared to Monmouth's feeble Guinevere, who was completely enchained by the bonds of societal expectations and standards, our modern day Guinevere, bound by nothing and almost as strong as Arthur himself, is free of the mold that tried to control all her previous literary incarnations. Remembering that Guinevere is a mirror for the feminist movement in society, we realize that women have achieved equality with men and firmly grasp the steering wheel that Tennyson's Guinevere desired to control so badly. As *King Arthur* shows, women may even be in control. Hanna Rosin assures us, in her article "The End of Men," that in the near future, women who are beginning to dominate the American workforce will make men completely obsolete. Rosin explains:

> At the same time, a new kind of alpha female has appeared, stirring up anxiety and, occasionally, fear. In fact, the more women dominate, the more they behave, fittingly, like the dominant sex. Rates of violence committed by middle-aged women have skyrocketed since the 1980s, and no one knows why. (2)

Through the use of the only weapon Guinevere had, sex, she brought about change that pulled her from the depths of oppression and into a dominant position above those who enslaved her in the first place: men. In a similar way, women in Europe and North America fought for control of their own destiny, and ultimately won that destiny, potentially ushering in a new era of female dominance and male submission.

7   Guinevere, a pillar in Arthurian legend, personifies the feminist movement throughout history. She grows and struggles against the bonds of male oppression until, finally, she breaks free and joins the ranks of King Arthur and his knights—finally seizing control of her own life and attaining true freedom. In just under a millennium, women have moved from an extremely oppressed and socially limited status to one poised to be dominant in the world. The modern day Guinevere can teach us many things about our culture as she has transformed in perfect parallel with the female gender. Although women have been granted all the rights that men currently have, they are still mentally held in bondage by the expectations and standards of social media. Guinevere, in the film *King Arthur,* seems a victim of the same problem as women today—she appears scantily clad, flaunting her extremely skinny and, as it turns out, CGI-enhanced body. This mental prison, however, traps men as well. For the first time in history, it seems, men are under the same negative social restraints as women, as all but one of the knights in the movie is also extremely fit. As Guinevere finally reaches equality with King Arthur in modern day retellings of Arthurian legend, the only question left to be answered is whether King Arthur himself will begin a slow decline into the pit of cultural bondage—the same pit that his queen so recently escaped.

Works Cited

Ahern, Stephen. "Listening to Guinevere: Female Agency and the Politics of Chivalry in Tennyson's 'Idylls'."*Studies in Philology* 101.1 (2004): 88-112. Web. 20 November 2011.

Hobbs, Vivian L., "Guinevere: Unchristian, Invisible, Unvictorian." *The Negro Educational Review* 55.4 (2004). Web. 20 November 2011.

hooks, bell. "The Significance of the Feminist Movement." *Feminist Theory: From Margin to Center.* Cambridge: South End Press, 1984. 821-831. Print.

Malory, Sir Thomas. *Le Morte D'Arthur.* Ed. Janet Cowen. 2 vols. New York: Penguin Books, 2006. Print.

Rosin, Hanna. "The End of Men." *The Atlantic.* August 2010. Web. 20 November 2011.

Wilhelm, James J. *The Romance of Arthur: An Anthology of Medieval Texts in Translation.* Psychology Press, 1 Feb. 1994. Web. 20 November 2011.

Should universities offer students courses in moral and ethical development? Alex Menzel believes they should and uses detailed research into recent history to bolster his claim. Is this research convincing? Can such research offer guidelines for future behavior?

Ethics in All Aspects of Life
Alex Menzel

1   I am the first to admit that I sometimes acted unethically and cheated in my classes in high school. Cheating usually starts at an early age; "9 out of 10 middle schoolers admit to copying," and I was one of them ("75 to 98"). Through my deceitful methods, I was able to successfully keep my nose clean until my junior year when I was caught cheating on a Chemistry exam. While my incident was not documented on my transcript due to alternative punishment, I felt horrible because I had let my family, teachers, and friends down. Before my meeting with the vice principal, I apologized to my Chemistry teacher and promised him that I would work to regain his trust and not let him down again. The final examination was less than a month away, so I studied extremely hard, learned all the material from the entire year, and earned the highest grade out of all of his classes on that final. Before entering college, I reexamined my failures in high school and looked for ways in which to become a better man. To achieve my goals of becoming successful, I realized that in life things are either good or evil. All good is difficult, and all evil is easy. Losing, cheating, and mediocrity are easy. Since I have loftier ambitions than these, I determined from that point forward I would no longer act dishonestly. But because all cheating students do not arrive at my same realization on their immoral behavior, and since "75 to 98 percent of college students . . . admit to cheating," then moral and ethical development should be part of the university education for all students ("75 to 98").
2   Former Harvard president Derek Bok addresses the issues and possible solutions to fixing students' morals in "Building Character," the sixth chapter in his book, *Our Underachieving Colleges*. According to Bok, most Americans base their morals on the principle of moral freedom, a principle under which people develop their own standards for their behavior (Bok 150). When students look at the actions of others, they see moral corruption is rampant. Many students who are cheating, meanwhile, view their actions as justified. For instance, an honors student justified his honors class cheating when he said, "We were good, moral students; we weren't like unethical people or anything" ("75 to 98"). Despite all of the corruption and scandal negatively influencing students, professors should not detail what their students should believe. Rather, teachers should put their pupils in touch with other "human minds that your human mind needs to include" (Ciardi 17). In other words, students need to be exposed to philosophical

thinkers that can help shape their morals more positively and overcome some of the negative influences that surround them. Most cheating starts at an early age, so universities not only must develop the students' ethics, but they also must "abandon easy dogmatisms and rethink their previous ethical positions" (Bok 151). Many undergraduates find college to be an opportunity to "discover themselves"; for that reason, universities should seize this opportunity to carefully mold students' minds and teach moral and ethical development (Karabell 223-224). Although universities cannot force proper morals into students' minds, universities can require students to take classes that will enhance their understanding of the good, which in turn, will make students more likely to do good.

3   Sports have always played a significant part in American culture. Even from an early age, children learn to love sports and often idolize many professional sports players, teams, and universities. Typically, sports positively influence children because they teach them many life lessons and generally focus on individual accomplishments. But, sports are also filled with unethical and immoral behavior. Students at SMU know all too well about corruption in university athletics. During the 1970s, the Southwest Conference was highly competitive and full of money that was ready to be spent on recruits. After SMU alumni grew tired of being shown up by their rivals, the university took cheating to a whole new level, which tarnished "the integrity of the whole university" (The Honor Code). The university started by hiring the defensive coordinator from the recent Super Bowl champions, the Dallas Cowboys. SMU's athletic department also set up a slush fund from notable alumni that allowed the coaches to purchase the best recruits money could buy. But, the corruption was not just at the coaching level. The main conspirators in the scandal included the governor of Texas, Bill Clements; the SMU President, L. Donald Shields; the athletic director, Bob Hitch; and the head coach, Bobby Collins. After the investigation of SMU, the NCAA handed out the harshest penalty they have ever issued: the so-called "death penalty." SMU football was obliterated by the cancellation of its 1987 season.

4   Just like Division I athletic programs, today's students are under the same types of pressure from teachers and family to earn high grades that will allow them to obtain a high-paying job after graduation (Patterson 75). But, these students are losing their moral sense by adapting to the old SMU football way of thinking and doing whatever it takes to be successful. According to *The New York Times* reporter, Joe Nocera, "If a university—and its community—can't treat players and coaches the same way everyone else is treated, then what is it really teaching? Surely the lessons it is imparting are the wrong ones" (Nocera). Universities must act ethically in every aspect of their business and maintain high standards to set a positive example for students. But instead of prescribing morals for students to abide by, teachers must guide their students through challenging, thought-provoking discussions of real world events. Students'

retention of material greatly improves when they can relate to the material that they are learning. When students are provoked to think critically about ethical dilemmas repeatedly in class, they become better suited to identify unethical behavior more easily and expediently. Teachers, meanwhile, can best approach the subjects of moral dilemmas by having students view issues from different sides to build "empathy—a feeling of genuine concern for the needs and feelings and sufferings of others" (Bok 159). Possessing the skills to solve moral issues outside the classroom, where their application is vital, allows individuals to solve the moral dilemmas quicker, before they compound (Patterson 77).

5   Students at the university level must also learn to behave ethically before graduating college for their businesses to achieve long-term growth. In business, people typically believe acting ethically is more expensive; therefore, they also believe that companies are only cost-efficient when they are acting immorally. However, the recent crisis on Wall Street has disproven this misconception. A business research organization, The Ethisphere Institute, recognizes companies that demonstrate real and sustained ethical leadership within their industries, putting into real business practice Ethisphere Institute's credo of "Good. Smart. Business. Profit" ("2011 World's"). After the debacle on Wall Street, Vivek Wadhwa from *Bloomberg Businessweek* decided to compare the return on investment between Ethisphere's World's Most Ethical companies (WME) against the S&P 500, an index comprised of 500 of the most commonly traded stocks in America that is considered to be the benchmark of the overall U.S. stock market (Wadhwa). The study found that if, five years ago, a person had invested in a portfolio of WMEs, that portfolio.

6   *Bloomberg Businessweek* writer Vivek Wadhwa's analysis focuses specifically on Wall Street banks CEOs' inability to change their narrow-minded business strategies and, more generally, on American business ethics. Wadhwa notes the three main reasons companies on Wall Street failed during the 2008 financial crisis: "the firms lacked higher purpose, lacked a clear strategy, and mismanaged their risks" (Wadhwa). Many of these failing companies' goals were primarily to make money for themselves and for their shareholders. Many large Wall Street investment banks, such as Bank of America and Citigroup, were asking their employees to sell unethical mortgages to customers who were unable to afford them. The investment banks' moral sense was overpowered by an irrational focus on short-term profits and whatever scheme would augment those profits. Other investment banks, like Charles Schwab & Co. and US Bancorp, have avoided the fallout by maintaining ethical business cultures in which customer service, honesty, and transparency are the main focuses. As a result, Charles Schwab & Co. and US Bancorp are now recognized as among the World's Most Ethical Companies (Wadhwa).

7   Ethical business success does not only apply to banks on Wall Street. Other notable WMEs include Starbucks, The Timberland Company, Whole

Foods Market, and Costco (Daniel). Some Wall Street analysts have ridiculed companies such as Costco for paying high wages to lower-level employees and keeping them around for a long time. The norm in the grocery industry is to pay easily replaceable employees low wages to minimize input costs. But Costco CEO Jim Sinegal does not act according to this norm. Instead, he maintains that "keeping good employees is strategic for the long-term success and growth of Costco" (Wadhwa). As a result, Costco maintains quality products that consumers want to buy because of happy, alert employees who feed up-to-date information from the ground level up the chain of command to headquarters. Costco's moral culture and ethical habits flow downward from Sinegal to his employees and, ultimately, to the customers. Other leaders, CEOs, presidents, and similar important figures must exhibit high ethical and moral standards so that these traits will carry through to the rest of their followers. The World's Most Ethical companies have soared through tough economic times and show a clear understanding of the financial implication of their actions: to be ethical means to be profitable. Universities could learn a great deal from such companies as these.

8   In life, talent, luck, and ability will help students achieve temporary success, but they need character to remain on top. After reflecting on my academic dishonesty during high school, I finally understood that each instance of cheating, regardless of whether or not I was caught, exhibited poor character and that an individual's character is defined by the actions he performs when no one is watching. Students must learn to delay instant gratification to achieve long-term success in every aspect of life. Coming to the realization that the repetition of ethical habits builds a solid virtuous base will prove to be extremely beneficial for my future. However, distractions can often lead people astray from their conscience. Universities should engrain students with strong morals and ethics by initiating frequent, repeated, thought-provoking discussions of real world problems. These discussions will challenge them to maintain strong character both in and out of the classroom.

Works Cited

"75 to 98 Percent of College Students Have Cheated." *Education-portal.com.* 29 June 2011. Web. 28 February 2012.

"2011 World's Most Ethical Companies." *Ethisphere: Good. Smart. Business. Profit.* January 2012. Web. 28 February 2012.

Bok, Derek C. *Our Underachieving Colleges: A Candid Look at How Much Students Learn and Why They Should Be Learning More.* Princeton, NJ: Princeton UP, 2006. 146-171. Print.

Ciardi, John. "Another School Year-What For?" *Criteria 2011-2012: A Journal of First-Year Writing.* Eds. Mary K. Jackman and Lee Gibson. Dallas: 2011. 17-19. Print.

Daniel, Susanna. "Ethical Companies Shown to Be More Profitable Over Time." *Bakersieldnow.com.* 30 November 2006. Web. 28 February 2012.

"The Honor Code." *Southern Methodist University.* 27 June 2011. Web. 28 February 2012.

Karabell, Zachary. "Society and Higher Education." *What's College For?: The Struggle to Define American Higher Education.* New York: Basic, 1998. 220-226. Print.

Nocera, Joe. "It's Not Just Penn State." *The New York Times.* 2 December 2011. Web. 28 February 2012.

Patterson, Trenton. "Let 1987 Be a Reminder." *Criteria 2011-2012: A Journal of First-Year Writing.* Eds. Mary K. Jackman and Lee Gibson. Dallas: 2011. 75-79. Print.

Wadhwa, Vivek. "Why Be an Ethical Company? They're Stronger and Last Longer." *Bloomberg.com. Bloomberg Businessweek.* 17 August 2009. Web. 28 February 2012.

Alex Mirabile's 1302 class studied American cultural myths shaped by religious, social, ethnic, and economic influences. Mirabile's research essay examines clothing carrying "Made in the USA" labels and alerts students to the manner in which these garments are produced. What is the true cost of this clothing? Does Mirabile convincingly show that this cost matters?

Sweatshops: A Look at America's Clothing Industry
Alex Mirabile

1   Sewing machines begin to buzz as the clock strikes eight. Women sit obediently behind their machines as they sew garment after garment. By lunchtime, the workers are starving, but in this factory they have no time to eat. The floors are dirty and windows are sealed shut. In a factory like this, filled with undocumented workers located somewhere in Queens, the risk of being caught lingers in the back of everyone's mind. As the clock ticks its way to five o'clock, the women round up their work for the day. Today is a special day; it's payday. On their way out, women collect their checks, only to be disappointed at their net earnings. Two hundred dollars is all these women have received for the week. But it's better than nothing and will keep them from starving. As the women exit the sweatshop, they know they will have to return tomorrow to the same seat in front of their sewing machine. *This* is America's clothing industry. Beautiful storefronts decorated with lavish clothing are nowhere near the reality. The real sources of clothing industry lie in the sweatshops where people slave away each day for hours with little to no pay.

2   That sweatshops exist in the United States comes as a surprise to most Americans. It is hard for people to realize that the sweatshop industry is operating in our own backyard. Americans don't recognize that these clothing factories operate because when thinking of a sweatshop, they think of impoverished countries overseas. Sweatshops there are not so surprising to Americans, but consumers do not realize that many of the clothes we trust as made in America are unethically produced in sweatshops. Surprisingly enough, "There are an estimated five thousand illegal, unregistered sweatshops in Los Angeles alone that label their products "Made in the USA" (Rogers 3). If more people were aware of this fact, perhaps people would stop supporting the companies using sweatshop labor. Unfortunately, companies do a good job at hiding their factories and tricking consumers into thinking they are being responsible buyers.

3   One of the biggest issues with sweatshops today, however, is not spreading awareness, but punishing the operators of these vile places. According to Tara Radin and Martin Calkins, "today's sweatshops violate our notions of justice, yet they continue to flourish. This is so because we have not yet settled on criteria that would allow us to condemn and do away with them and because the poor

working conditions . . . [are] preferable to . . . no job at all" (261). People may acknowledge the wrongs of sweatshops, but no significant steps have been taken against them. In fact, simply by dressing in our favorite brand, we are supporting these sweatshops. While conditions in sweatshops have improved little over the years, they still remain dangerous and unethical. Sweatshops continue to exist because companies are constantly demanding a cheaper way to manufacture their products. Americans need to recognize that sweatshops are undeniably occurring in our own backyard. The mistaken beliefs behind the origins of our clothing represent a frightening cover up of the unethical practices that exist in America today.

4   In the 19th century, seamstresses and dressmakers were common occupations. Their work was similar to today's in that "Dressmakers were responsible for producing an entire garment and could earn a decent wage. Seamstresses, however, were poorly compensated for work that was both physically demanding and unpredictable" (Liebhold and Rubenstein). These conditions were the initial steps toward the development of sweatshops. By the 1880s, the garment industry had become popular and production increased. Immigrants to America began to set up shop in their small apartments and created an environment with low wages and long hours. Although the pay was minute, it provided these workers with something; and similar to the argument today, something is better than nothing.

5   At that time, some people were able to work their way up from these workshops. These early sweatshops "provided many new arrivals a transition into American society and a more prosperous future for themselves and their families" (Liebhold and Rubenstein). As the 1960s rolled around, so did the growth of sweatshops in America. The growing economy, the greater demand for fashion, and the larger number of immigrants were all major factors that led to this resurgence. Sweatshops were no longer just for producing clothes; they now manufactured a variety of products, from household items to children's toys.

6   Many assumptions about sweatshops contribute to the hardships workers face behind factory doors each day. While most people recognize that these workshops are incredibly unethical, others do not think twice about the repercussions. At first glance, sweatshops may not seem as harmful as they are. Many people assume that sweatshops are merely factories producing clothing for big name labels around the world. It is hard for people to recognize the reality. At a time when the fashion industry is booming more than ever, the reality that these sweatshops are "promulgat[ing] mental and/ or physical abuse and contradict[ing] our considered notions of basic morality and strategic business purposes" (Radinand Calkins 261) disappears. Getting caught up in the latest trends and styles makes it hard to pay attention to those suffering behind the factory doors. The women and children forced into these horrible labor situations do not exist to those consumers mesmerized by fashion. Whether it is through guilt or ignorance, consumers seem to choose to avoid the truth. These consumers

are usually the people who assume factories are safe and fair. When many major brands are using sweatshops to produce their clothing, however, consumers are unable to see the faults that the popular companies hide. Americans assume that well- respected brands are trustworthy since they are successful and profitable companies; this mistaken trust is where the myth behind the entire clothing industry rests.

7   Sweatshops overseas are tempting to American companies. These factories boost productivity but also degrade the quality of clothing manufacturing in a multitude of ways. In one way, they help large companies produce their clothing more cheaply, creating an ever-growing production rate. According to Peter de Simone, co-author of "The Sweatshop Quandary," "Competitive U.S. manufacturers, enticed by cheap labor, free trade agreements and lower transportation costs, are moving more and more production overseas" (qtd. in Braunstein). Companies are able to rake in more profit because they pay almost nothing to manufacturer their clothing. In the long run, companies are able to increase profit since their production cost is much less than the retail price. However, while these companies find many positives in using sweatshops, many negatives affect the industry as well. Although these factories make clothing at a low cost and at a speedy rate, they do not guarantee quality. But these extremely underpaid employees and their grueling working conditions are not companies' only problems. Peter de Simone believes that "Some manufacturers look the other way" when it comes to the quality of clothing their factories produce. Most companies that are guilty of using sweatshops lose track and "their supply chains get completely out of control, and they have no handle on who's making their goods" (qtd. in Braunstein). Unfortunately, these factories' doors remain open because "many of the labor practices in question are legal outside North America and Europe or are tolerated by corrupt or repressive political regimes" (Arnold 221).

8   Many labels with very recognizable names such as Nike, Wal-Mart, and Disney have been proven guilty of using or operating sweatshops overseas at some point. These three brands are not the only guilty ones. Here in the United States, other respected companies and organizations have been caught in the act. Some of the most surprising pieces of clothing produced in these American sweatshops are uniforms worn by United States military and by upcoming London Olympic athletes. Shockingly, American tax dollars operate sweatshops where "most workers who make the uniforms worn by American soldiers are paid below poverty-level wages, have no health coverage or retirement plans and are forced to rely on government aid" ("U.S. Military"). This appalling truth is yet another example of how sweatshops are an unacceptable form of clothing production.

9   Companies that continue to hide their use of sweatshops contribute to this never-ending cycle each day. They are the factories, like those in Queens, New York, who devise ways to keep their secret in the factory by coaching their workers. While making apparel for stores like Victoria's Secret, The Gap, Banana

Republic, and Macy's, one sweatshop "handed out instructions to its workers telling them to give false answers about working conditions when government inspectors visited" (Greenhouse). Those who work in sweatshops give up their freedom and fall victim to psychological coercion. Owners force their employees to work hour upon hour and trick them into believing nothing is wrong with their work situation.

10   Workers are not drawn to work in sweatshops because of low wages and disgusting work conditions. Unfortunately, most people who suffer in these situations do so because they have no other choice. While they are being treated unfairly, they are still receiving pay. In some communities, sweatshop wages are greater than wages in other local businesses. Some economists argue that persons who work in sweatshops "are often paid better when compared with local wages; they are fortunate to have such work" (Arnold 221). They also believe that if wages were to be increased, companies would find it necessary to lay off factory workers to compensate for the pay raise. Also, for an immigrant, obtaining a working visa is a complicated process. Working in a sweatshop appears to be easier for immigrants to support themselves, even if the income is low. These immigrants are willing to do the work that most Americans are not. Without these workers, sweatshops in America would not be functioning; but unfortunately they accept the horrible working conditions because the immigrants trying to make it in America have no other choice.

11   In many ways, "sweatshops are much better than a sharp stick in the eye" (Neiman). Yes, these factories do provide work and a small amount of pay for people, but they also provide a never-ending problem. Working in a sweatshop is not "a pathway out of poverty; they create an asymmetric [and] unsustainable global economy" where a person has no chance at ever climbing up the success ladder (Neiman). Sweatshops may be providing work for people, but they are also providing a never-ending cycle of horrible labor conditions. The problem concerning undocumented workers in the United States is largely due to the operation of sweatshops. For many immigrants, accepting the poor conditions proves to be better than trying to get a legitimate job and risk being deported. Undocumented workers are a never-ending problem; and as they continue to sew away in factories, the problem only gets worse.

12   As one of these workers walks home, she passes by a storefront. She recognizes the display in the window. It's a design that she sewed a few months back. Looking into the store, she sees an array of happy shoppers perusing the merchandise. In the back, she recognizes smiles, as the customer is pleased with the outfit she tries on. The woman tries to smile as well, but all she can think about is the truth. She knows where the clothes come from and how they are made, but the people in the store are completely oblivious. The happy customers are blind to the fact the woman staring into the window has slaved over the clothes they now decide to purchase.

13   Americans need to become informed consumers to put an end to sweatshops. Every day, consumers making purchases are practicing sweatshop advocacy whether they realize it or not. As Americans, we rely so heavily on the perceptions of others, which causes our "closets of clothing [to be] stuffed with the changing demands of fashion" (Ross 2). Consumers are responsible for the unethical practices that happen each day behind factory doors. Assuming that sweatshops do not exist will not make the problem disappear, and this is why Americans must take responsibility. It is easy for consumers to believe that "we are not supposed to have sweatshops, places of work so bad that they remind us of the bad old days that we were supposed to have left behind" (Ross 10). To most people, this shocking reality is something they have either chosen to deny or to which they have been completely oblivious. Unfortunately, even though it is rarely addressed, a plethora of sweatshops still exist and continue to produce clothing we have in our wardrobes. The biggest issue about sweatshops is that their existence remains unknown. Educating the American public about sweatshops will result in more initiatives to help this worsening problem.

Annotated Works Cited

Arnold, Denis G., and Norman E. Bowie. "Sweatshops and Respect for Persons." *Business Ethics Quarterly* 13.2: 221-42. JSTOR. Web. Apr. 2012.

> According to Immanuel Kant, persons ought to be respected because persons have dignity. This article uses Kant's view of ethics to argue against sweatshops by proving that they violate the Kantian doctrine. Companies such as Nike, Wal-Mart, and Disney have proved to be the most controversial cases of offshore sweatshops. Economists argue that the people working in these sweatshops should be considered fortunate that they receive what they do and overlook the horrible conditions. They also believe that improving working circumstances and offering better pay would raise unemployment rather than help it. Psychological coercion is also discussed in the article and appears widespread among sweatshops. An example of psychological coercion is that many workers are told that if they don't work long hours and do what they are told they will lose their job.

"Between a Rock and a Hard Place: A History of American Sweatshops, 1820 Present." *History Matters: The U.S. Survey Course on the Web.* Web. Apr. 2012.

> This article focuses on the history of sweatshops in the United States. It gives important dates and information about unsafe conditions and how sweatshops in history compare to those of today. I will use this article in my paper to talk about the history of sweatshops and their differences from the past.

Ellen Braunstein. "From Sweatshops to Shopping Malls."*Shopping Center World* 30.9 (2001): 42. Print.

According to this article, Wal-Mart's merchandise, specifically its "Kathie Lee" goods, were produced by enslaved 13-year-olds in Honduras. These young teenagers were forced to work 13-hour days with almost no compensation. Other companies such as Nike and Foot Locker have also historically been in the spotlight regarding labor abuses. However, in the 1990s, nine companies, including Nike, joined the Fair Labor Association. This association is responsible for holding companies accountable for their labor standards and working conditions. These nine companies are Adidas, Eddie Bauer, Levi's, Liz Claiborne, Nike, Patagonia, Phillips-Van Heusen, Reebok and Gear for Sports. Still, many competitive US manufacturers seem to "look the other way" when it comes to cheap and unfair overseas production. This leads to companies having no control over who is making their garments and where they are being produced. A major abuser of this was Liz Claiborne until the company corrected itself and started to enforce improved labor standards.

Greenhouse, Steven. "Apparel Factory Workers were Cheated, State Says." *New York Times (1923-Current file)*: B2. *ProQuest Historical Newspapers: The New York Times (1851-2008)*.Jul. 24 2008. Web. Apr. 2012 .

In this article, Greenhouse speaks about a certain factory who gave their workers instruction sheets with details for how to answer questions to keep the sweatshop safe. Remarkably enough, this sweatshop made women's apparel for Banana Republic, The Gap, Macy's, Urban Apparel, and Victoria's Secret, all very popular companies; "most employees, virtually all of them Chinese immigrants, were paid just $250 when they worked their typical 66-hour, six-day weeks, amounting to $3.79 an hour, far below the state's $7.15-an-hour minimum wage." The information in this article is helpful to my research involving the companies that use sweatshops and how they cover up their use of them. It also helps to give me a better mental picture of what a sweatshop looks like on the inside.

Neiman, Adam, "Is a Sweatshop Better Than Nothing?" *New York Times* 19 Jan. 2009: A24(L). *Academic OneFile*. Web. Apr. 2012.

This article is a response to another article that states why sweatshops are good. While sweatshops do provide jobs and pay to impoverished people, they still do not possess healthy working environments. "When jobs aren't a pathway out of poverty, they create an asymmetric, unsustainable global economy of producer countries and consumer countries that can stand on its head only so long." This article is helpful to my research because it reveals the myth behind sweatshops.

Radin, Tara J., and Martin Calkins. "The Struggle Against Sweatshops: Moving Toward Responsible Global Business."*Journal of Business Ethics* 66 (2006): 261-72. Spring. Web. Apr. 2012.

This article explores the constant contradiction and struggle to punish sweatshop affiliates. Even though sweatshops prove to have horrible working conditions, people still choose to work in them because they lack any other job opportunity. Since there are no clear regulations against sweatshops,punishing their supporters is difficult. Radin and Calkins focus on the conditions in sweatshops, and they prove to be morally incorrect. Although such working conditions are unethical, people still chose to wear the clothing that these sweatshops produce. Wal-Mart and Kathie Lee Gifford are also exposed in the article for their involvement with sweatshops. The constant media attention and negative press coverage continue to inform people, but the absence of a definition proves to be the major reason for the continued existence of sweatshops.

Ross, Robert J. S. *Slaves to Fashion: Poverty and Abuse in the New Sweatshops*. Ann Arbor: University of Michigan Press, 2004. Print.

This book covers all aspects of sweatshops ranging from the history to ways we can stop these factories. Author Robert Ross is serious about his subject and makes a good point when he explains, "[T]hroughout the developed world, in Europe and North America, closets of clothing are stuffed with the changing demands of fashion." He is passionate that people are focused on keeping up with fashion and believes that this causes consumers to invest in sweatshop-produced clothing. It is hard to believe that there are sweatshops in America because "we are not supposed to have sweatshops, places of work so bad that they remind us of the bad old days that we were supposed to have left behind." I will use this information to support my conclusion and explain that consumers are responsible for the unethical practices that happen each day behind sweatshop doors.

Rogers, Joel ,et al. *Can We Put An End To Sweatshops?*. Beacon Press, 2002. eBookCollection (EBSCOhost).Web. 24 Apr. 2012.

The main focus of this book is the fight to eliminate sweatshops. Joel Rogers makes a valid point when he explains that "Even "buying American" can mean paying for sweatshop labor. There are an estimated five thousand illegal, unregistered sweatshops in Los Angeles alone that label their products 'Made in the USA'." Americans needs to think twice about where their clothes are coming from since the clothing industry nowadays is quite sketchy. This information is valid to my research because it supports my argument about sweatshops in America and how we should be more skeptical when buying.

"U.S. Military Uniforms Made in Sweatshops, Union Says." *The Nation* [Washington (Reuters)] 16 Mar. 2006. Web. Apr. 2012.

Shockingly enough, this article explains the use of sweatshops in making U.S. military uniforms. The report uncovers a host of abuses at factories supported by the U.S military. Workers are paid poverty wages to sew military uniforms. It also suggests that with better oversight and accountability of contractors, sweatshops can be eliminated from the military uniform supply chain. It is shocking that our tax dollars support these factories and "most workers who make the uniforms worn by American soldiers are paid below poverty-level wages, have no health coverage or retirement plans and are forced to rely on government aid." This article is helpful to my research to serve as a shock factor to the reader and prove that even the military is guilty of using sweatshops.

Marquelle Smith's class identified and researched debatable issues concerning the influence of reality TV shows on the viewing public. Each student then had to "make a case," or argue in support of a specific position, synthesizing primary and secondary sources. Does Smith make his case? How? As citation conventions recommended by the American Psychological Association are more common in the field of communications and media, Smith uses APA rather than MLA notations.

Race and Reality TV

Marquelle D.B. Smith

1   Reverend Martin Luther King, Jr. dreamed of the day when his "children [would not be] judged by the color of their skin but by the content of their character." He spoke those words in 1963. Has that day arrived? No. We can only imagine a world where people do not distinguish themselves as whites, blacks, or Hispanics but instead only as Americans. While recent legislation has helped to abolish discrimination, the media still have not done enough on their part to abolish racial stereotyping.

2   During the 1960s, Martin Luther King and the Civil Rights Movement advanced the concept of eliminating racial discrimination. Television followed with scripted dramas and comedies that encouraged Americans to disregard racial stereotypes. Shows such as *The Cosby Show* and *The Jeffersons* included positive images of black men who were strong fathers and families of color who were middle class. Unfortunately, the emergence of the genre of reality TV in the 1990s reversed the progress of these positive portrayals of minorities. Comedies and dramas that had broken down barriers were replaced with a genre that required no scripts and no message. In fact, however, this genre deserves criticism for the way it presents race in stereotypical and disrespectful ways.

3   Shows similar to *The Cosby Show* and *The Fresh Prince of Bel-Air* still remain the favorites of many viewers because they depicted positive images. No one will ever forget how the Huxtables represented the possibility of black professionals raising a normal family. We should thank Bill Cosby for creating a middle-class family composed of parents who were doctors and children with dreams of college. However, Leslie Inniss and Joe Feigan (1995) reveal that "some [black] viewers criticized the [Huxtables] because they were not like most black Americans," (p. 693), meaning that they were not poor. But the point was to show that the barrier of poverty could be broken. The Huxtables demonstrated to young black males a role model that encouraged them to go to college and, later, to become strong father figures. The show also encouraged young black women to embark upon the professional world. Like Martin Luther

King, *The Cosby Show* was aiming to remove not only racial stereotypes, but also discrimination between social classes.

4   The *Fresh Prince of Bel-Air* is another show that diminished the perceived gap between rich and poor blacks. In this show, Will Smith, a ghetto kid from West Philly, moves in with his aunt and uncle who live in a mansion in Beverly Hills. Not only does this show include a "Huxtable-like" family, but it also uses Will Smith to symbolize blacks leaving the ghetto and exploring affluent lifestyles in wealthy neighborhoods. The rivalry between Smith and his cousin, Carlton, was hilarious, but it also highlighted the most important theme in the show. Will and Carlton initially despised each other but later realized that they had much in common despite their different backgrounds. Towards the end of the show, they set their differences aside by helping each other in college so that they could be like Uncle Phil, the most popular judge in Beverly Hills. Even though these were scripted dramas, these shows used humor to overcome negative stereotypes.

5   Times have changed dramatically as reality TV has exposed the worst images of minorities. Unlike the Cosby and Smith shows, programs like *Cops, The Real World*, and *Flavor of Love* all degrade people of color. Katrina Bell-Jordan (2008), a journalist and media specialist from Ohio State, argues that these shows "promote a politics of difference, emphasize conflict, and dramatize scenarios that reinforce cultural codes and stereotypes" (p. 353). On *Cops,* it seems as if the objective is to grab as many black and Hispanic males off inner-city streets as possible. *The Real World* always casts some large, athletic black guy whose goal is to have sex with every woman while everyone else is supposed to fear him. Western Michigan communications professor Mark Orbe (2008), who has studied the show, argues that *The Real World* "reinforces societal fears of Black men" (p. 350).

6   One particularly offensive example of this trend is *Flavor of Love,* a "ghetto" version of *The Bachelor*. Rachel Dubrofsky and Antoine Hardy (2008), both in cultural studies at the University of South Florida, characterize the term "ghetto" as "a label for allegedly dysfunctional behavior (hypersexual, uncouth, criminal, violent, loud) and values (nontraditional family values, materialism) of Black people from urban neighborhoods" (p. 373). The show implies that people of color do not deserve to appear on *The Bachelor*. Notice how "Flavor Flav" wears pimp suits and hands out gaudy clocks to the contestants, whereas on *The Bachelor* the men wear formal attire and distribute roses to the women. Obviously, reality TV is segregated into the "classy only section" for whites and the "ghetto" section for minorities.

7   Reality television is defended by many critics as contributing to viewers' education on politically sensitive issues. Michael Hirschorn (2007), a producer of reality television shows, argues that reality TV "engage[s] hot-button cultural issues—class, sex, and race—that respectable television . . . rarely touches"

(p. 138). Other defenders argue that reality television gives groups of people "historically under- and/or misrepresented within television" an opportunity to "participate in representations of self" (as cited in Orbe, 2008, p. 349). However, Orbe himself believes that "reality-based programming has strengthened . . . stereotypical portrayals" and that this is especially bad because people see these "images as more 'real' than others" (p. 350).

8   The producers of reality TV should not take all the blame for this racial issue despite their broadcasts. We must question ourselves as the viewers who fund these shows and the contestants who present themselves in this way. Barry Brummett (2011), a communications professor at UT, believes that "media texts are sites of struggle over meaning and that we engage in an unconscious yet powerful struggle over how to interpret them" (p. 92). As America continues to struggle with the meaning of race, this curiosity fuels our appetite for reality TV. Thus, reality television is giving viewers what they want to see. Dubrofsky and Hardy (2008) argue that reality TV is "shaped and offered for sale like any other consumer product" (p. 374). This means that networks will show whatever sells, not caring who gets offended. What is sad is that black people themselves watch these segregated and demeaning shows.

9   The Civil Rights Movement along with the classic dramas accelerated a future where race is not an issue. Proof can be seen in President Obama's election in 2008. However, problems still exist in American society regarding race. The scripted dramas of the past helped Americans make progress in understanding each other's similarities and in moving beyond prejudicial stereotypes, whereas reality TV drags Americans' perspectives back to what they were at the time Martin Luther King gave his famous speech.

References

Bell-Jordan, K. (2008, Oct). *Black. White.* and a *Survivor of The Real World*: Constructions of race on reality TV. *Critical Studies in Media Communication*, 25(4), 353-372. doi: 10.1080/15295030802327725

Katrina Bell-Jordan teaches in the areas of media culture, news writing/ journalism, as well as rhetorical theory and criticism, persuasion and public address at Northeastern Illinois University. The *Critical Studies in Media Communication* is a scholarly journal, a credible source. Bell-Jordan argues that reality TV's success is fueled by racial stereotypes and cultural misrepresentations. She uses specific observations of the three TV shows named in her article's title. This source has a references list. The article can be accessed through Academic Search Complete.

Brummett, B. (2011). Rhetoric in popular culture (3rd ed.) Thousand Oaks, CA: Sage Publications, Inc.

Barry Brummett is a professor of communications at the University of Texas. He studies the ways in which popular culture creates attitudes and dispositions in people so as to affect the management of power. His book, *Rhetoric in Popular Culture*, explains various concepts of semiotics and rhetoric and how they can be applied to pop culture. The audience is of course college students, since this was a textbook for rhetoric classes. His view of television shows is that they influence people's attitudes and can work to empower and disempower groups of people. In regards to race and reality TV, the view makes perfect sense.

Dubrofsky, R.E. & Hardy, A. (2008). Performing race in *Flavor of Love* and *The Bachelor*. *Critical Studies in Media Communication,* 25 (4), 373-392. doi: 10.1080/15295030802327774

Rachael E. Dubrofsky is an assistant professor of critical/cultural studies at the University of South Florida. Antoine Hardy is a graduate student in the same program. Their research focuses on critical/cultural studies of communication and feminist media studies with a specialization in TV studies and surveillance. This article comes from the same volume of *Critical Studies in Media Communication* as the Bell-Jordan source, above. These authors draw a comparison between *Flavor of Love* and *The Bachelor* to prove how reality TV is racially biased. One could counter this argument because it does single out just these two shows. However, these shows have received some of the best ratings and they are based on the same concept, so the comparison seems valid. The source can be accessed through Academic Search Complete.

Hirschorn, M. (2007, May). The case for reality TV. *Atlantic Monthly*, 299(4), 138-143. Retrieved from: http://www.theatlantic.com/magazine/archive/2007/05/the-case-for-reality-tv/5791/

Michael Hirschorn is a contributing editor and writer for *Atlantic Monthly* magazine and founder of a TV production company behind many reality TV series. As the title indicates, his bias is in favor or reality TV in general. He is defending reality TV in general against arguments that it is a cheap substitute for scripted TV. This source leads to no others because his only evidence is his own observations and interpretations of various shows. This source can be accessed on-line through Google.

Inniss, L. & Feigan, J. (1995, July). *The Cosby Show*: The view from the black middle class. *Journal of Black Studies*, 25 (6), 692-711.

When this article was published in 1995, Leslie B. Inniss was a professor of African American Studies at Florida State University and Joe Feigan was at University of Florida. They are sociologists whose research is centered on controversial subjects in African American culture. The audience is most likely college students and other scholars studying black culture. The article was written after the final episode of *The Cosby Show* in 1992; the authors' purpose is to explore middle class blacks' responses to criticisms, especially among black viewers, that the Huxtables were too "white" and wealthy to represent real black families. The research showed that most middle class blacks thought that the positive images, fake or real, left a positive impact on Americans' minds. This article has references and can be found in JSTOR database.

Orbe, M.P. (2008). Representations of race in reality TV: Watch and discuss. *Critical Studies in Media Communication,* 25 (4), 345-352. doi: 10.1080/15295030802327790

Mark P. Orbe is a communications professor at Western Michigan University. He is the editor of the *Critical Studies in Media Communications* special edition on race and reality TV. This article is his introduction to the other essays in the volume. He gives a brief overview of each essay's topic and argument. This is a good source because it introduced me to several other good articles. It can be accessed through Academic Search Complete.

For a 1302 class research paper on American popular culture, Jessie Craft selected the figure of Lady Gaga to represent the many ways Americans engage the concept of celebrity in their media-drenched environment. Can such celebrity figures reveal important truths about ourselves and our society? Does Craft show that these figures matter?

Lady Gaga: Just a Thing in Our Imaginations
Jessie Craft

1   "Stefani Joanne Angelina Germanotta (born March 28, 1986), better known by her stage name Lady Gaga, is an American singer and songwriter. Born and raised in New York City, she primarily studied at the Convent of the Sacred Heart and briefly attended New York University's Tisch School of the Arts before withdrawing to focus on her musical career." This passage begins the *Wikipedia* entry on Lady Gaga. In contrast, on Lady Gaga's official web site the first paragraph of her biography reads in part:

> LADY GAGA CAME TO PROMINENCE FOLLOWING THE RELEASE OF HER DEBUT STUDIO ALBUM THE FAME (2008) . . . [SELLING] OVER 15 MILLION COPIES. . . . [EARNING] . . . SIX GRAMMY NOMINATIONS . . . TWO WINS [AND] THIRTEEN MTV VIDEO MUSIC AWARD NOMINATIONS. GAGA IS THE FIRST ARTIST . . . TO CLAIM FOUR #1 HITS FROM A DEBUT ALBUM.

Nowhere in this first paragraph or in the entirety of the official Lady Gaga web page biography does any mention of Stefani Germanotta appear. This is because the life and history of Stefani Germanotta is completely irrelevant to Lady Gaga. This pre-Lady Gaga history is "unimportant to the point of being inconvenient for the success of Lady Gaga's career...[and] what potentially tarnishes her image is the fact that Lady Gaga has any history prior to her rise to fame" (Bedard "Can't Read My Poker Face"). Many people have tried to answer the question "What is Lady Gaga?" Journalists have spent hours trying to define Lady Gaga and dissect her identity, but Lady Gaga is not one thing. She cannot be pinpointed and assigned one identity. She is merely a reflection, a mirror of what her fans are and what they want her to be.

2   Many of Lady Gaga's early music videos still contain an element of Stefani Germanotta. In the "Eh, Eh, Nothing Else I Can Say" music video, Lady Gaga appears as an excessively tanned American girl who is clearly of Italian descent. In this fairly ordinary video, Gaga successfully fulfills the role of a typical young pop star. Her costume, including her heels and white lingerie, which she scampers in throughout the music video, reflects the typical elements of a female celebrity and representation of girlhood.

3   The "Born This Way" video marks the beginning of Lady Gaga's disappearance as an identifiable human being. This video features two separate Lady Gagas: the mortal Lady Gaga and the immortal, goddess-like Gaga. The video details the odyssey of mortal Lady Gaga's demise and the rise of the new immortal Lady Gaga and represents the division between Gaga's body and the projection that is Lady Gaga now. This new Gaga is a projection of her fans. Lady Gaga emphasizes the importance of this relationship with her fans in her "Manifesto of Little Monsters" that she opens "Born This Way" with on tour: "We are nothing without our image. Without our projection. Without the spiritual hologram of who we perceive ourselves to be, or become rather, in the future" (Lady Gaga "Manifesto of Little Monsters"). Lady Gaga is nothing without her fans because her fans create her image and her image is everything.

4   Lady Gaga embraces both the good and bad opinions of her fans and detractors, incorporating them into her image. In 2009 when rumors about Lady Gaga being a hermaphrodite surfaced on the Internet, Lady Gaga used this attention, which most stars would consider to be negative, to further her connection with her fans. When asked about this rumor in a French TV interview, Lady Gaga answered, "I love the rumor that I have a penis... In fact, it makes me love my fans even more that this rumor is in the world because 17,000 of them come to an arena every night and they don't care if I'm a man, a woman, a hermaphrodite, gay, straight, transgendered, or transsexual" ("Lady Gaga: I love the Rumors that I have a Penis"). This rumor inspired elements of her music video "Telephone." In this video, Lady Gaga is brought into a Prison for Bitches. After throwing her into a holding cell, one of the guards says to the other, "I told you she didn't have a dick" (Lady Gaga "Telephone"). This exchange directly addresses the rumor questioning Lady Gaga's gender. All of Lady Gaga's actions and identities, in one way or another, are a reaction to the media and her fans. She reflects and encompasses their thoughts and their identities in her music, her performances, and ultimately in her own identity.

5   Lady Gaga is no longer represented as two Gagas in her "Telephone" video. The video is so fragmented and confusing that no identity can be assigned to Lady Gaga. She is just a collection of images flashing on the screen. Ella Bedard pinpoints this idea in her article, "Trajectory of the Monster," saying, "The ambiguities that surround Gaga reflect the myriad of contradicting sources that inform her identity...Gaga *is* only the collage of photos and Internet rumors that constitute her celebrity. She is a reflection of the pluralized and fragmented field of information through which she appears for our consumption" (Bedard "Trajectory of the Monster"). "Telephone" embodies the frenzied Gaga image as a product of her fans and their identities perfectly at this stage in her career. As quickly as Gaga squashes the penis rumor in her "Telephone" video by grinding almost completely naked against the prison bars, she turns it completely upside down and portrays herself as a man. Gaga invents her alter ego "Jo

Calderone" to represent yet another fragmented version of herself and, more importantly, to attract more attention. Jo Calderone was first discovered on the cover of *Vogue Hommes Japan* in June 2010. He is a mechanic from New Jersey with roots in Sicily. Jo Calderone even has his own Twitter account. It was not until August 2010, two months after the *Vogue Hommes Japan* cover release, that suspicions were confirmed: Jo Calderone is Lady Gaga. Instead of letting this alter ego die when the secret was revealed, Lady Gaga embraced Jo even more once the world saw that Jo was Lady Gaga. Jo came to the 2011 MTV Awards instead of Gaga. Then Gaga took it a step further by using photos of Jo as the cover photo for her new single: "You and I."

6   "You and I" began as an exclusive live performance song. It revealed a softer side of Lady Gaga. Instead of her typical hysterical performances, Lady Gaga usually sang the entire song while sitting at the piano. Then "You and I" was brought to one of America's biggest stages, *American Idol*, by Lady Gaga's producer Joe Irvine. At the time, it may have seemed like a brilliant suggestion to help contestant Haley Reinhart steal the show's spotlight and stand out from the other singers. But, while the performance backfired for Haley, Lady Gaga gained a great deal of attention from this unique publicity stunt with her producer. The Idol appearance sparked new curiosity about the song across the nation and fans eagerly awaited the radio release of "You and I." The new hit single's video, released on August 16, 2011 and starring both Lady Gaga and Jo Calderone, focuses on the unique relationship between her two personas. Journalist Roland Betancourt tries to dissect the meaning of this relationship: "[Gaga] is a creation of the lover, but the lover creates various images or permutations of Gaga" (Betancourt). That is, Jo Calderone both reflects Lady Gaga and creates various images of Lady Gaga. This is true in many senses; Jo Calderone is a rough around the edges Italian guy, which reflects Lady Gaga's heritage and aspects of her personality. This relationship between Gaga and Calderone also epitomizes Gaga's message to "love yourself." The music video finishes with the union of Lady Gaga and Jo Calderone. This lover relationship also goes beyond just Lady Gaga and Jo. It applies to Lady Gaga's relationship and coexistence with her fans as well. Lady Gaga is the creation of her fans and her fans create the various images that encompass Lady Gaga. Although there is some conclusion to the music video, many critics wonder what is next for Jo. Lady Gaga successfully leaves her audience in suspense, wanting more from Jo.

7   So what will come next for Jo aka Gaga? Do not look at Lady Gaga's projection for an answer; look at her fans and the media. That is what Lady Gaga is; "She is subversive and commercial, gendered and not, original and derivative. By continuously switching roles, she complicates these dualities and reveals how her identity, like any identity, is a contingency and a performance" (Bedard "Can't Read My Poker Face"). She is a reaction, a reflection, a projection, a mirror of her fans. And for those who wonder when the reign of Lady Gaga

will end, the answer to that question is up to the media and her Little Monsters. Gaga's fame is based on her coincidence with her fans. Gaga will decline when the world loses interest and stops anxiously awaiting her next move. When we stop hanging onto Gaga's every move, her every word, then she will come to an end. But will Gaga let this happen? In her interview with Anderson Cooper, Lady Gaga says, "That's what everyone wants to know, right? What's she gonna look like when she dies... Everybody wants to see the decay of the superstar" (Lady Gaga "Lady Gaga & the Art of Fame"). Foreshadowing the future? For someone craving so much attention, she just might rather die than lose her stage.

Works Cited

Bedard, Ella. "The Trajectory of the Monster: Some Musings on the Ascendance of a Myth and the Decay of the Female Celebrity." *Gaga Stigmata* (Mar. 2011): n. pag. Web. 6 Feb. 2012.

_____. "The Trajectory of the Monster: Some Musings on the Ascendance of a Myth and the Decay of the Female Celebrity." *Gaga Stigmata* (Mar. 2011): n. pag. Web. 6 Feb. 2012.

Betancourt, Roland. "The Perceptual Marriage: Notes on You and I and Future Work." *Gaga Stigmata* (Aug. 2011): n. pag. Web. 3 Feb. 2012.

Durbin, Kate. "Gaga Stigmata Interview with Spex Magazine." *Gaga Stigmata*. N.p., 30 June 2011. Web. 2 Feb. 2012.

Kaiser. "Lady Gaga's Male Alter Ego Jo Calderone is a Depression Era Mechanic." *Celebitchy*. N.p., 26 Aug. 2010. Web. 6 Feb. 2012.

Lady Gaga, perf. "Bio." *Lady Gaga*. Interscope Records, n.d. Web. 6 Feb. 2012.

Lady Gaga. "Born This Way." *Born This Way*. YouTube. Web. 6 Feb. 2012.

_____. "Eh, Eh Nothing Else I Can Say." *The Fame*. YouTube. Web. 6 Feb. 2012.

_____. "Lady Gaga & the Art of Fame." Interview by Anderson Cooper. *60 Minutes*. CBS. 13 Feb. 2011. *CBS News*. Web. Transcript. 6 Feb. 2012.

_____. "Manifesto of Little Monsters." *Gagapedia*. N.p., n.d. Web. 7 Feb. 2012.

_____. "Telephone." *The Fame Monster*. YouTube. Web. 6 Feb. 2012.

"Lady Gaga." *Wikipedia*. Wikimedia Foundation, 4 Feb. 2012. Web. 6 Feb. 2012.

Lady Gaga. "You and I." *Born This Way (Bonus Track)*. YouTube. Web. 6 Feb. 2012.

"Lady Gaga: I Love The Rumors That I Have A Penis." *Huffington Post*. N.p., 24 May 2010. Web. 6 Feb. 2012.

Place, Vanessa. "WAT IS GAGA?" *Gaga Stigmata* (Sept. 2010): n. pag. Web. 2 Feb. 2012.

A Tribute to Earlier SMU Writing Students and to the Instructors Who Taught Them

The following works, including head notes, come from SMU's first-year writing program spanning the 1990s. Faculty and students may recognize assignments and texts still being used in the program today.

1990–91
Arguments, not Facts, Have Persuasive Power: A Theory of Knowledge
Xiaofeng Xu

After reading several essays that conveyed, either implicitly or explicitly, an epistemology, or theory of knowledge, students in Xiaofeng Xu's 1302 class were asked to synthesize information from these essays and from personal experience to come up with their own epistemology. Xiaofeng draws from a recent event in China and from geological theory to support his definition of knowledge.

1 Many people remember what happened at Tiananmen Square in Beijing last June. We all saw the picture on CBS news and in the *Dallas Morning News*. Photography preserves a twinkling fact forever, and the pictures on the news and in the newspapers recorded the fact that students standing on a truck were displaying guns for the Beijing people to see. The U.S. news media and the Chinese government, however, explained the fact differently. CBS explained that the students, demonstrating peacefully for their freedom, had found the weapons, which had been brought to the city clandestinely by soldiers to suppress the students' demonstration. The Chinese government, however, attempted to convince us that the student ruffians had purposely seized the weapons from the soldiers in order to create trouble. People around the world saw the pictures and were persuaded by the argument voiced by CBS. The pictures captured facts, but those facts did not speak for themselves; people were persuaded not by the facts but by the interpretations that put the facts within a context.

2 Facts are less important than thought, and facts alone do not constitute knowledge. Our interpretation of the facts we collect from others and the facts we witness ourselves is subject to bias because we can never gather all the facts and because we will select facts from our experience and from reports in accordance with our prior experience and likes and dislikes. N.P. Birk and G.B. Birk call the phenomenon "the principle of selection." They state that "before it is expressed in words, our knowledge, both inside and outside, is influenced by the principle of selection" (103).

3   If facts, although a part of knowledge, are not the core of knowledge, what should we learn at school? We should learn to think independently. Knowledge derives from collecting facts and making sense of facts. With the development of scientific technology, computers collect facts today even better than we do; the computer, however, can't escape its enslavement to human design. Therefore, the ability to think independently, as W.C. Booth points out, distinguishes human beings from machines and animals. Booth emphasizes that "the education that a man must have is . . . liberal education. The knowledge it yields is the knowledge or capacity or power of how to act freely as a man" (279). He further claims that "a man can be ignorant even of Shakespeare, Aristotle, Beethoven, and Einstein, and be a **man for a' that**—if he has learned how to think his own thoughts, experience beauty for himself, and choose his own actions" (283). Undoubtedly, for Booth, thinking is more important than remembering facts, even those most important facts.

4   Some students are interested in thinking logically and independently; others pay attention only to remembering facts. Which kind of student should our schools develop? William G. Perry, Jr., gives us an excellent example. Driven "by a surge of curiosity and puckish glee" (269), a Mr. Metzger took an exam in a course he was not enrolled in. Metzger was able to write an essay about a book he had never read and received "his honor grade A–" (270). What is the magic? He was able to think independently and organize his ideas logically to relate the given evidence to some facts he did know. Those poor students who remembered only the facts received C+s because they were not able to put facts within a frame of reference and were not able to think for themselves. Thinking independently, Mr. Metzger completed his essay successfully without a lot of facts, but the facts were no help to those poor students who couldn't think independently.

5   Students need to know that facts change as people's perspectives change. In her "America Revised," Frances FitzGerald writes that history texts change as time passes and authors change, and that "each historian in some degree creates the world anew and . . . all history is in some degree contemporary history" (243). Historical texts change because historians think for themselves. They do not simply repeat the facts of their predecessors. We don't need to worry about changes in historical perspectives, but we do need to worry about whether or not we can think for ourselves and understand why the changes took place.

6   FitzGerald reports of the shift in perspective of United States history texts from the 1950s to the 1970s. Whereas the history texts of the 1950s told their readers of America's greatness, glory, and perfection in order to arouse the readers' love for the country and to make the country better, the history texts of the 1970s revealed social problems so that people could understand that many things still need to be changed. Which is better? God only knows. But one thing is sure—the Chinese Communist Government always tells its people how perfect its political system is and how happy its people are under its leadership.

When the country opened its doors to the world, the people finally found that the facts were not as the government had said. This realization partly accounts for the bloody event at Tiananmen Square last June. A historical book recording only pleasant things is not perfect. Students' historical pictures should not be unchangeable because the unchangeable picture means only that they never think independently. As thinkers, they should seek new ways to accommodate the new facts and to adjust continuously to new historical pictures.

7   In geology—my working field—there are many examples to prove that thinking, not facts, is the core of knowledge. Even if you get exactly the same facts as others, you can't see that the truth is in front of you if you can't think independently. The origin of the Plate Tectonics Theory is one of the best examples. The origin comes from a map of the world! It may sound ridiculous, but it is true. A famous geophysicist, A. Wegener, lying on a bed in a hospital around the 1910s, found a fact that he had never paid any attention to before—that is, the similarity in shape between the coastlines of North and South America and those of Euro-Africa. After having thought about it, he claimed that the Americas and Euro-Africa had been a supercontinent in geohistory and the separation between them occurred later. The view was totally different from the popular idea that the movement of the Earth's crust is mainly vertical. Ridiculed for nearly a half century, Wegener's idea was finally proved right, and more and more data from paleomagnetism, seismology, geophysics, paleontology, geochemistry, and sedimentology are supporting the theory. Almost everyone reads a world map frequently, but only Wegener thought about it independently. Plate Tectonics has today become the dominant theory in geology. Why did such a simple fact cause a revolution in geological theory? Because of the power of thinking.

8   Facts are important, but the power to connect facts logically to your ideas is much more important. The power of your knowledge doesn't depend on how many facts you collect, but on how you select and think about the facts. By themselves facts have little to say; combined with logical thought they become knowledge.

Works Cited

Birk, N.P. and G.B. Birk. "Selection, Slanting, and Charged Language" *Language Awareness*. Eds. Eschholz, et al. 4th. ed. 103-155.

Booth, Wayne C. "Is There Any Knowledge That a Man Must Have?" *The Norton Reader*. Eds. Arthur M. Eastman, et al. 7th ed. 268-283.

FitzGerald, Frances. "America Revised" *Fields of Writing*. Eds. Nancy R. Comley et al. St. Martin's Press. New York. 237-244.

Perry, William G., Jr. "Examsmanship and the Liberal Arts: A Study in Educational Epistemology" *A Short Course in Writing*. Kenneth A. Bruffee. 3rd ed. 266-277.

1991–92
Two Views on Imperialism: Victim and Victimizer
Christopher Kenniff

In the process of working to construct convincing texts, students examine the techniques of other writers. Such textual analysis also occurs in peer editing sessions, and ideally, in the writer's revisions of his or her own work. Chris Kenniff examines two texts in his essay, observing that writers' purposes determine some of the choices that they make in writing.

1   George Orwell's essay "Shooting an Elephant" and N. Scott Momaday's essay "The Way to Rainy Mountain" demonstrate that authors may successfully address a common issue through dissimilar means. Common to both essays is a disdain for imperialism. Orwell's essay reveals the futility of empire and tyranny through an incident in which Orwell, a policeman in Lower Burma, shoots an elephant in front of a Burmese crowd "solely to avoid looking like a fool" (97). Momaday's essay examines the result of American imperialism of the nineteenth century through the tragic demise of the Kiowa Indians and the tragedy of his grandmother's life. Although Orwell represents the imperialist/victimizer while Momaday presents the victim, both authors manipulate the emotions of the reader in order to influence him/her to question the motives and results of imperialism.

2   Orwell manipulates the readers' emotions by using terse, stark language that reflects his own personal response to the political and circumstantial realities which led him to shoot an elephant which had trampled a native. Orwell's hatred for the Burmese natives as well as his disillusionment with the politics of imperialism is appropriately reflected in statements such as, "I thought that the greatest joy in the world would be to drive a bayonet into Buddhist priest's guts" (93), and "when the white man turns tyrant it is his own freedom that he destroys" (95). These emotions are also evident through Orwell's word choice. The British are called "oppressors" (92) and the Burmese, "evil spirited little beasts" (93) and "coolies" (94). Through these graphically biased accounts of the Burmese and British, Orwell emotionally involves readers by asking them to go beyond mere sympathy and actually to empathize with him. Thus, the reader is drawn into Orwell's predicament: being convinced on an intellectual level that imperialism is wrong, yet feeling so bitter towards what he perceives as the less than human Burmese that it becomes virtually impossible to side

with them. Indeed, Orwell is not alone in hating the Burmese or in resenting their insistence that he shoot the elephant.

3   Momaday, on the other hand, manipulates the emotions of the reader through the use of highly romantic and poetic language. Whether he is describing Kiowa tradition, his grandmother's life, or a landscape, Momaday's word choice always reflects these qualities; houses, for instance, are described as "sentinels" (89) and the prairie as "an anvil's edge" (86). Momaday's moving use of language is also evident in his striking descriptions of the American midwest: "At a distance in July or August the steaming foliage seems almost to writhe in fire" (86) and "a dark mist lay over the Black Hills, and the land was like iron" (87). Momaday succeeds in evoking a variety of moods and emotions, ranging from awe, inspired by detailed descriptions of the land and the Kiowas' reverence for it, to nostalgia created by the author's passionate descriptions of his grandmother's life. Ultimately, the reader is left with a feeling of sadness and regret that colonization of the American west meant the death of Kiowa culture and tradition. Through his highly poetic and romantic language, Momaday encourages the reader's emotional connection to the Kiowa people, and in doing so emphasizes the tragic nature of their demise.

4   Although Orwell and Momaday share a common purpose in writing their essays, differences in their writing styles reflect the contrasting ways in which this purpose is revealed. For instance, Orwell's straightforward, unambiguous writing style immediately informs the reader of his purpose, "to relate the motives for which despotic governments act" (93), and his attitude towards his subject matter. Statements such as, "I had already made up my mind that imperialism was an evil thing but the sooner I chucked up my job and got out of it the better" (92) can leave no doubt that he, at the very least, does not endorse imperialism. This hard-edged style, combined with his concise language, leads to a powerful and convincing attack on imperialism.

5   In contrast, Momaday's romantic language contributes to a far subtler writing style in which the author's purpose is implicitly revealed. Instead of overtly attacking imperialism, Momaday suggests his purpose in an understated way that reflects his grandmother's outlook on the decline of Kiowa society. For instance, when Momaday writes that, "without bitterness, and for as long as she lived, she [his grandmother] bore a vision of deicide [the killing of a deity]" (88), he succeeds in illustrating the unjustness of the colonial expansion through the ultimate desecration of Kiowa culture and society: the killing of its god. That Momaday makes such powerful and convincing points without bitterness and without openly passing judgment on American colonialism adds great strength to his essay because it inspires the readers to ask their own questions, reach their own conclusions, and experience their own emotions. Through subtlety and imaginative writing, Momaday succeeds in evoking the sympathy of the reader, who is left with the sense that an awful injustice has been committed towards

the Kiowa peoples. In direct contrast to Orwell, what is left unsaid often speaks loudest in this essay.

6   Orwell's and Momaday's essays reflect different perspectives on imperialism. Orwell's first person account of shooting the elephant in front of the Burmese crowd reveals that Orwell is viewing imperialism in progress while Momaday's mostly third person accounts of his grandmother's life and the decline of Kiowa society reveal that he views imperialism after the fact. This difference in perspective may account for the two authors' dissimilar styles and uses of language. Orwell was an active participant in the British colonization of Burma and experienced first hand the emotions he wishes to convey to the reader. Therefore, he does not have to create an emotionally charged story for the audience; he simply must recreate his own experience as truthfully and vividly as possible. Orwell effectively and appropriately uses strong, unequivocal language and an up-front style to recount his strong, unequivocal emotions. Momaday, on the other hand, was not present when the U.S. Cavalry defeated the Kiowas at Palo Duro Canyon and never knew first hand "the dark brooding of old warriors" (87). Therefore, he must rely upon creativity and imagination to augment his knowledge of Kiowa history in order to convince the audience of the tragic nature of the tribe's demise. Momaday's subtle, suggestive style, coupled with his romantic use of language, is highly effective in achieving this goal; he actively engages the reader's imagination, evokes thought, and ultimately succeeds not only in questioning imperialism, but also engendering respect for Kiowa society and culture.

7   Aside from sharing a common purpose, Orwell's and Momaday's essays are similar in terms of their intended audience. Both authors address a very broad audience with no apparent expectations as to their knowledge or familiarity with the topic. However, each essay will have a greater impact on an audience familiar with the author's specific topic. Orwell's essay, for example, will undoubtedly mean more to a British audience who may feel strongly about or may be more familiar with British colonial history, particularly as it relates to Burma. Similarly, Momaday's essay will be more meaningful to an American audience. An American somewhat familiar with Indian issues will find Momaday's essay to be particularly powerful and effective. His topic and purpose represent a very sensitive issue that remains unresolved and that is considered by many to be a source of national disgrace.

8   The similarities between Orwell's essay and Momaday's lead me to wonder: is there really as big a difference as I normally perceive between the trials of the victim and the trials of the victimizer? After all, Orwell's essay clearly shows the immense emotional struggle that the author faced in dealing with the natives whom he secretly sides with. From his essay, I can well imagine a U.S. Cavalry soldier at Palo Duro Canyon struggling with his conscience while actively engaged in killing the Kiowa Indians. Similarly, I can imagine the Burmese

civilization eventually entering into a state of utter decline due to British colonization. So, while they firmly establish imperialism as evil, neither essay offers nor even hints at a solution. Perhaps a second essay by Orwell would be appropriate—one in which he stands up to the status quo of imperialism and spares the elephant, declaring, "Though I may have looked like a fool, I did not act foolishly," instead of wimpishly cowering to the will of the natives and his fear of embarrassment. So yes, there is a very big difference between the trials of the victimizer and of the victim because the victimizer possesses the means to affect a change in the trials of the victim and not vice versa. Perhaps the greatest strength of these essays is that they challenge the reader to experience the trials of both sides and through essentially leaving matters unresolved, challenge the reader to resolve them. Powerfully and finally they imply the question, "Will you too be the victimizer?" We are all challenged to answer "no."

Works Cited

Comley, Nancy R., et al. *Fields of Writing: Readings Across the Disciplines.* 3rd ed. New York: St. Martin's Press, 1990.
Momaday, N. Scott. "The Way to Rainy Mountain." Comley, et al. 86-90.
Orwell, George. "Shooting An Elephant." Comley, et al. 92-97.

1992–93
The Death Penalty: Revenge Disguised as Punishment
Diane Miller

1   In May of 1990, the Government took Jesse Joseph Tafero's most precious possession—his life. Tafero was sentenced to death for killing two police officers fourteen years before. John Horgan, in *Scientific American,* gives a graphic account of Tafero 's execution.

When a prison officer threw the switch, a sponge delivering electricity to Tafero's skull burst into flames. The executioner cut the current for six seconds—during which Tafero, smoke pouring from his head, moved and breathed, according to eye witnesses—and then shocked him again. After a total of six minutes and three jolts, Tafero was pronounced dead (19).

Currently, more than 2,400 men and women are on Death Row, awaiting their executions (Smolowe 69). For a country to condone this horrible, torturous death is terrible, but for a government actually to cause it is appalling.
2   Supporters of the death penalty believe that killing criminals will reduce the rate of recidivism. Advocates say that killing the criminal prevents him from committing any more crimes. As Ernest Van den Haag, a supporter of the death penalty puts it, "Death is the surest way to bring about incapacitation . . . the person who suffered it will not commit other crimes" (266). Although this is true, the same result can be achieved through less drastic means. The government does not need to kill people to keep them from committing more crimes. The less severe and more humane way to prevent criminal actions is life imprisonment. Behind bars, the prisoner is no longer a threat to society.
3   Advocates also believe that the death penalty will be a deterrent to homicidal crimes. Van den Haag says that "Deterrence may prevent the potential [murderers] from becoming actual murderers" (267). The problem with this argument is that it is based on assumptions, not on facts. As Van den Haag points out, there is no empirical evidence to prove that capital punishment works as a deterrent, and there is no experiment that could prove the truth of such speculation (265). Although the idea that a person would be too scared of his own execution to kill another person sounds reasonable, individuals committing such horrible crimes usually do not weigh the consequences beforehand. Even if a person who is contemplating murder does consider the consequences, the threat of a lifetime in jail would be a significant deterrent in itself. David Cockburn, who addresses

the issue in *Philosophy,* says that "A long prison sentence might involve more suffering on the part of the prisoner than does execution" (180).

4   Many supporters of capital punishment claim that executing criminals saves the government money. People say that their tax money should not be used to house, clothe, and feed someone who has committed such a horrible crime as murder. They would rather put the criminal to death than pay to keep him or her alive. This thinking is based on misconception. Capital punishment actually costs tax payers more money than keeping a prisoner in jail for life. Christy Hoppe writes in the *Dallas Morning News* about just how expensive the death penalty is. Hoppe explains that the average trial and appeal process takes about 75 years and costs taxpayers in Texas an average $2.3 million per case. Rick Halperin, in the *Daily Campus,* writes that Ted Bundy's execution cost Florida taxpayers over six million dollars (5). To imprison someone in a maximum security single cell for forty years only costs about $750,000. The economic argument, then, cannot be used to support the death penalty.

5   Since the death penalty does not deter homicide, nor does it reduce taxpayers' cost, one may wonder why capital punishment is imposed in the United States. One disturbing possibility is that people want retribution. Some people are not satisfied that murderers are locked up, even though the public is safe from them. People want to get even. Some think that when a person commits a horrible crime, he or she deserves to die. An editor for *America* magazine recognizes that it is understandable for people to have a "fierce desire for vengeance" for violent crimes ("Let Death Penalty" 538), but he continues to say that "the desire for revenge is itself evil temptation to be resisted," and that people must "reject vengeance as an acceptable reason for executions" (539).

6   Those who support capital punishment do so for reasons they think are good, but in fact they are doing something evil. In *The Plague,* Camus explains that "The evil that is in this world always comes from ignorance, and good intentions may do as much harm as malevolence, if they lack understanding" (131). So when people say a man should be put to death, they see it to be "necessary to protect society" (Halperin), rather than recognizing the evil that it is In an ignorant attempt to do good, proponents of capital punishment are allowing the government to take human lives.

7   Capital punishment should not be legal in the United States. None of the supporting arguments stand. It does not decrease the murder rate, and it costs the government more money than imprisoning the criminals for life. The underlying reason that the death penalty is practiced is that many people want retribution. The government should not concede to some people's desire for vengeance, a desire that is clearly wrong. The worst part is" . . . that in taking a life the state makes all of us accomplices" ("Let Death Penalty" 539). So long as capital punishment is practiced in this country, all citizens are responsible for each and every death.

Works Cited

Camus, Albert. *The Plague*. Trans. Stuart Gilbert. New York: J.B. Lippincott Co., 1958.

Cockburn, David. "Capital Punishment and Realism." *Philosophy* 66 (1991): 177-91.

Halperin, Rick. "Tide Turning Against Death Penalty." *Daily Campus* 29 Jan. 1992: 5.

Hoppe, Christy. "Death Penalty Called Costly and Inefficient." *Dallas Morning News* 8 March 1992: 12A.

Horgan, John. "Science and the Citizen: the Death Penalty." *Scientific American* July 1990: 17-19.

"Let the Death Penalty Die." *America* 2 June 1990: 538-39.

Smolowe, Jill. "Race and the Death Penalty." *Time* 29 April 1991: 68-69.

Van den Haag, Ernest. "The Deterrent Effect of the Death Penalty." *Effective Argument*. Eds. Nicholas J. Carl and James R. Nichol. New York: Simon and Schuster, 1991. 264-268.

1993–94
SMU: Supporting Human Rights or Human Debasement?
Robin Rasnake

1 "The University will not tolerate the disrespect for the rights of anyone. ... All members of the University community are protected from harassment, including but not limited to members according to their race, ethnicity, age, gender" (*Peruna* 90). This quotation comes from the student code of conduct, and it relates directly to the issue at hand: should SMU allow an exhibition of art which is considered obscene by a presidential commission? After doing much research and weighing the importance of this particular section of the code of conduct, I see numerous reasons to keep the exhibition off campus, if not completely out of existence. If the presidential commission found the exhibit obscene, then it obviously contains material which may be considered pornographic. SMU must take the commission's opinion seriously, especially since pornography has such a detrimental effect on society and on this university community. Numerous studies point to pornography as a catalyst for sexually violent acts committed against all people, in particular, women. Pornography debases women's bodies, relationships, and equality in society. Thus, SMU should not sponsor the exhibition because it promotes the degradation and abuse of women.

2 One of the most damaging ways that pornography degrades women is that it "tells the viewer to treat another human being as a thing, not a person" (Osanka and Johann 263). A woman defines herself by her "person," how she feels about issues, what kind of job she has, what kind of family situation she is in, and other dynamics of her life. Pornography, though, totally destroys this "person." In Irving Kristol's essay, "Pornography, Obscenity, and the Case For Censorship," he writes that, "pornography's whole purpose ... is to treat human beings obscenely, to deprive them of their specifically human dimension" (527). Pornography breaks up the human as a whole being and focuses on specific body parts. Even F.M. Christensen, a supporter of pornography, admits that "most pornography has a limited scope; it contains little else besides sex" (537). In addition, during Christensen's interview with *Playboy*, when asked if pornography reduced people to mere body parts, he did not answer "no" (537). Pornography hurts the human aspects of women, and SMU has the responsibility to prevent an exhibit from doing just that.

3 Not only does pornography debase a woman's being, but it also debases her relationships, in particular, her sexual relationships. Most women in healthy

sexual relationships hold sex in high regard because it represents genuine caring feelings between two people. However, pornographic material depicts sex in an almost inhuman way. "When sex is public, the viewer cannot see the sentiments and the ideals, but sees only the animal coupling" (Kristol 528). This dangerous characteristic of pornography ruins the image of sex as a loving act and strips it of every human component. It suggests to viewers of pornography that a woman's sexual relationships are not worthy of the same respect as a man's. Susan Brownmiller also recognizes this danger in her book, *Against Our Will: Men, Women, and Rape,* and adds that pornography "is a cynical exploitation of female sexual activity through the device of making all such activity and consequently all females, 'dirty'" (533). This view of women not only denies their human worth, but it also encourages a perception of women as a group that can and should be victimized.

4   Almost every day there is a report on the news about a woman being sexually assaulted, and too often pornography is a causative factor in crimes like these (Brownmiller 534). There are many reasons why pornography is a factor in sex crimes, but one of the most important reasons is that "pornography is the philosophy of rape" (533). Rape is a violent denial of someone's self-worth, and when committed against a woman, rape is an expression of woman-hating. In Andrea Dworkin's *Letters from a War Zone,* she makes an interesting connection between pornography's promotion of woman-hating and violent sexual behavior like rape. She writes:

> Pornography is hate propaganda against women. . . . It is also behavior training. People say, "Oh, well, pornography—that's for masturbation, nobody can get hurt that way." But orgasm is a very serious reward, isn't it? Think of Pavlov's little dogs, right? They don't just think about salivating, they salivate. They do it because they learned it. Period. Now think about pornography. The dehumanization is a basic part of the content of all pornography without exception. (148)

In other words, some people who view pornography don't just think about abusing women sexually, they actually go out and abuse them. This is not just an assertion that Dworkin makes in her essay. Studies show that 65 to 70 percent of the women in pornography are victims of incest or child abuse, and almost all of these victims say their abusers used pornography (Osanka and Johann 273).

5   The findings of these studies are not only shocking; they are also relevant to SMU's consideration of the art exhibit. Because the exhibit has a pornographic angle, it will have a harmful effect on the students who view it. SMU must consider this effect because pornography has proven in various studies to be a powerful agent of socialization for men and boys, many of whom learn most of what they believe about women and sex through pornography (Osanka and

Johann 267). If male students view the exhibit, they may come away from it with a false, lesser view of women. SMU cannot chance such a result. Moreover, because the University has such an influential voice in the community, it has a responsibility to everyone in that community, especially to its female members, to prevent an exhibition that would present men with a degrading view of women. SMU must realize that:

> Pornography is more than images. Rape, battery, sexual harassment, prostitution, and child abuse are pornography. These acts become justified and reinforced by two myths—women like being violated and men have the right to violate them. Men learn how to abuse women from porn and come to believe that abuse is something women want. (Osanka and Johann 268)

Students, if given the opportunity to view the exhibit in question, may come closer to accepting these myths. SMU should not host an exhibition on campus that would allow students to view materials that have no redeeming value except as tools for debasing women.

6   Many people today think the women's movement has come to a stop or, perhaps, just quieted down a bit. They do not see anything else that women need to fight for; women supposedly have equal pay, equal jobs, equal everything, right? But apparently, a woman does not have the right not to be abused, violated, or used by pornography. Instead, a vocal group of people cites the First Amendment as enough reason to push women's rights to the back of the line of importance and put the rights of pornographers, molesters, and rapists in the front. This is a sickening reality, but one that women live with every day. Andrea Dworkin sums up the situation when she writes:

> Here's the reality of it, and I beg you to think about this when you hear all the shit that you hear about the First Amendment. I beg you to think about this Constitution that was crafted to protect the institution of slavery; crafted not to interfere with the buying and selling of human beings. It is not a surprise then that this state, regulated by this Constitution, is deeply insensitive to crimes against people that involve buying and selling them. ("Woman-Hating" 36)

7   Unless SMU wants to earn a reputation for promoting the virtual enslavement of women, which is what pornography does, then it has no choice but to ban the exhibition. Not only would the University be tarnishing its reputation, it would also be blatantly disregarding the promise that is made in the code of conduct, "The University will not tolerate the disrespect for the rights of anyone." This promise suggests a responsibility on the part of the University not to deny women their basic rights even in favor of something called "art."

Works Cited

Brownmiller, Susan. "Pornography Hurts Women." *Writing Arguments*. Eds. John D. Ramage and John C. Bean. 2nd ed. New York: Macmillan, 1992. 532-35.

Christensen, F. M. "A Philosopher Looks at the Porn Debate." *Writing Arguments*. Eds. John D. Ramage and John C. Bean. 2nd ed. New York: Macmillan, 1992. 536-38.

Dworkin, Andrea. *Letters from a War Zone*. London: Seeker & Warburg, 1988.

_____. "Woman-Hating Right and Left." *The Sexual Liberals and the Attack on Feminism*. Eds. Dorchen Liedholdt and Janice G. Raymond. New York: Pergamon Press, 1990. 28-40.

Kristol, Irving. "Pornography, Obscenity, and the Case for Censorship." *Writing Arguments*. Eds. John D. Ramage and John C. Bean. 2nd ed. New York: Macmillan, 1992. 526-29.

Osanka, Franklin Mark and Sara Lee Johann. *Sourcebook on Pornography*. Canada: Lexington Books, 1989.

Peruna Express 1992-93. Dallas: Southern Methodist University, 1992.

1994–95
Banning Smoking: Our Only Hope
James Box

James Box, an avowed nonsmoker, anticipates that much of his audience will resist his proposed government prohibition of smoking. Consequently, he supplies abundant factual evidence to support his assertion that smoking threatens everyone, and he appeals to the audience's emotions by stressing the potential harm to children. Moreover, he is careful to counter major points of opposition and to cite precedents to show that his proposal is reasonable. His Annotated Works Cited and Works Consulted illustrate the variety of sources he examined and the decisions he made about which ones most effectively supported his argument.

1   As a nonsmoker, I do not like the unpleasant odor of cigarette smoke, and it annoys me to smell this way when I come home from a party. But smoking does not merely irritate—it kills. Smoking is one of the most important health issues in this country. It has been for quite some time, and it will continue to be important as long as people keep smoking. Former U.S. Surgeon General C. Everett Koop says that the issue of smoking has been his number one priority for most of his career (U.S., *Smoke*). He has constantly urged us to stop smoking so that we don't endanger ourselves and others. Still, many Americans continue to "light up" every day.

2   Some things have been done to protect us. Restaurants such as McDonald's, most airlines, and many workplaces have banned smoking. Unfortunately, however, smoking extends beyond the workplace or other public places. Smoking happens everywhere, affecting all of us, and these current individual policies aren't enough to protect everyone from the health hazards of smoking. Consequently, I propose that the government ban the smoking of cigarettes in the United States.

3   Obviously, the ban on cigarette smoking would be a drastic change, one that would not be pleasant for the large and powerful tobacco industry. Nearly 47,000 people would lose their jobs as a result of a ban. The tobacco companies' annual revenues from cigarette sales are about $48 billion. Also, tobacco produces about a $4 billion trade surplus ("Should" 36). So, what happens to the tobacco industry? These companies are already looking into their futures by diversifying their businesses. Philip Morris, which produces the popular Marlboro cigarettes, also owns Kraft, a food company, and Femsa, a Mexican beer company (Haas 53). They may be able to place their tobacco workers into other jobs. Moreover, the government could help people find other jobs before

the ban begins. Banning smoking in the United States won't necessarily shut down the state of North Carolina.

4   Moreover, there may actually be some economic gains produced by a ban on smoking. Since smoking leads to illness, people miss work because of smoking. If we consider that health problems will decrease due to an end to smoking, then people will not have to miss as much work. According to government estimates, companies could gain an additional $8.4 billion due to the decrease in smoking related absenteeism ("Should" 36). Additionally, smoking adds to the cost of business due to the lack of productivity on the job. Studies show that workers would increase productivity if smoking breaks were eliminated, saving businesses about $4,000 per former smoker (Weis 339-41). Clearly, these economic gains are secondary to the health gains, but concern about health could lead to greater productivity.

5   Many argue that a person has a right to smoke in this country. Naturally, this is an important issue, for our country is centered around freedom and rights. But, does the right to smoke exist? According to Dr. Koop, "If you smoke, you are playing a kind of Russian roulette with your health, and perhaps, with your life" (U.S., *Smoke*). Many smokers say that they have the right to do whatever they want to their bodies, but many current laws do protect us from ourselves. For example, the law makes it illegal to drive without wearing a seatbelt. This law protects us from the risk of injury in an accident. Similarly, a law against smoking would protect people from harming themselves. Perhaps more importantly, the seatbelt laws protect people other than the driver from possible harm in an accident; they protect crash victims from another person's actions. A law against smoking would also prevent possible harm due to someone else's actions. In particular, the seatbelt laws protect children from the risk of injury due to their caretakers' actions. A ban on smoking would also save children from the risk of injury.

6   So why not ban other harmful substances such as alcohol? Drinking isn't healthy, either. However, smoking is a much bigger problem because it directly affects so many people. If I sit in a crowded bar where other people are smoking, then I could be physically harmed by the smoke. On the other hand, if people around me are drinking, their consumption does not directly harm me. Although they may later crash into me while driving drunk, their beer does not go down my throat.

7   Let's look at the facts. Cigarettes first harm the people who smoke them. Every year, there are new reports about the health risks of smoking. The Public Health Service reports that a smoker has a risk of sudden cardiac death three times greater than that of a person who does not smoke. About 85% of all lung cancers in the United States are caused by smoking. People who smoke two packs a day have a lung cancer death rate twenty-five times greater than the rate for people who don't smoke at all. Moreover, cigarette smoking is the major cause of

chronic obstructive lung disease, especially emphysema and chronic bronchitis. Emphysema, common among older people who have smoked, is rarely found among older nonsmokers. Women who are pregnant have an increased risk of delivering their babies prematurely, or of aborting the fetus spontaneously (U.S., *Smoke*).

8   While smokers may choose to assume a risk despite the facts, they cannot be permitted to place nonsmokers at risk. "Passive smoking" is probably the most important issue in the ban on smoking. Here are some facts about passive smoking as reported by the U.S. Office on Smoking and Health: Nonsmokers exposed to tobacco smoke in the air absorb nicotine, carbon monoxide, and other elements of tobacco smoke. Contaminants from tobacco smoke in homes, worksites, and in public places may reach levels that exceed those allowed by environmental and occupational regulations. Basically, smoking pollutes the air. Tobacco smoke is physically irritating to many people, and it can provoke the symptoms of asthma, chronic bronchitis, and allergies. Exposure to tobacco smoke may cause disease, including lung cancer, in otherwise healthy adults. Reports show that the number of deaths due to passive smoking could be as many of 5,000 a year (U.S., *Statement*). And, there is new evidence that passive smoking can reach a fetus. A recent report of the American Medical Association states that harmful elements of cigarette smoke can reach a woman's fetus if she is routinely exposed to secondhand smoke ("Passive"). Again, a ban on smoking would alleviate these health problems.

9   In the home, where current antismoking regulations have no influence, secondhand smoke does the most harm. John F. Banzhaf, III, executive director of Action on Smoking and Health, gives disturbing information on smoking and its effects on children. First, he states that the smallest level of exposure to the cancer-causing elements of smoke (group-A carcinogens) can be potentially deadly. He insists that kids are hurt the worst by passive smoking: "'Young children are most susceptible to all sorts of illnesses because they have smaller airways, breathe more rapidly, and have more lung area per body than adults'" (Israeloff 54).

10   According to the U.S. Office of Smoking and Health, many studies by the Environmental Protection Agency (EPA) and other national agencies have been conducted about the effects of Environmental Tobacco Smoke (ETS) on children. The studies show that ETS exposure causes between 150,000 and 300,000 cases a year of bronchitis and pneumonia in children under eighteen months old. The EPA also says that 200,000 to one million asthmatic children experience more frequent attacks when exposed to ETS, and between 8,000 to 26,000 children will develop asthma each year if their parents smoke ten or more cigarettes a day. The National Center for Health Statistics says that infants who are exposed to ETS are two times more likely to die of Sudden Infant Death Syndrome than children whose parents don't smoke. Finally, the EPA says that children are

exposed to the harm of cigarette smoke not only in public places but also in the places they consider the safest: their homes and family automobiles (Israeloff 54-55). A ban on smoking would end smoking in the home, which causes so much harm to children. Like the child seatbelt laws and other safety regulations, an antismoking law would protect children from possible health risks caused by their parents' actions.

11 Some steps are already being taken to protect our children. Cases related to passive smoking and children are already making their way into the courtroom. Last year, in a ground breaking court decision in California, a woman lost custody of her daughter to her ex-husband. The eight-year-old girl had asthma, and her health problems became worse due to her mother's chain smoking (Sachs). The mother's argument was that a parent should only lose custody because of abuse or neglect. Since smoking is legal, she said, she was not doing anything wrong. But let's face it—smoking in the presence of a child is abuse, and the courts seem to now be classifying parental smoking as abuse or negligence. Eleven other states have addressed the same issue, and their decisions have usually been in favor of the nonsmoking parent (Sachs). Also, more than sixteen court orders have been issued across the nation to stop parents from smoking in the presence of their children (Israeloff 54). With these decisions, our courts are telling us that smoking does threaten people. Basically, these court decisions are already banning smoking in some instances. So, we might as well save the courts time and money.

12 These are the facts, folks. Nonsmokers have been trying to convince smokers that they are hurting everyone by their actions. These efforts have helped, but there is still much more to be done. Dr. Koop says that we cannot be satisfied until we are a completely smoke-free society. Without a ban on smoking, things can only get worse. Just think about Grandpa suffering through cancer treatments in the hospital, only to return there later to rot away in a hospital bed, breathing in oxygen through a mask. If Grandpa had not smoked a pack a day, maybe he would be fishing now. Just think about little Suzy sitting in a classroom while her friends are outside playing. Poor Suzy cannot play because she has chronic asthma due to her parents' smoking. We can put an end to these horrible stories. A ban on smoking is our only realistic hope.

Annotated Works Cited

Haas, Nancy. "Fighting and Switching." *Newsweek* 21 Mar. 1994: 52-53. Useful in treatment of the opposition. Provides current information on the tobacco companies, including statistics on their income. Also shows that tobacco companies are diversifying their businesses to cope with drops in domestic tobacco income.

Israeloff, Roberta. "How Secondhand Smoke Hurts Kids." *Parents Magazine*

Aug. 1993: 54-57. This is a very detailed article about secondhand smoke and the harm to children. Gives statistics and details on these effects, including several current reports by the EPA and other national health research agencies. Extremely helpful in showing the possible harms to children caused by parental smoking.

"Passive Smoking Is Found In Newborns." *New York Times* 23 Feb. 1994: C12. Provides the results of studies by the AMA on the presence of cigarette smoke in the fetus. Helped in my discussion of the harm of passive smoking.

Sachs, Andrea. "Home Smoke-Free Home." *Time* 25 Oct. 1993: 56. Shows the current legal battles related to parental smoking. The case presented shows that the government does consider smoking to be abuse. Helpful in showing that smoking hurts kids and that steps are already being taken in favor of nonsmokers.

"Should Cigarettes Be Outlawed?" *U.S. News and World Report* 18 Apr. 1994: 32-38. Shows the pros and cons of a ban on smoking. This source helped in giving me a background on smoking-related issues and helped me to look for items to research in more detail.

United States. Dept. of Health and Human Services. Public Health Service. Office of the Surgeon General. *A Smoke Free Society*. Washington: GPO, 1988. Letter by former Surgeon General Koop urging Americans to quit smoking. Gives details of the health hazards caused by cigarettes. Very helpful in establishing the need to stop smoking. The health facts were helpful in showing the effects of passive smoking.

―――――. Dept. of Health and Human Services. Public Health Service. Office on Smoking and Health. *A Statement on the Health Effects of Passive Smoking*. Washington: GPO, 1985. Provides facts and statistics about the possible harms caused by passive smoking. Extremely helpful in my argument on how a ban would end the harm caused by passive smoking.

Weis, W.L. "No Ifs, Ands, or Butts: Why Workplace Smoking Should Be Banned." *Management World* Sept. 1981 : 339-344. Explores the economic issues related to smoking in the workplace and shows business losses due to cigarette smoking. Helpful in showing how a ban would lead to economic gains.

Annotated Works Consulted

Doyle, Nancy. *Involuntary Smoking: Health Risks for Nonsmokers*. New York: Public Affairs Committee, 1987. Designed to show nonsmokers the health hazards of passive smoking. Gives facts about passive smoking, as well as suggestions for dealing with it Informed me both about health issues and about how people feel about the issue.

Tollison, Robert D., and Richard E. Wagner. *The Economics of Smoking*. Norwell: Kluwer Academic Publishers, 1992. Explores the economic issues related to smoking, including cigarette taxes and smoking in the workplace. It helped me explore the economic benefits due to a ban on smoking and gave me references related to the issue.

Troyer, Ronald J., and Gerald E. Markle. *Cigarettes: The Battle Over Smoking.* New Brunswick: Rutgers University Press, 1983. Explores the history of the debate on smoking. Covers the health, economic, and psychological aspects of smoking. Helpful in providing necessary background information for my argument.

United States Dept. of Health, Education, and Welfare. Public Health Service. *Smoking and Health: A Report of the Surgeon General.* Washington: GPO, 1979. Provides background information on the health hazards of smoking, as well as steps for prevention. Helped me understand the effects of smoking and the Surgeon General's view on smoking. The source is actually designed to convince people to quit smoking and then to help them quit.

Viscusi, W. Kip. *Smoking: Making the Risky Decision.* New York: Oxford University Press, 1992. Explores all the issues related to smoking and gives views on both sides of these issues. Also gives background information to help prepare my proposal and argument.

1995-96
Homosexuality and Baptist Ideals
Katherine Echols

Religious leaders often use the Bible to support their positions on social issues. In this essay, Katherine Echols uses close Biblical textual analysis to substantiate her argument that some Baptists are unnecessarily harsh in their condemnation of homosexuality.

1   On a sunny April afternoon in Topeka, Kansas, mourners gather inside a church to attend the funeral of a loved one who died of AIDS. However, this funeral is no ordinary funeral. Instead of being allowed to grieve in peace, those attending are interrupted on their way in and out of the church by cries of "Fags in hell" and "God hates fags—Romans 9:13." Picketers carrying signs march around the church, around the parking lot, and even around the mourners themselves. The leader of these cruel and unfeeling demonstrations is the Reverend Fred Phelps, pastor of Westboro Baptist Church in Topeka. Phelps devotes the majority of his time and ministry to proclaiming his hate for homosexuals. His children and grandchildren support him in his efforts, helping him distribute flyers bearing hate messages to known homosexuals in town, several of whom are prominent members of the community.

2   To repeat a bumper sticker philosophy, "Hate is not a family value." Although most instances of discrimination are not as severe as those demonstrated by Phelps, the members and general teachings of the Baptist church actively discriminate against homosexuals. Homosexuals are almost always denied ordination, denied membership, and denied the kingdom of heaven (Geis 42). Christians should not condemn homosexuals; this is not in accordance with God's will. Jesus Christ taught his followers to love one another, to reach out to one another, and not to hate. His apostle Paul wrote to the Galatians that Christians must love their neighbor as themselves. Because homosexuals are valuable members of society, and because they are no less valuable in God's sight than heterosexuals, the Baptist church, in its effort to become like Christ, should reconsider its present stance regarding homosexuality.

3   In order to observe Baptist discrimination against homosexuality, one only has to examine the statements of the Reverend Jerry Falwell: "Homosexuals represent the devil, Satan" (Gomes 497). Activists expressed a similar outlook in a 1977 campaign to abolish homosexual civil rights in Dade County, Florida. A Baptist minister in Dade County stated, "We are facing the devil himself in homosexuals." Cars in the Dade County area carried bumper stickers that

read."Kill a queer for Christ" (Scanzoni & Mollenkott 2). These attitudes seem to be relatively common among Baptists and other religious fundamentalists in America. From the pulpits of many Baptist churches, one often hears that homosexuals may not enter the kingdom of God, that they are condemned to hell. Churches often refuse self-avowed homosexuals membership, and almost always deny them ordination in the Southern Baptist Church (Geis 43). Can these attitudes of discrimination and intolerance be allowed to continue in the Baptist denomination? Can these prejudices be ignored, permitting the church members to continue to convey these philosophies of utter hatred? Clearly they cannot.

4   Several causes contribute to this discriminatory point of view, foremost being interpretation of the original Greek and Hebrew texts of the Bible and the context in which those texts were written. Members and ministers such as Phelps and Falwell serve as perpetuating causes, keeping the issue and their prejudiced opinions in the forefront of church members' minds. While adherence to tradition and fear of change are causes that are not easily provable or observable, they still contribute to the problem of discrimination. In order to develop the points of interpretation and context, the scriptures which scholars commonly interpret to condemn homosexuality will be examined in two parts: Old Testament passages and New Testament passages.

5   Perhaps the most common Biblical passage used to condemn homosexuality is the story of Sodom and Gomorrah, found in Genesis 19:4-11: (This and all subsequent Biblical references not otherwise noted are from *The Student Bible, New International Version*.)

> But before they lay down, the men of the city, the men of Sodom, both young and old, all the people to the last man, surrounded the house; and they called to Lot, 'Where are the men who came to you tonight? Bring them out to us, that we may know them.' Lot went out of the door to the men, shut the door after him, and said, 'I beg you, my brothers, do not act so wickedly. Behold, I have two daughters who have not known man; let me bring them out to you, and do to them as you please; only do nothing to these men, for they have come under the shelter of my roof.' But they said, 'Stand back! 'And they said, 'This fellow came to sojourn, and he would play the judge! Now we will deal worse with you than with them.' Then they pressed hard against the man Lot, and drew near to break the door. But the men put forth their hands and brought Lot into the house to them, and shut the door. And they struck with blindness the men who were at the door of the house, both small and great, so that they wearied themselves groping for the door.

6   The problem with the story of Sodom and Gomorrah is a question of context. Lot's visitors were messengers of God, sent to warn Lot and his family of the impending destruction of Sodom. God decided to destroy Sodom because of the

people's inhospitality (Luke 10:10-13), greed, and failure to care for the poor (Ezekiel 16:49-50), not because of homosexual sins (Gomes 498). The homosexual assault in this passage is merely evidence of the inhospitality for which God condemned the Sodomites, rather than the cause itself. The *yadha*, which means "to know," appears in this passage. According to D.S. Bailey, author of several books addressing homosexuality and Christianity, *yadha* emerges 943 times in the Old Testament; only ten of the 943 refer to sexual acts, and those ten refer exclusively to heterosexual acts (Jones 68). In this instance, the author uses *yadha* to indicate intellectual and social knowledge (Mickey 55). Another similar passage in the Old Testament, Judges 19:22-25, is often used along with the story of Sodom and Gomorrah in order to denounce homosexuality. This passage deals with the destruction of Gibeah, a town that was also destroyed because its people were inhospitable. The words and circumstances of this passage are similar to those in Genesis 19, and for the same reasons one can conclude that the passage also has been interpreted incorrectly.

7   The Holiness Codes, found in Leviticus 18:19-23 and 20:10-16, also appear to condemn homosexuality. In these passages, homosexuality is referred to among a list of other sexual "sins." At the same time, however, the codes speak out against wearing clothing made of a mixed blend of fabric, cross-breeding animals, eating rare meat, and planting two different kinds of seed in the same field (Gomes 498). These laws were given to the children of Israel by God before the birth of Christ. The Reverend L. Robert Arthur points out in his book that the Mosaic Laws of the Old Testament "should be interpreted in the light of the theology of St. Paul, explained in his letter to the Galatians, 3:23-25: 'But before faith came, we were kept under the law, shut up unto the faith which should afterward be revealed. Wherefore the Law was our schoolmaster to bring us unto Christ, that we might be justified by faith. But after that faith is come, we are no longer under a schoolmaster'" (Arthur 5). In its doctrine, the Baptist church affirms that Christ fulfilled the laws of the Old Testament, that these laws were no longer needed for redemption. Along with this principle, the church also asserts that the old laws are no longer enough to "save" mankind, that Jesus Christ is the only way to "come to the Father" (John 14:6). The Holiness Codes are therefore rendered unnecessary and ineffective to the Christian faith.

8   The writings in the New Testament deal somewhat differently with the issue of homosexuality. Jesus Christ himself never expressed his views on the subject (Gomes 498). Paul wrote about homosexuality in three different passages: Romans 1:27, I Corinthians 6:9, and 1 Timothy 1:10. Only in Romans does the scripture directly deal with homosexuality:

> Because of this, God gave them over to shameful lusts. Even their women exchanged natural relations for unnatural ones. In the same way the men also abandoned natural relations with women and were inflamed with lust

for one another. Men committed indecent acts with other men, and received in themselves the due penalty for their perversion (1:26-27).

9   In this passage, Paul is speaking out against the people's rejection of God, and their subsequent worship of people and things. These verses speak out against idolatry, and cannot be applied only to homosexuals. According to Scanzoni and Mollenkott:

> What seems 'natural' in any culture is often simply a matter of accepted social custom, and sometimes Paul spoke of nature in that way. For example, in 1 Cor. 11:14-15, Paul raises the question, 'Does not Nature herself teach you that while flowing locks disgrace a man, they are a woman's glory?' However, in Greek and Roman culture, homosexuality was at least to some extent part of accepted social custom, and no doubt it seemed as natural as anything else to many persons. Thus, in Rom. 1:26-27, it is doubtful that Paul is speaking of nature in the sense of custom, unless he is referring to a violation of Jewish custom and law (64).

10 From the same passage, the fact that "men also abandoned natural relations with women" must also be addressed. Scientists and theologians alike define homosexuality in terms of those who are inverts, and those who are perverts. An invert, according to Sigmund Freud, is "attracted exclusively to members of his own sex, with absolutely no desire for heterosexual relationships" (Jones 16). On the other hand, a pervert is one who "knowingly and self-consciously" engages in sexual behaviors that violate known values, socialization influences, and so on. These could include both heterosexual perversions as well as homosexual perversions, but clearly they would be a self-conscious departure from a psychologically and sociologically perceived and experienced norm (Mickey 66). Romans clearly implies that these men and women were perverts, rather than inverts, who lusted after others and "gave up natural relations."

11 In the two other passages in the New Testament that speak out against homosexuality, 1 Corinthians 6:9 and 1 Timothy 1:8-11, homosexuality appears among a list of other sins. Arthur argues that the words in the original texts that have traditionally been interpreted to mean homosexuality in these passages have no association with homosexuality whatsoever. The word *arsenokites* meant "temple prostitutes" in the first-century translations of the Bible. Arthur explains the use of *arsenokites* in light of the fact that the people of that day offered sexual offerings to the gods, and prostitutes, both male and female, remained at the temple to receive the offerings. The other word, *malakos,* which translators also interpreted to mean homosexuality, actually means "spineless." Paul was speaking out against those who were without the backbone to stand up for what they knew was right (Arthur 8).

12 Throughout the years, the church has chosen to single out the homosexual as particularly offensive. Even if fundamentalists are correct in their interpretation

of the Bible as condemning homosexuality, Biblical authors did not single out homosexuality as being more offensive than any of the other sins with which it appears in the New Testament passages. The homosexual in the fundamentalist church has become ostracized and deemed unworthy of membership in the fellowship of believers. According to Helmut Thielicke, a contemporary Christian theologian, the church should not simply tell the homosexual that he "is a sinner and is thus 'unsuited for the kingdom of God.' . . . What we must do is study the problem at great depth and listen carefully to what the homosexual has to say, recognizing that he is no greater a sinner than any of us and that his deviation is 'a kind of symptomatic participation in the fate of the fallen world'" (Jones 76). The church must remember its assertion that God's grace is available to us all, according to the scriptures, and it must be realistic in facing the facts about homosexuality, welcoming those whom society ostracizes and educating the members of the church. Christians should also remember its affirmation that Christ himself healed, taught, and ate with sinners.

13 The following, taken directly from *The Book of Discipline of the United Methodist Church*, could be a model for Christians dealing with the question of homosexuality:

> Homosexual persons no less than heterosexual persons are individuals of sacred worth. All persons need the ministry and guidance of the Church in their struggles for human fulfillment, as well as the spiritual and emotional care of a fellowship which enables reconciling relationships with God, with others, and with self. Although we do not condone the practice of homosexuality and consider this practice incompatible with Christian teaching, we affirm that God's grace is available to all. We commit ourselves to be in ministry for and with all persons (96).

14 Overcoming the stereotypes of homosexuality and the fears and traditional teachings of the church is not an easy task. It is not proposed that the Baptist church radically change its views regarding homosexuality. However, the church should consider adopting a more open-minded philosophy, one that would allow homosexuals to become members of the church, to worship as others do, and to feel welcome in a loving body of believers.

Works Cited

Arthur, L. Robert. *Homosexuality in the Light of Biblical Language and Culture.* Los Angeles: The Universal Fellowship Press, 1977.

Associated Press. "Minister plans to continue picketing AIDS victims." *The Dallas Morning News* 10 April 1993: 7A.

Geis, Sally B. and Donald E. Messer, eds. *Caught in the Crossfire: Helping Christians Debate Homosexuality.* Nashville: Abingdon Press, 1994.

Gomes, Peter J. "Homophobic? Reread Your Bible." *The Aims of Argument*. Eds. Timothy W. Crusius and Carolyn E. Channell Mountain View, California: Mayfield Publishing Co., 1995. 497-499.

Jones, Kimball. *Toward a Christian Understanding of the Homosexual.* New York: Association Press, 1966.

Mickey, Paul A. *Of Sacred Worth*. Nashville: Abingdon Press 1991.

Patterson, Ronald P., et al., eds. *The Book of Discipline of the United Methodist Church*. Nashville: The United Methodist Publishing House, 1988.

Scanzoni, Letha, and Virginia Ramey Mollenkott. *Is the Homosexual My Neighbor?* San Francisco: Harper & Row, 1978.

The Student Bible. New International Version. Grand Rapids, Michigan: Zondervan Bible Publishers, 1990.

1995–96
La Vida Loca
(The Crazy Life)
Eddie Frazer

Eddie Frazer writes movingly about his years as a member of a Dallas gang. He analyzes the reasons he believes gangs and gang violence are spreading so rapidly in our culture and suggests ways to overcome the problem.

1   At 12:00 noon I stepped outside for the lunch break. I walked toward the brick wall of the schoolyard where my friends Noe, Julian, and the others stood. Noe asked, *"Esta listo, carnal?"* (You ready, brother?) I nodded, but I couldn't stop shaking. I felt like vomiting because I was so scared. When our enemies, a group of approximately 15 guys, came toward us, my legs trembled involuntarily. I had fought many times, but I had also been severely beaten, and the fear never left me. I had to stand my ground: I was new and had to prove myself. If I did not, I would be marked as spineless and would have to be on guard every day. This time, fate intervened. A school security guard broke us up and sent us inside. Rarely, however, did such a savior appear. As the years passed, I took part in many bloody battles, both in and out of the schoolyard.
2   In five years I had become one of the gang leaders: my friends and I stood on the front line as a fight was about to begin. The less-experienced waited with respect behind us for our signal. By now, my body trembled not with fear but with anger and determination to fight and win. I fought hard and enjoyed watching the fear in my opponents' eyes as they went down. Over the years, I had developed into someone to be feared. I never forgot the beating I had received and vowed that neither I nor anyone I loved would ever again suffer such a humiliation. I liked to live this way: the more respect we earned, the less we had to fight and be on the lookout. Even so, if one of us walked home alone, he might be attacked. Luckily, nobody decided to shoot at us.
3   Although my best friend, Raul, and I were fighters, we were also above average students. We knew that college was the best way to get out of *la vida loca,* or the crazy life, before it destroyed us. We were not the toughest or the craziest. Our lives were easy compared to the lives of many of our friends who had joined the gangs that were spreading rapidly throughout Dallas. Raul and I had loving families to support us. The real gangsters had only their gangs to rely on. Gangs function as families for many young people. Not finding love in their families, they devote themselves to their *clika,* or gang.

4   Gangs all basically operate in the same way. To enter, you must prove that you will be loyal and can take a beating or even die for your *carnales* (brothers). The initiation is usually a timed fight, depending on the individual's fighting ability. A small, young initiate might have to fight three gang members for one minute each, while an older person might have to fight up to seven people for seven minutes each. Sometimes there is no time limit. Gangs also test bravery. The test might be stealing a car or participating in a drive-by shooting. Members usually feel no guilt for their actions: if someone tries to harm one of the "homeboys," he deserves to be crushed.

5   In my former gang, the Oak Cliff Syndicate (O.C.S.), the members took nicknames to conceal their identities from the police. "Too Tall," "Jason," "Puppet," "Wilo," and "Lucifer" were just a few of my associates. If a witness said, "I saw Puppet do it," the police would have nothing to go on because the nicknames are so common.

6   Most gangs have dress codes. They wear their "colors" or have *placas,* or tattoos, that symbolize their gangs. My mom told me that when she was growing up in the projects in West Dallas, the lowriders, or *cholos,* wore khakis, house shoes, T-shirts, and flannels. Back then, this was not strictly a dress code, but was the only dress they could afford. The clothes were inexpensive, but the *cholos* would press them and keep them clean to turn their appearance into something honorable because it was all they had. Today a dress code is popular with most gangs.

7   The two most notorious gangs in America are the Bloods, who wear red, and the Crips, who wear black or blue. Michael B. Green, a former Crip, reports that the Crips also wear British Knights brand clothing, with the BK standing for "Blood Killer" (Green 46). The color for the Oak Cliff Syndicate is green. As members, we proudly wore green, even though we knew we could be killed by rival members of other gangs just for doing so. Gangs also devise identifying hand signals, or form letters with their fingers. These signs are used to greet other gang members, and as Ice-T put it, "You can tell another gang member to f--- off by throwing up your signals" (Ice-T 64). Wearing colors and throwing hand signals is dangerous for anyone. My fellow gang member, Lucifer, so-called because of his ferocious nature, told me once, "You should wear your colors, throw up your signs, and be ready to fight and go down for your *clika.* This ain't no game, this is the real thing, and if you can't hang with us you better not even think of joining."

8   Many teenagers join gangs to feel wanted. According to *Aztlan* magazine, most gang members are rebellious because of a stressful environment and their minority status (Moore and Vigil 27). Many feel trapped in the ghetto. They think they will never be able to get out, so they feel they should have pride and protect their neighborhoods. One Hispanic male commented, "We can't compete with whites because we know our place. Other *barrios,* they're our

competition. We take pride in our little nation and if any intruder enters . . . we feel our community is being threatened" (Moore and Vigil).

9   For teenagers, puberty is a very confusing time. I remember feeling lost. I was not a child, but I wasn't a man either. Even though I very much wanted to grow up, I felt no one would let me. Most children entering their teens feel the same way, and those who live in poverty or have one or no parents have a larger burden. Some are fortunate enough to have parents or others to steer them in the right direction and love them, but those who don't often turn to gangs. In a gang, one is not a child but a man responsible for his new family. To many such teens, the gang is the only entity that loves and cares for them. They don't want to return to being alone without love, so if their gang is threatened, they naturally become violent and protective. Without their gang, many feel no love, only thoughts of hate and suicide.

10   Last year, I brought my friend Puppet to SMU to encourage him to go to college. As we drove home, he told me that he felt he was not wanted and was looked down upon by SMU students. "They acted like I was gonna stab 'em or something," he said. "I get treated a lot better back in the 'hood" I still push him to study, but I feel his discouragement also.

11   The gang problem today is not the gangs themselves. The problem is violence. Most gangsters live in poverty and feel they have nothing left to lose. As James Baldwin says, a man with nothing to lose is "the most dangerous creation of any society" (Baldwin 76). In the ghetto, if you sit there and do nothing, you will go crazy. If you depend on the police to serve justice, most of the time you will lose. Those who live in the ghetto believe, rightly or wrongly, that the police want the ghetto to destroy itself. They believe also that if one gang member kills another, the police won't pursue the killer.

12   Gang violence has been growing for years, so it will take more than one step to solve it. Teenagers who turn to gangs for love often look up to murderers and drug dealers. Since the gangs are their only source of love, it is natural for the teens to want to become like the people they admire. Teens need better role models to show them better ways to survive. They need to understand that education will help them. Raul and I were taught these things by our parents, so we were blessed. Some of our friends have not been as fortunate, so we try to be good role models for them. Many have looked up to us and are following in our footsteps. Puppet is now a soccer player at Cedar Hill High School and wants to play for SMU. Lucifer, once a coldhearted murderer, has turned to God for forgiveness. His dream is to become a policeman and help children stay out of gangs. He, like many others, is trying to resist *la vida loca*—the crazy life.

13   Gang life is tempting, and like the taste for sex, drugs, or alcohol, the longing for gang life will always burn inside any former gangster. As Ice-T has said, the ultimate rush for any man is power (Ice-T 139). The power a gangster possesses is more addictive than any drug. Teenagers must be taught better ways to resist

the temptation of gang life. The best way is to teach a child right from wrong from the beginning. Help can also come from those who have made it out of the ghetto and those who have never been there. Looking down on victims of poverty will only add fire to their frustration. Looking away achieves nothing. Most of America does not see what kids are going through, and their eyes must be opened. Instead of ignoring violence on the street, we should do what we can to help. America needs all the help it can get. A boy is murdered on the street. He has been shot and run over by a car numerous times. His homeboys see this and enter their cars crying. Then they go out and murder. If no one lifts a finger to stop all the violence, it will spread rapidly, and many of our children will be consumed by *la vida loca*.

Works Cited

Baldwin, James. *The Fire Next Time*. New York: Vintage, 1963.
Green, Michael B. "You see a red flag, shoot." *Sports Illustrated* May 1994: 46.
Ice-T. "To Live and Die in L.A." *Playboy* February 1994: 64, 139, 140.
Moore, Joan W. and James Diego Vigil. "Chicano Gangs: Group Norms and Adult Factors Relating to Adult Criminality." *Aztlan* Fall 1987: 27, 31.

1996–97

In their essays, Bruce A. Lynch and Theresa Stefanko show how careful analysis of a writer's techniques can shed light on a text's purpose and meaning. Lynch also demonstrates how a strong thesis can "redeem" a five paragraph essay.

How King Changed Time
Bruce A. Lynch

1   Martin Luther King, Jr.'s "Letter from Birmingham Jail" is a response to criticism of his tactics by white clergymen. Although the letter has been widely read, its target audience was the specific group of white clergymen who had urged him to adopt a more passive stance in the struggle for civil rights. Each paragraph is like a wave pounding away at the shoreline of white resentment. And as with waves, it is the structure that gives each paragraph its strength. However, no two paragraphs are identical in structure. One of the most powerful paragraphs in the letter is paragraph twenty-six. This paragraph can be divided into three parts. It begins with King's explanation of the argument of the white clergymen; King then refutes the argument; and finally, he states his vision of the future in relation to this argument. What makes this structure unique is that King discusses the recurring theme of "time" in each portion. However, he changes its meaning in each segment. By doing this, King is able to sway the opinion of the white clergymen toward his viewpoint. He begins the paragraph with a definition of time that is comfortable to his audience. He then gradually shifts the meaning to a more neutral context. And finally, he convinces the readers to accept a definition of time totally contrary to the definition with which they began the paragraph.

2   Paragraph twenty-six begins with an explanation of the white clergymen's opposition to one of King's ideas. The white clergymen have expressed the belief that blacks have not waited long enough for their civil rights and that it is just a matter of time and patience before they receive them. To solidify their view, they refer to the fact that the Christians waited thousands of years for their civil rights and the blacks have waited only several hundred. In this context, time is a gradual catalyst; when allowed to go forward on its own accord, it will, without doubt, provide a positive result. King captures the true essence of the white clergymen's beliefs when he writes that "there is something in the very flow of time that will inevitably cure all ills"(120). This is a view that was accepted by many whites at the time. They knew that eventually blacks would

attain equal rights; they just did not want it to occur yet. But near the end of this section, King begins to wean the reader off the concept of time as a positive entity. Here, he refers to the beliefs of the white clergymen as a "misconception of time"(120). The choice of the word "misconception" is very important because King is trying gradually to pull the white clergymen toward his ideology rather than simply pushing his views down their throats. "Misconception" implies that King can see where the idea came from, but he also can see a small mistake in the reasoning behind it. It has a much more amicable connotation than if he had simply said this idea is wrong. The readers can feel King's interest in their beliefs and ideas. Thus, King has achieved his first step in getting the white clergymen on his side. He has gotten them to trust him.

3   Now that King has his target audience trusting him, he chooses to present time as a more neutral entity in an attempt to bring their thinking even closer to his before he presents his true argument. Time, he says "can be used either destructively or constructively" (120). With this statement, the readers are introduced to the fact that it is up to an individual to change time. Any person has the ability to alter the course of human history in either a positive or negative direction. King also continues to push away slowly the idea that racial equality is an inevitable function of time, as he argues that "human progress never rolls in on wheels of inevitability"(120). He stresses that for a positive change to occur, all of the people must ask for the help of God. In this way he downplays the possibility of positive changes occurring simply by chance. This assertion only helps to boost the readers ' confidence in King, because hi s statement makes them feel that God will help them make this move toward racial equality, and if God will help them , it must be a just and righteous cause. At this point in the paragraph, King has a rock-solid rapport with his readers. He has made it easy for them to "step away" from their beliefs as to the nature of time, and now has them thinking of time as something that their righteous actions control.

4   In the final portion of the paragraph, King uses the base that he has established to propel his argument toward a consensus. He begins his argument with the presentation of time as a limitation or a negative factor. King urges his readers to "use time creatively" (120). He suggests that it is the time to take real steps toward racial equality and justice, and this argument is well accepted by these readers, who have already been convinced that time can be used either positively or negatively. Knowing this, King is able to scare his readers to action without even mentioning one thing to scare them, because by suggesting that time is critical, he knows that the readers will assume that if they do not change time in a positive direction, someone else will change it in a negative direction. In this sequence, King employs an abstract scare tactic that allows him to achieve the desired effect without the risk of losing some readers. He ends the third segment as well as the paragraph with a call to action aimed at everyone: "Now is

the time to lift our national policy from the quicksand of racial injustice to the solid rock of human dignity" (120).

5   The three-tiered structure of paragraph twenty-six is a masterwork in emotional persuasion. King gently guides his target audience away from their own views on the relationship between time and racial equality through an intermediate layer and then finally to his views on the subject. The diction that King employs allows these readers to feel comfortable throughout the change and constantly solidifies their trust in him. As it was for the white clergymen, it would be difficult for anyone to read this paragraph and not believe in King's ideas afterwards.

Work Cited

King, Martin Luther, Jr. "Letter from Birmingham Jail." *The Aims of Argument.* Eds. Timothy W. Crusius and Carolyn E. Channell Mountain View, CA: Mayfield Publishing Company, 1995. 112-135.

1998-99

Before responding to a writer's argument, students should demonstrate an understanding of his or her message. In the following two selections, Carrye Rudolph presents a detailed summary of Mark Edmundson's controversial essay "On the Uses of a Liberal Education: As Lite Reading for Bored College Students," and Ashley Asel responds to that article. In her final essay examination, Ashley makes use of several course readings to support her evaluation. These readings can be found in the next section of Criteria, "A Community of Scholars." Mark Edmundson's article can be found online at <http://www.westminster.edu!staff/muthmp/Edmundsonl.html>.

Analysis of the Present Day University
Carrye Rudolph

1 As the children of the baby boomers become the students of the university, Mark Edmundson evaluates the purpose of a liberal education. "On the Uses of a Liberal Education: As Lite Reading for Bored College Students" critiques the higher education system of today and defines the individual's role in reforming them.

2 As the baby boomers opened the floodgate of the university with the GI Bill, the universities grew to accommodate this influx in students. As our parents passed through, in order to maintain the prosperous trend, universities turned to promotional strategies to keep enrollment high. College became a competitive market, and students and parents became the informed consumers. The student is the consumer, and his or her buying power controls the university. The students' annual evaluation day reveals to Edmundson the present role of the university: to cater to students and their expectations of college. He detests the results that portray his function as entertaining, diverting, and presenting material in "an enjoyable and presentable way" (40). Instead of an education focused on challenging students and encouraging them to understand themselves, it is a university culture (and American culture) focused on entertainment and consumption.

3 The new generation, Generation X, is one concerned with blending in. The fear of being ostracized results in little original thinking or action. Therefore, the population becomes "low-key and non-assertive" (41). There is no passion or strong emotion, neither in life nor in school. The fire to learn to overcome ignorance is extinguished. "The central thrust of current consumer culture—to buy in order to be" stresses the concept of college as the manufacturer of the cool, nonchalant youth (41). Change is unwelcome, so consumers do not challenge the system but rather expect constant catering to the students. Parents raise sheltered Students with endless flattery, and they assume flattery will continue in college.

4   "Teach what pulls the kids in, or walk"; this is the unspoken principle governing many universities these days (45). A consumer-oriented university means students who dislike a professor can avoid him or her, regardless of their reasons, be it tough grading or radical views. This puts professors at the mercy of a student's whim. Professors must work toward the "new classroom," conducive to the students' ideas but lacking that perspective of teachers to provide new ideas and information. Precautionary measures must also be taken to avoid offensive comments to students, and teachers can no longer "defy student conviction and affront them occasionally" (49). Political correctness has led to cultural studies which are little more than uncritical discussion of students' tastes, not intellectual analysis of culture; "the customer is given what they [sic] most want—easy pleasure" (48). The new fad of television celebrities as speakers for commencement addresses illustrates the move towards entertainment versus challenging intellect, regardless of controversy or disturbance. Because they refuse to acknowledge lack of knowledge, students no longer come to school to destroy ignorance, but instead they want to be entertained, not en lightened.
5   Not only does the current generation control the university, but money matters also play a role. Students are always conscious of the competitive workplace after their college days. They do not want to drop a class, for they know how ominous that drop looks on their transcript, so they take only those "easy" classes. To serve the paying parents and students, colleges have devised the two-week floating period, when one can drop and add and shop for classes. They also allow pass-fail courses to be taken. The consumer-dominated school produces places where "almost no one fail[s] and everything [is] enjoyable" (44). The humanities have begun grading easier, and have relaxed requirements in order to compete with sciences for students. Colleges use nonacademic advertisement to bring in the best, brightest, and richest to the school. The brochures portray nice dorm rooms, state-of-the-art recreational facilities, and aesthetically pleasing campuses, not descriptions of hard, intellectually challenging courses or future prospects of overcoming ignorance. College recruiters are marketing and luring buyers, just like car salesmen.
6   The idea of genius has disappeared in the present culture. Everyone wants to slip into the norm and not be exalted for a brilliant distinguishing characteristic. Our political system requires great minds to interpret our present to propose possibilities for the future. Therefore, we must challenge ourselves and our beliefs and look beyond ourselves. Teachers need to be able to encourage this individuality, or "intelligent students [will] never learn to strive to overcome who they are" (49). This will result in a generation that thinks only of money and lives for easy pleasure. Colleges need to reclaim their status of institutions of higher learning, not of multi-purposed entertainment facilities. Universities need to raise standards to instill a challenging environment, conducive to learning. Students need to become individuals against current opinion and find that

passion for life and learning; thus, "we can become freer—freer to be ourselves, to be what we most want and value" (49). Genius needs to be recognized and praised, and universities need to adapt to the new millennium.

Work Cited

Edmundson, Mark. "On the Uses of a Liberal Education: As Lite Reading for Bored College Students." *Harper's* Sept. 1997: 39-49.

On Education, Discernment, and Discourse

In the following works, educators, writers, and statesmen raise discerning questions about the state, quality, and purpose of university education, particularly the role of the humanities in our ever-changing world. They urge us to think for ourselves, "to claim" an education, and to consider not only what education can do for and to us, but also what we can do with it for ourselves and others. May these works, coming from books, essays, articles, letters, and speeches, and employing rhetorical strategies that deserve attention, invite you to raise your own questions in the never-ending discourse that is higher education.

Columnist and historian Zachary Karabell's survey of American universities and their students offers many instances, including some here at SMU, to support his claim that the educational process has been "dumbed down" in recent years to suit the demands of both students and parents.

From *What's College For?*
Zachary Karabell

1   Although there are no reliable studies on the reading workload of students, anecdotal evidence suggests that students are doing less reading than ever before. Students will no longer read what they used to. Comparing syllabi from thirty years ago with those of today, it's clear that reading assignments are much lighter than they once were. Too much can be made of this. After all, students have been using Cliffs Notes and other "condensed" sources, including *Reader's Digest* books, for quite some time. But students are now more vocal in their refusal to read beyond a very limited number of pages, as little as thirty to forty pages a week in some courses. Students offer a variety of excuses, but the most difficult one to counter is the claim that they simply don't have the time. If they are working a full-time job and caring for a family, then several hundred pages a week in each of three or four courses can become untenable.

2   At the same time, students, like most human beings, don't necessarily like to work. Fear of failure may not be the best motivation, but it is often an effective one. Knowing that you will be evaluated negatively if you do not do the required work is a spur to doing it. If, however, students use both appeals to administrators and harsh teacher evaluations, and if the nature of academic employment now means that these are effective tools to put pressure on professors, then the ability of a professor to get students to do the work is hampered.

3   Some professors resort to the most juvenile, hand-holding techniques to get their students to read. Some go as far as reading out loud to their students on the theory that otherwise they'll never do the assignment. Others trim more and more pages off their syllabi each year. The result is that in many places education is, in effect, "dumbed down."

4   This "dumbing down" is particularly prevalent in the humanities, where the courses are harder to justify to students and parents, both of whom view college almost entirely in job-oriented terms. One business major at Southern Methodist University told me that she took an occasional English course in order to give herself a break from numbers. Most of her friends, however, couldn't understand why she bothered. At SMU, the business school is awash in money, and the connections between it and the Dallas business community are well established. Many students go to SMU to major in business, join a fraternity or sorority, and then find a good entry-level position through the contacts they've made in their four years. Humanities courses are seen as a luxury at best, and for many they're simply a waste of time.

Although Thomas Jefferson spent much of his later life developing plans for an institution of higher education—they eventually culminated in the University of Virginia—he did not consider systematic schooling for females in the same light as for males. Some of his thoughts on the subject were expressed in a letter to a very close friend, Nathaniel Burwell written March 14, 1818.[1]

Letter from Thomas Jefferson to Nathaniel Burwell on the Education of Women

Dear Sir,
1   Your letter of February 17 found me suffering under an attack of rheumatism, which has but now left me at sufficient ease to attend to the letters I have received. A plan of female education has never been a subject of systematic contemplation with me. It has occupied my attention so far only as the education of my own daughters occasionally required. Considering that they would be placed in a country situation, where little aid could be obtained from abroad, I thought it essential to give them a solid education which might enable them, when [they] become mothers, to educate their own daughters, and even to direct the course for sons, should their fathers be lost, or incapable, or inattentive. My surviving daughter accordingly, the mother of many daughters as well as sons, has made their education the object of her life, and being a better judge of the practical part than myself, it is with her aid and that of one of her *élèves*[2] that I shall subjoin a catalogue of the books for such a course of reading as we have practised.
2   A great obstacle to good education is the inordinate passion prevalent for novels and the time lost in that reading which should be instructively employed. When this poison infects the mind, it destroys its tone and revolts it against wholesome reading. Reason and fact, plain and unadorned, are rejected. Nothing can engage attention unless dressed in all the figments of fancy, and nothing so bedecked comes amiss. The result is a bloated imagination, sickly judgment,

---

[1]Head note is from *Encyclopedia Britannica*; footnotes added by *Criteria* editors:
[2]French for *pupils, students.*
[3]Jean-Francois Marmontel, French writer whose *Contes moreaux* (1761), or sentimental "moral tales," were widely read [*Encyclopedia Britannica*, eb.com].
[4]Maria Edgeworth, Irish writer whose first published writings argued for women's education (1795), and whose first novel, *Castle Rackrent* (1800), with its realistic portrayals of Irish peasantry, influenced later writers such as Sir Walter Scott [NNDB, © Soylent Communications 2011].
[5]Madame de Genlis, popular French writer of stern children's books (nothing fanciful; only "rational" tales); adult novels; and works about education and etiquette; in *Emma*, Jane Austen refers with some irony to a book by Mme. de Genlis [*Encyclopedia Britannica*, eb. com; *The New Criterion*, newcriterion.com; *Encyc. of the Exquisite*, © J. Jenkins 2010].

and disgust toward all the real businesses of life. This mass of trash, however, is not without some distinction; some few, modeling their narratives, although fictitious, on the incidents of real life, have been able to make them interesting and useful vehicles of a sound morality. Such, I think, are Marmontel's[3] new moral tales, but not his old ones, which are really immoral. Such are the writings of Miss Edgeworth,[4] and some of those of Madame Genlis.[5] For a like reason, too, much poetry should not be indulged. Some is useful for forming style and taste. Pope, Dryden, Thompson, Shakespeare, and of the French, Molière, Racine, the Corneilles, may be read with pleasure and improvement.

3 The French language, become that of the general intercourse of nations, and from their extraordinary advances now the depository of all science, is an indispensable part of education for both sexes. In the subjoined catalogue, therefore, I have placed the books of both languages indifferently, according as the one or the other offers what is best.

4 The ornaments, too, and the amusements of life are entitled to their portion of attention. These, for a female, are dancing, drawing, and music. The first is a healthy exercise, elegant and very attractive for young people. Every affectionate parent would be pleased to see his daughter qualified to participate with her companions, and without awkwardness at least, in the circles of festivity of which she occasionally becomes a part. It is a necessary accomplishment, therefore, although of short use for the French rule is wise that no lady dances after marriage. This is founded in solid physical reasons, gestation and nursing leaving little time to a married lady when this exercise can be either safe or innocent. Drawing is thought less of in this country than in Europe. It is an innocent and engaging amusement, often useful, and a qualification not to be neglected in one who is to become a mother and an instructor. Music is invaluable where a person has an ear. Where they have not, it should not be attempted. It furnishes a delightful recreation for the hours of respite from the cares of the day, and lasts us through life. The taste of this country, too, calls for this accomplishment more strongly than for either of the others.

5 I need say nothing of household economy, in which the mothers of our country are generally skilled, and generally careful to instruct their daughters. We all know its value, and that diligence and dexterity in all its processes are inestimable treasures. The order and economy of a house are as honorable to the mistress as those of the farm to the master, and if either be neglected, ruin follows, and children destitute of the means of living.

6 This, sir, is offered as a summary sketch on a subject on which I have not thought much. It probably contains nothing but what has already occurred to yourself, and claims your acceptance on no other ground than as a testimony of my respect for your wishes, and of my great esteem and respect.

Source: *The Writings of Thomas Jefferson,* Paul L. Ford, ed., 1892–1899, 10 vols.

Poet and educator Adrienne Rich first presented this text at the Douglass College Convocation of September 6, 1977. Though it is directly addressed to an audience of women, its injunctions "to claim," to be responsible for, one's own education are invaluable to every student.

Claiming an Education (1977)

Adrienne Rich

For this convocation, I planned to separate my remarks into two parts: some thoughts about you, the women students here, and some thoughts about us who teach in a women's college. But ultimately, those two parts are indivisible. If university education means anything beyond the processing of human beings into expected roles, through credit hours, tests, and grades (and I believe that in a women's college especially it might mean much more), it implies an ethical and intellectual contract between teacher and student. This contract must remain intuitive, dynamic, unwritten; but we must turn to it again and again if learning is to be reclaimed from the depersonalizing and cheapening pressures of the present-day academic scene.

The first thing I want to say to you who are students, is that you cannot afford to think of being here to receive an education; you will do much better to think of yourselves as being here to claim one. One of the dictionary definitions of the verb "to claim" is: *to take as the rightful owner; to assert in the face of possible contradiction.* "To receive" is *to come into possession of; to act as receptacle or container for; to accept as authoritative or true.* The difference is that between acting and being acted-upon, and for women it can literally mean the difference between life and death.

One of the devastating weaknesses of university learning, of the store of knowledge and opinion that has been handed down through academic training, has been its almost total erasure of women's experience and thought from the curriculum, and its exclusion of women as members of the academic community. Today, with increasing numbers of women students in nearly every branch of higher learning, we still see very few women in the upper levels of faculty

---

This talk was given at the Douglass College Convocation, September 6, 1977, and first printed in The Common Woman, a feminist literary magazine founded by Rutgers University women in New Brunswick, New Jersey.

"Claiming an Education," from *On Lies, Secrets, and Silence: Selected Prose 1966-1978* by Adrienne Rich. Copyright © 1979 by W. W. Norton & Company, Inc. Used by permission of W. W. Norton & Company, Inc.

and administration in most institutions. Douglass College itself is a women's college in a university administered overwhelmingly by men, who in turn are answerable to the state legislature, again composed predominantly of men. But the most significant fact for you is that what you learn here, the very texts you read, the lectures you hear, the way your studies are divided into categories and fragmented one from the other—all this reflects, to a very large degree, neither objective reality, nor an accurate picture of the past, nor a group of rigorously tested observations about human behavior. What you can learn here (and I mean not only at Douglass but any college in any university) is how *men* have perceived and organized their experience, their history, their ideas of social relationships, good and evil, sickness and health, etc. When you read or hear about "great issues," "major texts," "the mainstream of Western thought," you are hearing about what men, above all white men, in their male subjectivity, have decided is important.

Black and other minority peoples have for some time recognized that their racial and ethnic experience was not accounted for in the studies broadly labeled human; and that even the sciences can be racist. For many reasons, it has been more difficult for women to comprehend our exclusion, and to realize that even the sciences can be sexist. For one thing, it is only within the last hundred years that higher education has grudgingly been opened up to women at all, even to white, middle-class women. And many of us have found ourselves poring eagerly over books with titles like: *The Descent of Man; Man and His Symbols; Irrational Man; The Phenomenon of Man; The Future of Man; Man and the Machine; From Man to Man; May Man Prevail?; Man, Science and Society;* or *One-Dimensional Man*—books pretending to describe a "human" reality that does not include over one-half the human species.

Less than a decade ago, with the rebirth of a feminist movement in this country, women students and teachers in a number of universities began to demand and set up women's studies courses—to *claim* a woman-directed education. And, despite the inevitable accusations of "unscholarly," "group therapy," "faddism," etc., despite backlash and budget cuts, women's studies are still growing, offering to more and more women a new intellectual grasp on their lives, new understanding of our history, a fresh vision of the human experience, and also a critical basis for evaluating what they hear and read in other courses, and in the society at large.

But my talk is not really about women's studies, much as I believe in their scholarly, scientific, and human necessity. While I think that any Douglass student has everything to gain by investigating and enrolling in women's studies courses, I want to suggest that there is a more essential experience that you owe yourselves, one which courses in women's studies can greatly enrich, but which finally depends on you, in all your interactions with yourself and your world. This is the experience of *taking responsibility toward yourselves.* Our upbringing as women has so often told us that this should come second to our relationships and responsibilities to other people. We have been offered ethical models of the self-denying wife and mother; intellectual models of the brilliant but slapdash dilettante who never commits herself to anything the whole way, or the intelligent woman who denies her intelligence in order to seem more "feminine," or who sits in passive silence even when she disagrees inwardly with everything that is being said around her.

Responsibility to yourself means refusing to let others do your thinking, talking, and naming for you; it means learning to respect and use your own brains and instincts; hence, grappling with hard work. It means that you do not treat your body as a commodity with which to purchase superficial intimacy or economic security; for our bodies and minds are inseparable in this life, and when we allow our bodies to be treated as objects, our minds are in mortal danger. It means insisting that those to whom you give your friendship and love are able to respect your mind. It means being able to say, with Charlotte Brontë's *Jane Eyre:* "I have an inward treasure born with me, which can keep me alive if all the extraneous delights should be withheld or offered only at a price I cannot afford to give."

Responsibility to yourself means that you don't fall for shallow and easy solutions—predigested books and ideas, weekend encounters guaranteed to change your life, taking "gut" courses in stead of ones you know will challenge you, bluffing at school and life instead of doing solid work, marrying early as an escape from real decisions, getting pregnant as an evasion of already existing problems. It means that you refuse to sell your talents and aspirations short, simply to avoid conflict and confrontation. And this, in turn, means resisting the forces in society which say that women should be nice, play safe, have low professional expectations, drown in love and forget about work, live through others, and stay in the places assigned to us. It means that we insist on a life of meaningful work, insist that work be as meaningful as love and friendship in our lives. It means, therefore, the courage to be "different"; not to be continuously available to others when we need time for ourselves and our work; to be able to demand of others—parents, friends, roommates, teachers, lovers, husbands, children—that they respect our sense of purpose and our integrity as persons. Women everywhere are finding the courage to do this, more and more, and we are finding that courage both in our study of women in the past who possessed it, and in each other as we look to other women for comradeship, community, and challenge. The difference between a life lived actively, and a life of passive drifting and dispersal of energies, is an immense difference. Once we begin to feel committed to our lives, responsible to ourselves, we can never again be satisfied with the old, passive way.

Now comes the second part of the contract. I believe that in a women's college you have the right to expect your faculty to take you seriously. The education of women has been a matter of debate for centuries, and old, negative attitudes about women's role, women's ability to think and take leadership, are still rife both in and outside the university. Many male professors (and I don't mean only at Douglass) still feel that teaching in a women's college is a second-rate career. Many tend to eroticize their women students—to treat them as sexual objects—instead of demanding the best of their minds. (At Yale a legal suit [*Alexander* v. *Yale*] has been brought against the university by a group of women students demanding a stated policy against sexual advances toward female students by male professors.) Many teachers, both men and women, trained in the male-centered tradition, are still handing the ideas and texts of that tradition on to students without teaching them to criticize its antiwoman attitudes, its omission of women as part of the species. Too often, all of us fail to teach the most important thing, which is that clear thinking, active discussion, and excellent writing are all necessary for intellectual freedom, and that these require *hard work*. Sometimes, perhaps in discouragement with a culture which is both antiintellectual and antiwoman, we may resign ourselves to low expectations for our students before we have given them half a chance to become more thoughtful, expressive human beings. We need to take to heart the words of Elizabeth Barrett Browning, a poet, a thinking woman, and a feminist, who wrote in 1845 of her impatience with studies which cultivate a "passive recipiency" in the mind, and asserted that "women want to be made to *think actively:* their apprehension is quicker than that of men, but their defect lies for the most part in the logical faculty and in the higher mental activities." Note that she implies a defect which can be remedied by intellectual training; *not* an inborn lack of ability.

 I have said that the contract on the student's part involves that you demand to be taken seriously so that you can also go on taking yourself seriously. This means seeking out criticism, recognizing that the most affirming thing anyone can do for you is demand that you push yourself further, show you the range of what you *can* do. It means rejecting attitudes of "take-it-easy," "why-be-so-serious," "why-worry- you'll-probably-get-married-anyway." It means assuming your share of responsibility for what happens in the classroom, because that affects the quality of your daily life here. It means that the student sees herself engaged *with* her teachers in an active, ongoing struggle for a real education. But for her to do this, her teachers must be committed to the belief that women's minds and experience are intrinsically valuable and indispensable to any civilization worthy the name; that there is no more exhilarating and intellectually fertile place in the academic world today than a women's college—if both students and teachers in large enough numbers are trying to fulfill this contract. The contract is really a pledge of mutual seriousness about women, about language, ideas, methods, and values. It is our shared commitment toward a world in which the inborn potentialities of so many women's minds will no longer be wasted, raveled-away, paralyzed, or denied.

In the following excerpt from her 1989 book, Talking Back: Thinking Feminist, Thinking Black, *writer and professor bell hooks, in her customary, deft blend of the personal and professional, describes her first-year experiences at Stanford University as a minority, working-class, scholarship student, as well as her early experiences teaching at Yale University. She makes the argument that "education as the practice of freedom," while transformative and life-altering, nevertheless means maintaining strong connections with and deep respect for family, friends, neighbors, and others from our home communities.*

keeping close to home: class and education
bell hooks

1   We are both awake in the almost dark of 5 a.m. Everyone else is sound asleep. Mama asks the usual questions. Telling me to look around, make sure I have everything, scolding me because I am uncertain about the actual time the bus arrives. By 5:30 we are waiting outside the closed station. Alone together, we have a chance to really talk. Mama begins. Angry with her children, especially the ones who whisper behind her back, she says bitterly, "Your childhood could not have been that bad. You were fed and clothed. You did not have to do without—that's more than a lot of folks have and I just can't stand the way y'all go on." The hurt in her voice saddens me. I have always wanted to protect mama from hurt, to ease her burdens. Now I am part of what troubles. Confronting me, she says accusingly, "It's not just the other children. You talk too much about the past. You don't just listen." And I do talk. Worse, I write about it.
2   Mama has always come to each of her children seeking different responses. With me she expresses the disappointment, hurt, and anger of betrayal: anger that her children are so critical, that we can't even have the sense to like the presents she sends. She says, "From now on there will be no presents. I'll just stick some money in a little envelope the way the rest of you do. Nobody wants criticism. Everybody can criticize me but I am supposed to say nothing." When I try to talk, my voice sounds like a twelve year old. When I try to talk, she speaks louder, interrupting me, even though she has said repeatedly, "Explain it to me, this talk about the past." I struggle to return to my thirty-five year old self so that she will know by the sound of my voice that we are two women talking together. It is only when I state firmly in my very adult voice, "Mama, you are not listening," that she becomes quiet. She waits. Now that I have her attention, I fear that my explanations will be lame, inadequate. "Mama," I begin, "people usually go to therapy because they feel hurt inside, because they have pain that will not stop, like a wound that continually breaks open, that does not

heal. And often these hurts, that pain has to do with things that have happened in the past, sometimes in childhood, often in childhood, or things that we believe happened." She wants to know, "What hurts, what hurts are you talking about?" "Mom, I can't answer that. I can't speak for all of us, the hurts are different for everybody. But the point is you try to make the hurt better, to heal it, by understanding how it came to be. And I know you feel mad when we say something happened or hurt that you don't remember being that way, but the past isn't like that, we don't have the same memory of it. We remember things differently. You know that. And sometimes folk feel hurt about stuff and you just don't know or didn't realize it, and they need to talk about it. Surely you understand the need to talk about it."

3   Our conversation is interrupted by the sight of my uncle walking across the park toward us. We stop to watch him. He is on his way to work dressed in a familiar blue suit. They look alike, these two who rarely discuss the past. This interruption makes me think about life in a small town. You always see someone you know. Interruptions, intrusions are part of daily life. Privacy is difficult to maintain. We leave our private space in the car to greet him. After the hug and kiss he has given me every year since I was born, they talk about the day's funerals. In the distance the bus approaches. He walks away knowing that they will see each other later. Just before I board the bus I turn, staring into my mother's face. I am momentarily back in time, seeing myself eighteen years ago, at this same bus stop, staring into my mother's face, continually turning back, waving farewell as I returned to college—that experience which first took me away from our town, from family. Departing was as painful then as it is now. Each movement away makes return harder. Each separation intensifies distance, both physical and emotional.

4   To a southern black girl from a working-class background who had never been on a city bus, who had never stepped on an escalator, who had never traveled by plane, leaving the comfortable confines of a small town Kentucky life to attend Stanford University was not just frightening; it was utterly painful. My parents had not been delighted that I had been accepted and adamantly opposed my going so far from home. At the time, I did not see their opposition as an expression of their fear that they would lose me forever. Like many working-class folks, they feared what college education might do to their children's minds even as they unenthusiastically acknowledged its importance. They did not understand why I could not attend a college nearby, an all-black college. To them, any college would do. I would graduate, become a school teacher, make a decent living and a good marriage. And even though they reluctantly and skeptically supported my educational endeavors, they also subjected them to constant harsh and bitter critique. It is difficult for me to talk about my parents and their impact on me because they have always felt wary, ambivalent, mistrusting of my intellectual aspirations even as they have been caring and supportive. I want to speak about

these contradictions because sorting through them, seeking resolution and reconciliation has been important to me both as it affects my development as a writer, my effort to be fully self-realized, and my longing to remain close to the family and community that provided the groundwork for much of my thinking, writing, and being.

5   Studying at Stanford, I began to think seriously about class differences. To be materially underprivileged at a university where most folks (with the exception of workers) are materially privileged provokes such thought. Class differences were boundaries no one wanted to face or talk about. It was easier to downplay them, to act as though we were all from privileged backgrounds, to work around them, to confront them privately in the solitude of one's room, or to pretend that just being chosen to study at such an institution meant that those of us who did not come from privilege were already in transition toward privilege. To not long for such transition marked one as rebellious, as unlikely to succeed. It was a kind of treason not to believe that it was better to be identified with the world of material privilege than with the world of the working class, the poor. No wonder our working-class parents from poor backgrounds feared our entry into such a world, intuiting perhaps that we might learn to be ashamed of where we had come from, that we might never return home, or come back only to lord it over them.

6   Though I hung with students who were supposedly radical and chic, we did not discuss class. I talked to no one about the sources of my shame, how it hurt me to witness the contempt shown the brown-skinned Filipina maids who cleaned our rooms, or later my concern about the $100 a month I paid for a room off-campus which was more than half of what my parents paid for rent. I talked to no one about my efforts to save money, to send a little something home. Yet these class realities separated me from fellow students. We were moving in different directions. I did not intend to forget my class background or alter my class allegiance. And even though I received an education designed to provide me with a bourgeois sensibility, passive acquiescence was not my only option. I knew that I could resist. I could rebel. I could shape the direction and focus of the various forms of knowledge available to me. Even though I sometimes envied and longed for greater material advantages (particularly at vacation times when I would be one of few if any students remaining in the dormitory because there was no money to travel), I did not share the sensibility and values of my peers. That was important—class was not just about money; it was about values which showed and determined behavior. While I often needed more money, I never needed a new set of beliefs and values. For example, I was profoundly shocked and disturbed when peers would talk about their parents without respect, or would even say that they hated their parents. This was especially troubling to me when it seemed that these parents were caring and concerned. It was often explained to me that such hatred was "healthy and normal." To my

white, middle-class California roommate, I explained the way we were taught to value our parents and their care, to understand that they were not obligated to give us care. She would always shake her head, laughing all the while, and say, "Missy, you will learn that it's different here, that we think differently." She was right. Soon, I lived alone, like the one Mormon student who kept to himself as he made a concentrated effort to remain true to his religious beliefs and values. Later in graduate school I found that classmates believed "lower class" people had no beliefs and values. I was silent in such discussions, disgusted by their ignorance.

7   Carol Stack's anthropological study, *All Our Kin*, was one of the first books I read which confirmed my experiential understanding that within black culture (especially among the working class and poor, particularly in southern states), a value system emerged that was counter-hegemonic, that challenged notions of individualism and private property so important to the maintenance of white-supremacist, capitalist patriarchy. Black folk created in marginal spaces a world of community and collectivity where resources were shared. In the preface to *Feminist Theory: from margin to center*, I talked about how the point of difference, this marginality can be the space for the formation of an oppositional world view. That world view must be articulated, named if it is to provide a sustained blueprint for change. Unfortunately, there has existed no consistent framework for such naming. Consequently both the experience of this difference and documentation of it (when it occurs) gradually lose presence and meaning.

8   Much of what Stack documented about the "culture of poverty," for example, would not describe interactions among most black poor today irrespective of geographical setting. Since the black people she described did not acknowledge (if they recognized it in theoretical terms) the oppositional value of their world view, apparently seeing it more as a survival strategy determined less by conscious efforts to oppose oppressive race and class biases than by circumstance, they did not attempt to establish a framework to transmit their beliefs and values from generation to generation. When circumstances changed, values altered. Efforts to assimilate the values and beliefs of privileged white people, presented through media like television, undermine and destroy potential structures of opposition.

9   Increasingly, young black people are encouraged by the dominant culture (and by those black people who internalize the values of this hegemony) to believe that assimilation is the only possible way to survive, to succeed. Without the framework of an organized civil rights or black resistance struggle, individual and collective efforts at black liberation that focus on the primacy of self-definition and self-determination often go unrecognized. It is crucial that those among us who resist and rebel, who survive and succeed, speak openly and honestly about our lives and the nature of our personal struggles, the means by which we resolve and reconcile contradictions. This is no easy task. Within the

educational institutions where we learn to develop and strengthen our writing and analytical skills, we also learn to think, write, and talk in a manner that shifts attention away from personal experience. Yet if we are to reach our people and all people, if we are to remain connected (especially those of us whose familial backgrounds are poor and working-class), we must understand that the telling of one's personal story provides a meaningful example, a way for folks to identify and connect.

10 Combining personal with critical analysis and theoretical perspectives can engage listeners who might otherwise feel estranged, alienated. To speak simply with language that is accessible to as many folks as possible is also important. Speaking about one's personal experience or speaking with simple language is often considered by academics and/or intellectuals (irrespective of their political inclinations) to be a sign of intellectual weakness or even anti-intellectualism. Lately, when I speak, I do not stand in place—reading my paper, making little or no eye contact with audiences—but instead make eye contact, talk extemporaneously, digress, and address the audience directly. I have been told that people assume I am not prepared, that I am anti-intellectual, unprofessional (a concept that has everything to do with class as it determines actions and behavior), that I am reinforcing the stereotype of black people as non-theoretical and gutsy.

11 Such criticism was raised recently by fellow feminist scholars after a talk I gave at Northwestern University at a conference on "Gender, Culture, Politics" to an audience that was mainly students and academics. I deliberately chose to speak in a very basic way, thinking especially about the few community folks who had come to hear me. Weeks later, Kum-Kum Sangari, a fellow participant who shared with me what was said when I was no longer present, and I engaged in quite rigorous critical dialogue about the way my presentation had been perceived primarily by privileged white female academics. She was concerned that I not mask my knowledge of theory, that I not appear anti-intellectual. Her critique compelled me to articulate concerns that I am often silent about with colleagues. I spoke about class allegiance and revolutionary commitments, explaining that it was disturbing to me that intellectual radicals who speak about transforming society, ending the domination of race, sex, class, cannot break with behavior patterns that reinforce and perpetuate domination, or continue to use as their sole reference point how we might be or are perceived by those who dominate, whether or not we gain their acceptance and approval.

12 This is a primary contradiction which raises the issue of whether or not the academic setting is a place where one can be truly radical or subversive. Concurrently, the use of a language and style of presentation that alienates most folks who are not also academically trained reinforces the notion that the academic world is separate from real life, that everyday world where we constantly adjust our language and behavior to meet diverse needs. The academic setting is separate only when we work to make it so. It is a false dichotomy which suggests that

academics and/or intellectuals can only speak to one another, that we cannot hope to speak with the masses. What is true is that we make choices, that we choose our audiences, that we choose voices to hear and voices to silence. If I do not speak in a language that can be understood, then there is little chance for dialogue. This issue of language and behavior is a central contradiction all radical intellectuals, particularly those who are members of oppressed groups, must continually confront and work to resolve. One of the clear and present dangers that exists when we move outside our class of origin, our collective ethnic experience, and enter hierarchical institutions which daily reinforce domination by race, sex, and class, is that we gradually assume a mindset similar to those who dominate and oppress, that we lose critical consciousness because it is not reinforced or affirmed by the environment. We must be ever vigilant. It is important that we know who we are speaking to, who we most want to hear us, who we most long to move, motivate, and touch with our words.

13   When I first came to New Haven to teach at Yale, I was truly surprised by the marked class divisions between black folks—students and professors—who identify with Yale and those black folks who work at Yale or in surrounding communities. Style of dress and self-presentation are most often the central markers of one's position. I soon learned that the black folks who spoke on the street were likely to be part of the black community and those who carefully shifted their glance were likely to be associated with Yale. Walking with a black female colleague one day, I spoke to practically every black person in sight (a gesture which reflects my upbringing), an action which disturbed my companion. Since I addressed black folk who were clearly not associated with Yale, she wanted to know whether or not I knew them. That was funny to me. "Of course not," I answered. Yet when I thought about it seriously, I realized that in a deep way, I knew them for they, and not my companion or most of my colleagues at Yale, resemble my family. Later that year, in a black women's support group I started for undergraduates, students from poor backgrounds spoke about the shame they sometimes feel when faced with the reality of their connection to working-class and poor black people. One student confessed that her father is a street person, addicted to drugs, someone who begs from passersby. She, like other Yale students, turns away from street people often, sometimes showing anger or contempt; she hasn't wanted anyone to know that she was related to this kind of person. She struggles with this, wanting to find a way to acknowledge and affirm this reality, to claim this connection. The group asked me and one another what we do to remain connected, to honor the bonds we have with working-class and poor people even as our class experience alters.

14   Maintaining connections with family and community across class boundaries demands more than just summary recall of where one's roots are, where one comes from. It requires knowing, naming, and being ever-mindful of those aspects of one's past that have enabled and do enable one's self-development

in the present, that sustain and support, that enrich. One must also honestly confront barriers that do exist, aspects of that past that do diminish. My parent's ambivalence about my love for reading led to intense conflict. They (especially my mother) would work to ensure that I had access to books, but would threaten to burn the books or throw them away if I did not conform to other expectations. Or they would insist that reading too much would drive me insane. Their ambivalence nurtured in me a like uncertainty about the value and significance of intellectual endeavor which took years for me to unlearn. While this aspect of our class reality was one that wounded and diminished, their vigilant insistence that being smart did not make be a "better" or "superior" person (which often got on my nerves because I think I wanted to have that sense that it did indeed set me apart, make me better) made a profound impression. From them I learned to value and respect various skills and talents folk might have, not just to value people who read books and talk about ideas. They and my grandparents might say about somebody, "Now he don't read nor write a lick, but he can tell a story," or as my grandmother would say, "call out the hell in words."

15 Empty romanticization of poor or working-class backgrounds undermines the possibility of true connection. Such connection is based on understanding difference in experience and perspective and working to mediate and negotiate these terrains. Language is a crucial issue for folk whose movement outside the boundaries of poor and working-class backgrounds changes the nature and direction of their speech. Coming to Stanford with my own version of a Kentucky accent, which I think of always as a strong sound quite different from Tennessee or Georgia speech, I learned to speak differently while maintaining the speech of my region, the sound of my family and community. This was of course much easier to keep up when I returned home to stay often. In recent years, I have endeavored to use various speaking styles in the classroom as a teacher and find it disconcerts those who feel that the use of a particular patois excludes them as listeners, even if there is translation into the usual, acceptable mode of speech. Learning to listen to different voices, hearing different speech challenges the notion that we must all assimilate—share a single, similar talk—in educational institutions. Language reflects the culture from which we emerge. To deny ourselves daily use of speech patterns that are common and familiar, that embody the unique and distinctive aspect of our self is one of the ways we become estranged and alienated from our past. It is important for us to have as many languages on hand as we can know or learn. It is important for those of us who are black, who speak in particular patois as well as standard English to express ourselves in both ways.

16 Often I tell students from poor and working-class backgrounds that if you believe what you have learned and are learning in schools and universities separates you from your past, this is precisely what will happen. It is important to stand firm in the conviction that nothing can truly separate us from our pasts

when we nurture and cherish that connection. An important strategy for maintaining contact is ongoing acknowledgement of the primacy of one's past, of one's background, affirming the reality that such bonds are not severed automatically solely because one enters a new environment or moves toward a different class experience.

17 Again, I do not wish to romanticize this effort, to dismiss the reality of conflict and contradiction. During my time at Stanford, I did go through a period of more than a year when I did not return home. That period was one where I felt that it was simply too difficult to mesh my profoundly disparate realities. Critical reflection about the choice I was making, particularly about why I felt a choice had to be made, pulled me through this difficult time. Luckily I recognized that the insistence on choosing between the world of family and community and the new world of privileged white people and privileged ways of knowing was imposed upon me by the outside. It is as though a mythical contract had been signed somewhere which demanded of us black folks that once we entered these spheres we would immediately give up all vestiges of our underprivileged past. It was my responsibility to formulate a way of being that would allow me to participate fully in my new environment while integrating and maintaining aspects of the old.

18 One of the most tragic manifestations of the pressure black people feel to assimilate is expressed in the internalization of racist perspectives. I was shocked and saddened when I first heard black professors at Stanford downgrade and express contempt for black students, expecting us to do poorly, refusing to establish nurturing bonds. At every university I have attended as a student or worked at as a teacher, I have heard similar attitudes expressed with little or no understanding of factors that might prevent brilliant black students from performing to their full capability. Within universities, there are few educational and social spaces where students who wish to affirm positive ties to ethnicity—to blackness, to working-class backgrounds—can receive affirmation and support. Ideologically, the message is clear—assimilation is the way to gain acceptance and approval from those in power.

19 Many white people enthusiastically supported Richard Rodriguez's vehement contention in his autobiography, *Hunger of Memory*, that attempts to maintain ties with his Chicano background impeded his progress, that he had to sever ties with community and kin to succeed at Stanford and in the larger world, that family language, in his case Spanish, had to be made secondary or discarded. If the terms of success as defined by the standards of ruling groups within white-supremacist, capitalist patriarchy are the only standards that exist, then assimilation is indeed necessary. But they are not. Even in the fact of powerful structures of domination, it remains possible for each of us, especially those of us who are members of oppressed and/or exploited groups as well as those radical visionaries who may have race, class, and sex privilege, to de-

fine and determine alternative standards, to decide on the nature and extent of compromise. Standards by which one's success is measured, whether student or professor, are quite different for those of us who wish to resist reinforcing the domination of race, sex, and class, who work to maintain and strengthen our ties with the oppressed, with those who lack material privilege, with our families who are poor and working-class.

20 When I wrote my first book, *Ain't I A Woman: black women and feminism*, the issue of class and its relationship to who one's reading audience might be came up for me around my decision not to use footnotes, for which I have been sharply criticized. I told people that my concern was that footnotes set class boundaries for readers, determining who a book is for. I was shocked that many academic folks scoffed at this idea. I shared that I went into working-class black communities as well as talked with family and friends to survey whether or not they ever read books with footnotes and found that they did not. A few did not know what they were, but most folks saw them as indicating that a book was for college-educated people. These responses influenced my decision. When some of my more radical, college-educated friends freaked out about the absence of footnotes, I seriously questioned how we could ever imagine revolutionary transformation of society if such a small shift in direction could be viewed as threatening. Of course, many folks warned that the absence of footnotes would make the work less credible in academic circles. This information also highlighted the way in which class informs our choices. Certainly I did feel that choosing to use simple language, absence of footnotes, etc. would mean I was jeopardizing the possibility of being taken seriously in academic circles but then this was a political matter and a political decision. It utterly delights me that this has proven not to be the case and that the book is read by many academics as well as by people who are not college-educated.

21 Always our first response when we are motivated to conform or compromise with structures that reinforce domination must be to engage in critical reflection. Only by challenging ourselves to push against oppressive boundaries do we make the radical alternative possible, expanding the realm and scope of critical inquiry. Unless we share radical strategies, ways of rethinking and revisioning with students, with kin and community, with a larger audience, we risk perpetuating the stereotype that we succeed because we are the exception, different from the rest of our people. Since I left home and entered college, I am often asked, usually by white people, if my sisters and brothers are also high achievers. At the root of this question is the longing for reinforcement of the belief in "the exception" which enables race, sex, and class biases to remain intact. I am careful to separate what it means to be exceptional from a notion of "the exception."

22 Frequently I hear smart black folks, from poor and working-class backgrounds, stressing their frustration that at times family and community do not

recognize that they are exceptional. Absence of positive affirmation clearly diminishes the longing to excel in academic endeavors. Yet it is important to distinguish between the absence of basic positive affirmation and the longing for continued reinforcement that we are special. Usually liberal white folks will willingly offer continual reinforcement of us as exceptions—as special. This can be both patronizing and very seductive. Since we often work in situations where we are isolated from other black folks, we can easily begin to feel that encouragement from white people is the primary or only source of support and recognition. Given the internalization of racism, it is easy to view this support as more validating and legitimizing than similar support from black people. Still, nothing takes the place of being valued and appreciated by one's own, by one's family and community. We share a mutual and reciprocal responsibility for affirming one another's successes. Sometimes we have to talk to our folks about the fact that we need their ongoing support and affirmation, that it is unique and special to us. In some cases we may never receive desired recognition and acknowledgement of specific achievements from kin. Rather than seeing this as a basis for estrangement, for severing connection, it is useful to explore other sources of nourishment and support.

23 I do not know that my mother's mother ever acknowledged my college education except to ask me once, "How can you live so far away from your people?" Yet she gave me sources of affirmation and nourishment, sharing the legacy of her quilt-making, of family history, of her incredible way with words. Recently, when our father retired after more than thirty years of work as a janitor, I wanted to pay tribute to this experience, to identify links between his work and my own as writer and teacher. Reflecting on our family past, I recalled ways he had been an impressive example of diligence and hard work, approaching tasks with a seriousness of concentration I work to mirror and develop, with a discipline I struggle to maintain. Sharing these thoughts with him keeps us connected, nurtures our respect for each other, maintaining a space, however large or small, where we can talk.

24 Open, honest communication is the most important way we maintain relationships with kin and community as our class experience and backgrounds change. It is as vital as the sharing of resources. Often financial assistance is given in circumstances where there is no meaningful contact. However helpful, this can also be an expression of estrangement and alienation. Communication between black folks from various experiences of material privilege was much easier when we were all in segregated communities sharing common experiences in relation to social institutions. Without this grounding, we must work to maintain ties, connection. We must assume greater responsibility for making and maintaining contact, connections that can shape our intellectual visions and inform our radical commitments.

25 The most powerful resource any of us can have as we study and teach in

university settings is full understanding and appreciation of the richness, beauty, and primacy of our familial and community backgrounds. Maintaining awareness of class differences, nurturing ties with the poor and working-class people who are our most intimate kin, our comrades in struggle, transforms and enriches our intellectual experience. Education as the practice of freedom becomes not a force which fragments or separates, but one that brings us closer, expanding our definitions of home and community.

Perhaps best known for his award-winning book, The Courage to Teach, *Parker J. Palmer works with professionals in education, medicine, business, law, public service, and religion to actively encourage community and spiritual awareness among the various practitioners, ultimately leading to social change. He wrote the following afterword to a collection of essays honoring another academic activist, Ernest Boyer, who served sixteen years as president of The Carnegie Foundation for the Advancement of Teaching.*

The Quest for Community in Higher Education
Parker J. Palmer

1   Academic culture is a curious and conflicted thing. On the one hand, it holds out the allure and occasionally the reality of being a "community of scholars"—colleagues with common roots in the depths of the intellectual tradition working together to seek new insights into the world's wonders. On the other hand, it is a culture infamous for fragmentation, isolation, and competitive individualism—a culture in which community sometimes feels harder to come by than in any other institution on the face of the earth.

2   This cultural contradiction is vexing, partly because people feel resentful when they are promised one thing and given something quite different. When the academy fails to achieve sustained community in even minimal form, its capacity to pursue its core mission is weakened.

3   That mission can be summed up in three words: *knowing, teaching,* and *learning.* And all three of those words name enterprises that are essentially communal. This claim seems simple and straightforward, but the truth is that we tacitly understand the academy's three-fold mission in highly individualistic terms. Knowing is often regarded as an act of personal genius, something done by very smart people working largely in isolation. Teaching and learning are often regarded as a one-on-one exchange of information, a transfer of knowledge from a teacher who is quite smart to a student who is not—at least not yet!

4   However, when knowing, teaching, and learning are understood and pursued in these ways, we not only distort intellectual history but we fail to develop genuine intellectual capacity in the next generation. Knowing has always been and always will be a dialectic between individual insight and shared communal understandings—a back-and-forth of dissent and consent around what we see and what it means, without which our sight would be even dimmer than it is. Teaching and learning have always been and always will be a complex dance

---

"The Quest for Community in Higher Education," by Parker J. Palmer from *Creating Campus Community: In Search of Ernest Boyer's Legacy,* Wm. M. McDonald, Ed., by permission of John Wiley & Sons, Inc. Copyright © 2002 by John Wiley & Sons, Inc.

between teachers, students, and subjects, a communal engagement with each other and with the world without which authentic education cannot happen.

5   Community in higher education is not optional but essential if we wish to pursue our mission with full integrity. In service of that mission, I want to explore the quest for community on three levels of academic life: community across the entire staff of an institution; community in the classroom and other teaching and learning venues; and community between the academy and the world around it.

Community Across the Staff

6   I spent my undergraduate years at Carleton College in Minnesota, and among the remarkable teachers I had on that campus were Dacie and Roy Moses. Neither of them had a Ph.D., and I am not even sure whether either of them had graduated from high school. Dacie, who was in her sixties when I was a student, worked behind the desk in the college library. Roy had been a skilled carpenter in his younger years, but early on, while he was helping a neighbor build a barn, a huge beam had fallen on him, leaving Roy permanently disabled and largely homebound.

7   The Moses' house on the edge of campus was a home-away-from-home for many Carleton undergraduates, including me. If you were having trouble with a professor, trouble with romance, trouble with your parents, or—most likely—trouble with yourself, stopping by Dacie's and Roy's for a round of cribbage, coffee, cookies, and conversation was the best therapy you could get.

8   In what sense were Dacie and Roy my teachers? What I learned from them was the very incarnation of the abstract ideas we were studying in our liberal arts courses. I learned that generosity is stronger than arrogance. I learned about the dignity of common work. I learned about the value of honest relationships. I learned about the transcendence of the human spirit.

9   There are many things that make me proud of my alma mater and grateful to her. But nothing makes me prouder or more grateful than the fact that, after Roy and Dacie died, the college purchased their home and turned it into a permanent house of hospitality, honoring the fact that—rightly understood—everyone who works at a college is a teacher.

10   The notion that "we are all teachers" is not romanticism. Instead, it is a simple reality related to what educational researchers have called the hidden curriculum. What students learn in college comes not only—and certainly not principally—from lecturers, readings, and discussions, that is, from the content of the formal curriculum. It comes from the way individual and collective life is lived on a campus—from the way the people employed there do their work, conduct their relationships, make their choices, and otherwise reveal their true values, which may be quite at odds with the values espoused in the classroom.

11   We should celebrate the congruities we find between academic rhetoric and

practice, and we should be conscious and critical of the many incongruities. It is cause for celebration when we teach courses on ecological problems *and* have a buildings and grounds crew that takes leadership in a campus recycling program; when we exhort students to become good citizens *and* have a faculty that conducts its decision making in a civil manner; when we advocate good customer relations in business courses *and* have a registrar's staff that deals understandingly with students when they are trying to enroll in overcrowded courses.

12 But when we find incongruities at points such as these, we can be sure of one thing: students are learning at least as much from what we do as from what we say. We need to work hard on aligning the hidden curriculum with our educational purposes—as hard as we work on our formal course offerings. Above all, we must work to bring all staff into a shared sense of community and mission, for only so will people be willing to embrace the reality that we are all teachers.

13 This, in turn, requires a realistic understanding of what community among staff might mean. Every educational institutional has gaps, large and small, between administrative, academic, student services, and professional support staff—gaps in power, status, income, job security. Although some of these gaps can and should be narrowed or closed, others will always be with us. Community among staff cannot have a utopian meaning that flies in the face of reality, or the rhetoric will discourage rather than empower people.

14 So what might community mean in a real-life situation? I believe that certain experiential markers allow individuals to feel that they are in community with others despite any gaps that might exist. Here are five such markers that are within our reach, if we choose to reach for them:

1. I feel in community when I believe that I play a meaningful role in a shared educational mission, and others see me doing so. The first part—belief—is my own responsibility, and it often requires inner work to embrace the meaning of my own role. The second part is the responsibility of others: leaders who articulate the shared mission, staff development activities that assume a shared mission, and colleagues in other departments who act as if we had a shared mission.

2. I feel in community when I am affirmed for the work I do on behalf of the shared mission if it contributes to that mission. If what I do falls short, I am told about that as well and offered help to improve my performance. That is, I am not ignored in either the successes or the failures of the work I do.

3. I feel in community when I know that I can take creative risks in my work and sometimes fail—and still be supported. I understand that not any old risk will do. The risks must be worth taking to advance the shared mission, and the failures must be such that I can learn from them. But within those limits, the safety to fail in a good cause and still be supported is one of the marks that I am in community.

4. I feel in community when I am trusted with basic information about important issues relating to the shared mission. For example, instead of the silence that often surrounds budgetary cutbacks or realignments, I am told that decisions need to be made and why—and I am given adequate information about when, how, by whom, and on what basis they are being made. Nothing undercuts my sense of community more quickly than being kept in the dark about basic issues until "the day after."

5. I feel in community when I have a chance to voice my opinion on issues relating to the shared mission or my part of it—and I am given meaningful responses to what I have to say. I do not need to have my way all the time or even most of the time, but I need to know that my voice is wanted and heard.

15 In sum, I feel that I am in community when I feel seen, known, and respected—when I am taken seriously and appreciated, not just for the function I perform but for who I am as a person. Community is about power *and* rewards *and* relationships *and* meaning—and there will always be imbalances among us in those regards. But we can go a long way toward community by understanding that imbalances in one area can often be corrected, or at least relieved, by rebalancing in another.

16 There are many practical steps we can take to help community happen. This is not the place to spell them out in great detail, but here are three possibilities that can be realized either on small college campuses or within human-scale units of a large university:

- People often spend decades working alongside each other without knowing much, if anything, about who the others are, how they are, why they are here, or where they are going. The absolute minimum in building community is to learn at least a little bit about each other's stories. We could begin small staff or committee meetings with a simple autobiographical question that each person has a few minutes to answer aloud: "Tell us about an important older person in your life." "Tell us about the first dollar you ever made." "Tell us about the best vacation you ever took." Questions like these are nonthreatening and can be answered on any level of vulnerability a person chooses. But the cumulative effect of asking and answering them over a period of months and years is the growth of interpersonal understanding and a deepening sense of community.

- Though much of our work in institutions must be done through a division of labor, with different people pursuing different specializations, it is possible from time to time to find work that can be shared for the sake of community building. In a school where I once worked, there was an annual mass mailing to alumni and other constituents to solicit financial support. The mailing could have been done by a machine or by an outside "service provider." Instead, we gathered the entire staff once a year, for the better part of a day, and together we folded papers and stuffed envelopes, sang and laughed and told tales, and enjoyed each other's company.

- Every institution could profit from examining its own processes of information sharing and decision making through the lens of exclusion and inclusion. In many colleges and universities, for example, the proportion of adjunct faculty has increased dramatically over the past decade. But during that same decade, information sharing and decision making has proceeded apace, as if all the faculty were full-time, either tenured or on a tenure track. The good that would come from including adjunct faculty as trust holders of the institution cannot be overestimated—and its impact would be felt not only in improved morale but in teaching effectiveness as well.

Community in Teaching and Learning

17 Closely examined, the phrase "community in teaching and learning" is redundant; without community, there can be no teaching or learning worthy of the name. But it is a redundancy worth uttering because teaching and learning are so often reduced to a one-to-one exchange of information in which "community" is regarded as neither achievable nor desirable. Students are gathered in one place, called the classroom, not for the sale of community but merely to make it unnecessary for the professor to deliver the information more than once.

18 By now we have more than enough research (to say nothing of personal experience) to know that the fastest and deepest learning happens when there is a dynamic community of connections between teacher and student and subject. The student who feels related to a subject is motivated to do the hard work called learning. That relationship is often mediated by a professor to whom the student feels connected in the first place and strengthened by building relations with other students who are engaged in the process.

19 As I argue at length in my book *The Courage to Teach* (1998), the danger in insisting on making community a key component of teaching and learning is that people will try too quickly to translate community into a technique, for example, collaborative learning. But good teaching can never be reduced to technique. If you want to prove the point, simply collect a dozen student stories of good teachers they have had and notice how seldom technique is mentioned—and how, when it is mentioned, there is great variation among the techniques that good teachers use.

20 To say that community is key to teaching and learning and then translate that into small circles of students engaged in analyzing case studies or solving problems is to diminish the possibilities inherent in the idea and to marginalize faculty whose disciplines or personal gifts do not lend themselves to this approach.

21 We need a more capacious view of what community in teaching and learning

might mean, which is why I have found myself talking less about *community*—a word that is so easily reified—and more about a capacity for *connectedness*. If we could ask ourselves critical questions about our own capacity for connectedness and our strategies for developing that capacity in our students, we might discover more and more ways to create community in the classroom without confining the concept to its most conventional forms.

22 As an acid test of my point, let me take the much-maligned pedagogy called lecturing, which is often criticized these days as tragically anticommunal, little more than the egocentric performance of a "sage on the stage," as contrasted with the community-building mentoring of a "guide by the side." That caricature began to fall apart for me as I thought back over my own education, which was graced, from time to time, by a lecturer who created a palpable and powerful sense of community in session after session after session.

23 How can a lecture course create community when, for fifty minutes, the classroom is dominated by one voice? The answer, of course, involves the motivations of the lecturer, what he or she is saying, and the ends he or she intends to serve. A lecture that emerges from "a capacity for connectedness" and evokes that same capacity in the listener has certain characteristics that distinguish it quite clearly from a lecture that cuts the connections off.

24 The latter is exemplified by the lecturer who tells you what the right questions are and gives you all the right answers, asking only your assent. But when a lecturer generates new questions right before your eyes, giving you a glimpse of where questions come from, then wrestles with those questions in open and vulnerable ways, a sense of connectedness is created among the listeners, who find themselves engaged in their own inner dialogue.

25 Similarly, when a lecturer simply rehearses "the facts of the matter" in a given field of study, expecting the listeners to commit them to memory, connectedness is shut down. But when a lecturer portrays the human drama from which those facts were generated—when we learn not just the content of Marx's ideas but the personal and social dynamics that animated his mind—we are connected with the lecturer, the subject, and one another in surprising ways.

26 The communal consequences of a good lecture are much like those of good theater. When you attend a skillful production of a great drama, you are not a passive member of the audience. Far from it. You are deeply engaged in body, mind, and spirit with what is happening on stage. You need not be a member of the cast to be a participant in that community of meaning, for your own life is being evoked by the words of the playwright and the interpretations of the actors.

27 My insistence that a variety of teaching techniques have the potential to help create community should not be taken as a license to teach however one will. It should give us pause to note that the practice of lecturing is much more widespread in the academy than the practice of creating community through lecturing! There is a litmus test here, and it is a rigorous one. Does my pedagogy

come from a place of connectedness in me so it can evoke in my students those connections that make learning possible? Or am I using my pedagogy in a way that distances me from my subject and sets me apart from my students, thus diminishing the chances that my classroom will become a place of live encounter?
28 If we could ask those questions openly and answer them honestly, we would take a meaningful step toward creating more community among teachers and students at the heart of academic life—without reducing community to one size that fails to fit all.

Community with the World

29 From its very inception, higher education has had an uneasy, even hostile, relation to the world around it; we tend to hold academic values in ways that set us apart. In fact, we sometimes hold our values as weapons against the world—a tendency driven deep into our institutional DNA.

30 Here is how the Columbia Accountability Study (1995) characterizes the evolutionary starting point of the modern university:

> Since their medieval origins, universities have claimed special status, not as a privilege but as an essential prerequisite to carrying out their mission. Universities arose from non-institutional gatherings of scholars. A great teacher would attract a following, often from faraway places. Soon the out-of-towners found themselves in need of protection, and so they banded together in guilds to obtain immunities from local interference, service obligations, and taxation [Graham, Lyman, and Trow, p. 5].

31 Do we still need protection today, so many centuries later? I do not want to minimize the dangers of external assaults on academic freedom (though I agree with the wag who said that academic freedom in recent decades has meant little more than the freedom to be academic). But the protection we most need today is not from the outside world but from ourselves; from our own tendencies toward arrogance and isolation, from our own self-protective and self-defeating insularity, from our many ways of widening rather than closing the gap between the academy and the world around us.

32 We can hold our values in ways that connect us creatively with the world rather than set us apart. We can reach out for partnerships with others, and when we do, we may find that our values are more widely shared than we imagine.

33 "The world" is a very large place, so I need to be selective in illustrating the kinds of partnerships I have in mind. I will offer just one example as I bring this afterword to a close: the story of Princeton Project 55. It is a story that is not as well known as it deserves to be and is instructive on at least two fronts: it gives us a model of creating community between the academy and world, and it tells us something about transforming academic politics in order to get a job done.

34 As they approached their fortieth reunion, the Class of 1955 at Princeton

University decided to give their alma mater an unusual gift. Instead of a bell tower or a meditation garden or a major contribution to the endowment, they offered their influence and expertise in building a bridge between the university and the world—a bridge that would allow new generations of Princeton students to link their education with their emerging vocations and with a wide range of societal concerns.

35 The influence and expertise of the Class of '55 is considerable. Among their number are some who are quite visible in American public life, others who are not known publicly but who hold positions of real power, and still others whose lives have been quietly devoted to high purposes. Not every college could claim so many names in the first or second categories, perhaps, but every college has among its alumni countless people who know and serve the world well.

36 For several years prior to their fortieth reunion, members of the Class of '55 worked to generate both money for this project and, more important, administrative and faculty commitment to a partnership between the university and its alumni in the service of Princeton students. Using their connections, class members began to create internships and service-learning opportunities for undergraduates, and the faculty and administration began to explore the implications of such a program for finances, the academic calendar, course credit, curriculum, and pedagogy.

37 What ensued is impressive by any measure. In 1990, Princeton Project 55 launched its first initiative, with fourteen summer interns and eight year-long fellows being placed in significant positions with public interest organizations. Since that time, Project 55 has placed almost seven hundred students or recent graduates as interns and fellows in twenty cities around the country, while leveraging nearly $6 million in stipends and salaries for these students. The leaders of Project 55 estimate that these students, through their work with public interest organizations, have touched the lives of some five million Americans. (Supporting documents and additional information on Project 55 can be found on the Web at http://www.Project55.org/Index.html.)

38 These data are impressive. But even more impressive to me is that, from the outset, the Class of '55 started using its authority in the life of the university to open a new dialogue about curriculum and pedagogy—about community at the heart of academic life.

39 In 1995, the group—which had by then expanded to include alumni from every decade since the fifties—issued a discussion paper titled "Princeton University in the 21 Century: Paths to More Effective Undergraduate Education." In the preface, the writers announce their intentions in words both substantive and bold, words of a sort not often uttered by alumni to their alma mater:

> This paper makes the case for a new approach to undergraduate education at Princeton, an approach that takes account of research that:

- Increasingly illuminates how individuals learn most effectively;
- Reflects a growing consensus on what students need to know to function more effectively as individuals, citizens, and workers; and
- Suggests the curricular and pedagogical approaches most responsive to new knowledge and new needs.

It is time for even the greatest of our institutions of higher education and research to think in different ways. As they do so, the first requirement will be for clarity about, and a shared definition of, basic institutional purposes. So that readers will understand our perspectives in what follows, we note our belief that Princeton's purposes should be:

- Nurturing (not merely "teaching") reflective, caring, able citizens;
- Discovering important knowledge and truths; and
- Serving society's civic, economic, and social needs.

Secondly, we intend this paper to be a strong argument for experiential education at Princeton. The contemporary definition of experiential education is:

Learning activities that engage the learner in the phenomenon being studied. It assumes (and we cannot stress this point too strongly) that the experience is closely linked to a course, is overseen by a teacher, and is subjected to active, collaborative reflection with peers and others in the classroom and elsewhere on campus.

40 Exploring all that we might learn from Princeton Project 55 is beyond the scope of this book. But the most important insight the story offers, it seems to me, is this: among all the constituencies of our academic institutions, alumni may be in the best position to help us create more community between the academy and the world and to do so in ways that respect core academic values. They are also the constituency least often called upon for purposes such as these—or for any purpose other than financial support!

41 Ever since I learned about Princeton Project 55, I have been pondering a critical question: Why do we who care about educational reform either ignore the alumni or wait for them to approach us, as the Class of 1955 approached Princeton? Why do we not reach out to the graduates of our institutions for assistance in building bridges between the academy and the world?

42 What alumni can bring to this bridge building is not only energy, knowledge, contacts, and financial resources. They also bring a new force to the politics of academic reform, which is much in need of new forces! In very short order, Project 55 broke through the historic resistance of many academic institutions, especially elite institutions, to anything that takes them out of their comfort zone. They were able to do so for at least three reasons: (1) the alumni are a legitimate constituency of the university; (2) their approach to the university was deeply respectful of its integrity and yet appropriately critical of its limitations; and (3) they represent real power in the university's life.

43   As we pursue our efforts to fulfill the promise of the academy by deepening the communal relations of administrations, faculty, staff, and students, let us not forget the needs of the larger world—or our own need for the new perspectives and energies that exchange with that world can bring. Perhaps we have planted the seeds of our own transformation by educating generations of students who left the academy, became good citizens of that larger world, and can now turn around and help us become good citizens, too.

References

Graham, P.A., Lyman, R.W., and Trow, M. (1995). Accountability of colleges and universities: An Essay. In *The Accountability Study*. New York: Columbia University. Available at http://Info.library.emory.edu/FryeInstitute/Readings/17141501.pdf

Palmer, P.J.(1998). *The Courage to Teach*. San Francisco: Jossey-Bass.

Update, August 2003. Since members of the class of '55 launched Princeton Project 55 (PP55) in 1989, over 1,000 fellows and interns have been placed in nonprofit organizations, leveraging over $14 million in stipends. Most of the former fellows and interns continue to be actively involved in their communities through careers and/or volunteerism. PP55's discussion paper cited by Palmer let to the Princeton University Community-Based Learning Initiative. Also, PP55 has encouraged alumni of other colleges and universities to develop public interest efforts. PP55's "The Alumni Network" program, started in 1999, has 19 affiliates so far, including alumni groups from Bucknell, Dartmouth, Franklin & Marshal, Georgetown, Harvard, Syracuse, and Yale. For these and other PP55 programs, visit www.project55.org.

Abraham Lincoln
Second Inaugural Address
Saturday, March 4, 1865

Fellow-Countrymen:

1   At this second appearing to take the oath of the Presidential office there is less occasion for an extended address than there was at the first. Then a statement somewhat in detail of a course to be pursued seemed fitting and proper. Now, at the expiration of four years, during which public declarations have been constantly called forth on every point and phase of the great contest which still absorbs the attention and engrosses the energies of the nation, little that is new could be presented. The progress of our arms, upon which all else chiefly depends, is as well known to the public as to myself, and it is, I trust, reasonably satisfactory and encouraging to all. With high hope for the future, no prediction in regard to it is ventured.

2   On the occasion corresponding to this four years ago all thoughts were anxiously directed to an impending civil war. All dreaded it, all sought to avert it. While the inaugural address was being delivered from this place, devoted altogether to *saving* the Union without war, insurgent agents were in the city seeking to *destroy* it without war—seeking to dissolve the Union and divide effects by negotiation. Both parties deprecated war, but one of them would *make* war rather than let the nation survive, and the other would *accept* war rather than let it perish, and the war came.

3   One-eighth of the whole population were colored slaves, not distributed generally over the Union, but localized in the southern part of it. These slaves constituted a peculiar and powerful interest. All knew that this interest was somehow the cause of the war. To strengthen, perpetuate, and extend this interest was the object for which the insurgents would rend the Union even by war, while the Government claimed no right to do more than to restrict the territorial enlargement of it. Neither party expected for the war the magnitude or the duration which it has already attained. Neither anticipated that the *cause* of the conflict might cease with or even before the conflict itself should cease. Each looked for an easier triumph, and a result less fundamental and astounding. Both read the same Bible and pray to the same God, and each invokes His aid against the other. It may seem strange that any men should dare to ask a just God's assistance in wringing their bread from the sweat of other men's faces, but let us judge not, that we be not judged. The prayers of both could not be answered. That of neither has been answered fully. The Almighty has His own

purposes. "Woe unto the world because of offenses; for it must needs be that offenses come, but woe to that man by whom the offense cometh." If we shall suppose that American slavery is one of those offenses which, in the providence of God, must needs come, but which, having continued through His appointed time, He now wills to remove, and that He gives to both North and South this terrible war as the woe due to those by whom the offense came, shall we discern therein any departure from those divine attributes which the believers in a living God always ascribe to Him? Fondly do we hope, fervently do we pray, that this mighty scourge of war may speedily pass away. Yet, if God wills that it continue until all the wealth piled by the bondsman's two hundred and fifty years of unrequited toil shall be sunk, and until every drop of blood drawn with the lash shall be paid by another drawn with the sword, as was said three thousand years ago, so still it must be said "the judgments of the Lord are true and righteous altogether."

4   With malice toward none, with charity for all, with firmness in the right as God gives us to see the right, let us strive on to finish the work we are in, to bind up the nation's wounds, to care for him who shall have borne the battle and for his widow and his orphan, to do all which may achieve and cherish a just and lasting peace among ourselves and with all nations.

John F. Kennedy
Inaugural Address
Friday, January 20, 1961

1   Vice President Johnson, Mr. Speaker, Mr. Chief Justice, President Eisenhower, Vice President Nixon, President Truman, reverend clergy, fellow citizens, we observe today not a victory of party, but a celebration of freedom—symbolizing an end, as well as a beginning—signifying renewal, as well as change. For I have sworn before you and Almighty God the same solemn oath our forebears prescribed nearly a century and three quarters ago.
2   The world is very different now. For man holds in his mortal hands the power to abolish all forms of human poverty and all forms of human life. And yet the same revolutionary beliefs for which our forebears fought are still at issue around the globe—the belief that the rights of man come not from the generosity of the state, but from the hand of God.
3   We dare not forget today that we are the heirs of that first revolution. Let the word go forth from this time and place, to friend and foe alike, that the torch has been passed to a new generation of Americans—born in this century, tempered by war, disciplined by a hard and bitter peace, proud of our ancient heritage—and unwilling to witness or permit the slow undoing of those human rights to which this Nation has always been committed, and to which we are committed today at home and around the world.
4   Let every nation know, whether it wishes us well or ill, that we shall pay any price, bear any burden, meet any hardship, support any friend, oppose any foe, in order to assure the survival and the success of liberty.
5   This much we pledge—and more.
6   To those old allies whose cultural and spiritual origins we share, we pledge the loyalty of faithful friends. United, there is little we cannot do in a host of cooperative ventures. Divided, there is little we can do—for we dare not meet a powerful challenge at odds and split asunder.
7   To those new States whom we welcome to the ranks of the free, we pledge our word that one form of colonial control shall not have passed away merely to be replaced by a far more iron tyranny. We shall not always expect to find them supporting our view. But we shall always hope to find them strongly supporting their own freedom—and to remember that, in the past, those who foolishly sought power by riding the back of the tiger ended up inside.
8   To those peoples in the huts and villages across the globe struggling to break the bonds of mass misery, we pledge our best efforts to help them help themselves, for whatever period is required—not because the Communists may

be doing it, not because we seek their votes, but because it is right. If a free society cannot help the many who are poor, it cannot save the few who are rich.

9 To our sister republics south of our border, we offer a special pledge—to convert our good words into good deeds—in a new alliance for progress—to assist free men and free governments in casting off the chains of poverty. But this peaceful revolution of hope cannot become the prey of hostile powers. Let all our neighbors know that we shall join with them to oppose aggression or subversion anywhere in the Americas. And let every other power know that this Hemisphere intends to remain the master of its own house.

10 To that world assembly of sovereign states, the United Nations, our last best hope in an age where the instruments of war have far outpaced the instruments of peace, we renew our pledge of support—to prevent it from becoming merely a forum for invective—to strengthen its shield of the new and the weak—and to enlarge the area in which its writ may run.

11 Finally, to those nations who would make themselves our adversary, we offer not a pledge but a request: that both sides begin anew the quest for peace, before the dark powers of destruction unleashed by science engulf all humanity in planned or accidental self-destruction.

12 We dare not tempt them with weakness. For only when our arms are sufficient beyond doubt can we be certain beyond doubt that they will never be employed.

13 But neither can two great and powerful groups of nations take comfort from our present course—both sides overburdened by the cost of modern weapons, both rightly alarmed by the steady spread of the deadly atom, yet both racing to alter that uncertain balance of terror that stays the hand of mankind's final war.

14 So let us begin anew—remembering on both sides that civility is not a sign of weakness, and sincerity is always subject to proof. Let us never negotiate out of fear. But let us never fear to negotiate.

15 Let both sides explore what problems unite us instead of belaboring those problems which divide us.

15 Let both sides, for the first time, formulate serious and precise proposals for the inspection and control of arms—and bring the absolute power to destroy other nations under the absolute control of all nations.

17 Let both sides seek to invoke the wonders of science instead of its terrors. Together let us explore the stars, conquer the deserts, eradicate disease, tap the ocean depths, and encourage the arts and commerce.

18 Let both sides unite to heed in all corners of the earth the command of Isaiah—to "undo the heavy burdens . . . and to let the oppressed go free."

19 And if a beachhead of cooperation may push back the jungle of suspicion, let both sides join in creating a new endeavor, not a new balance of power, but a new world of law, where the strong are just and the weak secure and the peace preserved.

20 All this will not be finished in the first 100 days. Nor will it be finished in

the first 1,000 days, nor in the life of this Administration, nor even perhaps in our lifetime on this planet. But let us begin.

21 In your hands, my fellow citizens, more than in mine, will rest the final success or failure of our course. Since this country was founded, each generation of Americans has been summoned to give testimony to its national loyalty. The graves of young Americans who answered the call to service surround the globe.

22 Now the trumpet summons us again—not as a call to bear arms, though arms we need; not as a call to battle, though embattled we are—but a call to bear the burden of a long twilight struggle, year in and year out, "rejoicing in hope, patient in tribulation"—a struggle against the common enemies of man: tyranny, poverty, disease, and war itself.

23 Can we forge against these enemies a grand and global alliance, North and South, East and West, that can assure a more fruitful life for all mankind? Will you join in that historic effort?

24 In the long history of the world, only a few generations have been granted the role of defending freedom in its hour of maximum danger. I do not shrink from this responsibility—I welcome it. I do not believe that any of us would exchange places with any other people or any other generation. The energy, the faith, the devotion which we bring to this endeavor will light our country and all who serve it—and the glow from that fire can truly light the world.

25 And so, my fellow Americans: ask not what your country can do for you—ask what you can do for your country.

26 My fellow citizens of the world: ask not what America will do for you, but what together we can do for the freedom of man.

27 Finally, whether you are citizens of America or citizens of the world, ask of us the same high standards of strength and sacrifice which we ask of you. With a good conscience our only sure reward, with history the final judge of our deeds, let us go forth to lead the land we love, asking His blessing and His help, but knowing that here on earth God's work must truly be our own.

Appendix

with
The Revision and Editing Process
Revision Worksheet
Editing Worksheet
Correct Writing Basics

Appendix

Discernment and Discourse: Course Descriptions

DISC 1311: Foundations of Written and Oral Discourse
This course gives students practice in the reading, writing, and analytical skills necessary for the successful completion of DISC 1312 and 1313. Students will approach writing as a process of drafting, revising, and editing; and they will work on sentence-level and paragraph-level writing skills as they build toward essay-length writing projects. Students must earn a C- or better to proceed in the sequence of DISC courses.

DISC 1312: Introduction to Academic Discourse
This course introduces students to a variety of discipline-based modes of inquiry and expression. The texts students read and create will employ and exemplify the principles of academic discernment and discourse. Students must earn a C- or better to proceed in the sequence of DISC courses.
Prerequisite: DISC 1311 or 550 on the SAT Critical Reasoning or 24 on the ACT English section.

DISC 1313: Inquiry Seminar
This course is a topic-based seminar through which students continue to develop their critical reading and writing skills, employing analysis, evaluation, synthesis, and /or integration, while learning to employ research protocols for the discipline or various disciplines represented in the course. Students must earn a C- or better to complete their DISC requirement.
Prerequisite: DISC 1312.

ESL Discernment and Discourse Writing Sequence (DISC 1311, 1312, 1313) focuses on the special needs of non-native speakers of English, offering additional practice in reading comprehension, vocabulary development, grammatical accuracy, and conversational and compositional "fluency." The ultimate goal of these sections is to provide ESL students with the tools they need to produce written and spoken work that conforms to the standards applied to their native English-speaking peers. As in regular sections of DISC 1312 and 1313, a final grade of C- or above is required for successful completion of the ESL sections.

DISC 1315: Perspectives of Thought
This course focuses on analytical writing while exploring major modes of interpreting the world and defining what constitutes knowledge in the 21st Century.
Restricted to Hilltop Scholars and New Century Scholars placing out of DISC 1312.

DISC 2305: Honors Humanities Seminar I
Insights from literature, linguistics, philosophy, psychology, and science that became major modes of interpreting the world in the 20th Century and that

define what constitutes knowledge in the 21st Century. Open only to students in the University Honors Program.

DISC 2306: Honors Humanities Seminar II
A study of ethical questions derived from history, literature, psychology, and philosophy that focuses on what constitutes a meaningful life. The course also explores historical challenges to the bases of ethics.
Prerequisite: DISC 2305.

Class Attendance and Office Visits

Discernment and Discourse classes are workshop classes; therefore, attendance, preparation, and participation are both expected and required. However, since illnesses and crises do occur, you may need to miss a class or two. You may also need to miss class to observe a religious holiday per University Policy 1.9 or to participate in a legitimate University function. Inform your instructor—in advance whenever possible—if you must be absent. **Be prepared to provide documentation for absences you believe excusable, and be aware that it is your responsibility to ascertain that the instructor will, in fact, excuse the absence.** Whether your absence is excused or unexcused, you are nevertheless responsible for all work that is due and for all material covered or assigned in the class or classes you miss.

Attendance policy: If you have more than three unexcused absences in a MWF section or two in a TTH section, your grade will suffer a penalty of up to a full letter grade. And if you have more than six unexcused MWF absences or four in a TTH class, you should expect to fail the course. If you have more than one absence during a summer session, expect your grade to be lowered; if you have more than three absences, you risk failing the course. Because the University's General Education policies mandate that students be enrolled in the Discernment and Discourse sequence each semester until they satisfactorily complete the Written Fundamentals requirement, students may not drop courses with a Discernment and Discourse (DISC) prefix.

If you have a special problem with attendance, confer with your instructor. *Do not just stop attending your classes.* Your teachers will announce their office hours at the beginning of each semester; you can visit their offices during these hours or request an appointment for a conference. If you experience difficulties with any phase of the course, see your teacher immediately. *Do not wait until these problems become insurmountable.*

Awards and Honors
The *Criteria* Award for Distinction

The editors of *Criteria* consider for publication all outstanding written work submitted by DISC faculty from student writers in their classes. Student writers whose exceptional contributions merit distinction will be selected each year for the *Criteria* Award.

Recipients of the *Criteria* Award for 2012–2013 are Danielle Katz, Alex Mirabile, and Marquelle Smith.

The Laura Kesselman Devlin Award

The Devlin Award commemorates Laura Devlin, a first-year writing teacher distinguished for academic rigor, intellectual adventure, and human concern. This award for continuing excellence is presented annually to a full-time faculty member whose major teaching responsibility is in DISC.

The Devlin Lecturer for 2012–2013 is Vanessa Hopper.

The Writing Center

The Writing Center faculty would like to extend a personal invitation to visit SMU's Writing Center when you need help with a writing—or reading—project of any kind. The Writing Center is a resource free to all members of the SMU community: undergraduate and graduate students, faculty, and staff. Rhetoric faculty members will be available by appointment Monday through Friday afternoons to assist you.

Whether you need help understanding a writing or reading assignment, getting started in the writing process, revising a draft in progress, or applying your teacher's comments to subsequent assignments, we offer one-on-one tutorials that we hope will send you in the right direction. Of course, we can't do everything in one thirty-minute session, nor will we violate SMU's Honor Code by providing you with ideas or editing your papers, but we can provide strategies that will help you learn how to "decipher" reading and writing assignments, generate your own ideas, revise and edit more efficiently and effectively, and benefit as fully as possible from your teacher's suggestions. And if you think that you have a particular area of weakness, such as punctuation or predication, Writing Center faculty members can help you learn to identify and rectify these problems, thus making you a more confident writer. So, as you can see, while we won't work for you, we will definitely work with you!

We hope that this brief description of the Writing Center gives you some idea of our various services. We are here to help you, but you must take the first step by calling 214-768-3648 for a Writing Center faculty tutorial. If you are working on an essay for a course, it is a good idea to schedule your tutorial well in advance of the due date, thus allowing yourself ample time for revision, a conference with your teacher, and perhaps even a follow-up appointment with us.

Writing Center appointments fill quickly, so we recommend that you call at least 48 hours in advance to reserve a time for your half-hour tutorial. If you must cancel or reschedule a Writing Center appointment, please do so at least one day ahead of time so that we can make your appointment time available to others who call. To schedule, reschedule, or cancel a Writing Center appointment, please call 214-768-3648.

We look forward to seeing you soon in Room 202H Loyd Center.

Lee Gibson
Faculty Coordinator

Kristen Polster
Stephanie Amsel
Writing Center Faculty

The Altshuler Learning Enhancement Center

The Altshuler Learning Enhancement Center (LEC) provides a variety of services to support the academic success of SMU's undergraduates. Most students who arrive at SMU find that the learning strategies that worked for them in high school are in need of an upgrade. We're here to help. Students at all levels have found that work with the LEC can make a huge difference. All LEC services are offered without charge to SMU undergraduates.

Our programs include:

- **ORACLE/HDEV 1110:** A one credit elective course, ORACLE (Optimum Reading, Attention, Comprehension and Learning Efficiency) helps students improve reading comprehension and rate while developing a personalized system of strategic learning techniques. ORACLE can help you make a successful transition to college, whether you excelled in high school without ever studying, have multiple courses with heavy reading loads, or aim for a 4.0 in three majors while running for Student Senate.

- **Success Strategies/HDEV 1111:** A one credit elective course, Success Strategies introduces academically struggling students to specific approaches to help them achieve greater success in their academic, professional, and personal life. In this course, students will engage in ongoing self-assessment and journal writing to explore strategies and to identify academic challenges, as well as strengths they possess to overcome these challenges. Students will also be introduced to learning strategies and study skills, and they will have the opportunity to explore campus resources they can use to succeed at SMU.

- **Learning strategies workshops:** Students who can't take ORACLE can develop college-level learning strategies by attending one-hour drop-in workshops on a wide variety of topics including time management, note taking, study-reading, concentration, and test preparation, test taking, and test anxiety. Check the LEC web page for a complete schedule of this semester's workshops, and then drop in for one or all.

- **Individual academic counseling:** For one-to-one help with learning strategies, call the L.E.C. to make an appointment for individual academic counseling. We can help you assess your reading and learning skills, develop new strategies, and apply them to the demands of your courses.

- **Drop-in tutoring:** The LEC offers one-to-one or small group sessions, five afternoons and evenings a week, for most key first- and second-year courses and many higher-level ones. Use LEC tutoring to raise a B to an A or to repair a disaster. Tutoring works best when you start soon and come frequently, least well when you wait till the night before a test.

We invite you to check out our website at *www.smu.edu/alec* to learn more about our programs, or to stop by in person at 202 Loyd Center. We look forward to working with you to help you meet your academic goals.

Patricia Feldman
Associate Director, LEC

Central University Libraries: Ask a Librarian.

Fondren Library is the main library at SMU. It is open 24/5 to students, except for breaks and holidays. It has resources for your education and enjoyment, including feature films. You will find many great spaces to study, including group study rooms that can be reserved online at smu.edu/cul/rooms. WiFi is available throughout the facility and outside in the courtyard.

Circulation & Reserve   smu.edu/cul/flc/circ   214-768-2329
Circulation staff will assist you in checking out, renewing, and returning library materials, including items placed on reserve by faculty members.

Information Commons   Fondren East, 1st Floor
The Information Commons not only has plenty of computers for you to use, but also librarians on hand to help. The Research Services desk, Touch Learning Center (TLC), and Multimedia Center are located here.

ID Card
Your SMU ID is your library card; bring it whenever you come to the library. Use your ID to check out books and Pony Express Cash account to pay for printing and copying.

Research Resources

Research Services   askalibrarian.smu.edu   214-768-2326
For help from a research librarian, use our Ask a Librarian service to email, IM, call, or TXT the librarian on duty. Ask us anything, anytime, from anywhere.

Stop by (Fondren East, 1st floor) or call 214.768.2326 for on-the-spot research help. Our student assistants are often available to provide basic help during extended hours.

Research Guides   guides.smu.edu
Created by SMU librarians, these subject-specific research guides provide recommendations for where to start your research. Supplemental guides assist with creating annotated bibliographies, finding primary sources, and more.

Discover SMU Libraries   smu.edu/cul
Search most library online resources, including the library catalog, digital collections, and subscription databases all at once. This is especially useful for preliminary and multidisciplinary research.

Off-Campus Access to Resources
Current SMU faculty, staff, and students may use library resources from off-campus. Logging in is required in order to access these resources remotely, so be sure to start at smu.edu/cul.

Researching Like a College Student

In high school, you may have written at least one research paper. To write the paper, you reported evidence by authors who agreed with you. Your teacher probably had you turn in the assignment in stages, to help you plan your paper. In college, writing papers will be a different experience.

Research is a quest and a conversation.

A researcher questions the information that came before and responds to it. Research papers involve an inquiry on a specific issue and communicate the intellectual conversation you are having with other scholars. You will not simply tell what others have said; instead, you will give your standpoint with regard to the interpretation of text, data, or events. You will seek useful disagreements on a subject and show how your position is supported by experts, as well as where others interpreted the material differently. You may need to use primary sources (and find out the difference between primary and secondary sources). You will actively seek opposing viewpoints and consider these alternative perspectives. As you consider the evidence, you should learn to be open to rethinking your stance rather than simply digging in your heels and sticking with your initial position.

Research is a process.

A researcher gathers information, reviews it, and then seeks to fill information gaps. You will use only scholarly, peer-reviewed journals and books as resources, taking a variety of sources and analyzing or synthesizing the material into an integrated whole. Sometimes the most helpful part of an article will be the bibliography, so make sure you read the works cited thoroughly and get any useful sources. Not all sources will be available in SMU's libraries, but if you start researching early enough, then you can order them through interlibrary loan. For most of your classes, you will be responsible for planning your research/writing schedule. Remember that research will usually take at least twice as much time as you think it will so plan accordingly. As you progress through your academic career, you will learn that the most convenient and familiar resources are not necessarily the best choices. The best databases for an introductory course will not be adequate for an upper-level seminar.

Research is difficult, but rewarding. Ask a librarian for help. We are here to help you.

Rebecca Graff
SMU Central University Libraries
Research Librarian and Instruction Coordinator
askalibrarian.smu.edu

Computers on Campus

Computers can be effective tools in all stages of the writing process—from the first brainstorming notes, through global and local revision, to the final formatted essay. Using a computer allows the writer to make changes more easily and thus to produce a carefully considered essay.

Some DISC sections meet in computer classrooms, not to teach students computer skills, but to allow students to use networked systems to share ideas, comments, and drafts, and to learn online search strategies. Even those DISC sections that meet in traditional classrooms have access to display computers to demonstrate revision strategies.

For students who do not own a computer or whose computer malfunctions or crashes, SMU maintains several labs where students may use personal computers or receive assistance in using unfamiliar equipment or software. These labs are linked to local and campus networks and to the Internet; some are wireless. You'll find computer labs in Fondren Library West, 1st and 3rd floors; the Business Information Commons; the Altshuler Learning Enhancement Center; Hughes-Trigg Student Center (the CyberCafe is open 24 hours a day); basement of Hamon Arts Library; Laura Lee Blanton Building; and residence halls. Students may print in these labs from the public computers or from their laptops, using a copy card or Pony Express card.

For information on specific locations and hours of availability, check your new Owner's Manual for first-year students on "Academic Computing," or check the website: smu.edu/help/networking/labs.asp.

For computing help, call the Help Desk at 214-768-4357 or e-mail them at help@smu.edu or go to the Office of Information Technology, Fondren Library.

Blackboard

Blackboard is an online Course Management System, or CMS, that many professors at SMU use to post course material, make announcements, allow students to share ideas and drafts through online journals and blogs, and conduct conversations on discussion boards. Some DISC sections use Blackboard regularly. You can access Blackboard at: courses.smu.edu.

Use your eight-digit Student I.D. as your user name and password the first time you log on.

On Grading

I do not . . . grade on potential, talent, improvement, effort, motivation, intention, behavior, personality, weight, height, sex, race, accent, appearance. I grade on accomplishment. . . . As represent exceptional work, far above average. Bs represent good work, above average. Cs represent average work. Ds below-average work. And Fs exceptional work in the wrong direction.

It is the work I am grading, not the student. It is work that can be shown to the student, to colleagues, to administrators; it is work that relates directly to the quality of the reference that would be given for the student when that student applies to more advanced courses or for a job. It is a grade that represents my evaluation of what the student has accomplished and demonstrated at the end of the course after the student has had the benefit of extensive writing and extensive reaction to that writing.

From A Writer Teaches Writing, by Donald Murray

STANDARDS FOR EVALUATION

	Excellent (A)	Good (B)	Adequate (C)	Poor (D)	Failing (F)
C O N T E N T	Significant controlling idea or assertion supported with concrete, substantial, and relevant evidence.	Controlling idea or assertion supported with concrete and relevant evidence.	Controlling idea or assertion general, limited, or obvious; some supporting evidence is repetitious, irrelevant, or sketchy.	Controlling idea or assertion too general, superficial, or vague; evidence insufficient because obvious, contradictory, or aimless.	No discernible idea or assertion controls the random or unexplained details that make up the body of the essay.
D E V E L O P M E N T	Order reveals a sense of necessity, symmetry, and emphasis; paragraphs focused and coherent; logical transitions reinforce the progress of the analysis or argument. Introduction engages initial interest; conclusion supports without merely repeating.	Order reveals a sense of necessity and emphasis; paragraphs focused and coherent; logical transitions signal changes in direction; introduction engages initial interest; conclusion supports without merely repeating.	Order apparent but not consistently maintained; paragraphs focused and for the most part coherent; transitions functional but often obvious or monotonous. Introduction or conclusions may be mechanical rather than purposeful or insightful.	Order unclear or inappropriate, failing to emphasize central idea; paragraphs jumbled or underdeveloped; transitions unclear, inaccurate, or missing. Introduction merely describes what is to follow; conclusion merely repeats what has been said.	Order and emphasis indiscernible; paragraphs typographical rather than structural; transitions unclear, inaccurate, or missing. Neither the introduction nor the conclusion satisfies any clear rhetorical purpose.
S T Y L E	Sentences varied, purposeful, and emphatic; diction fresh, precise, economical, and idiomatic; tone complements the subject, conveys the authorial persona, and suits the audience.	Sentences varied, purposeful, and emphatic; diction precise and idiomatic; tone fits the subject, persona, and audience.	Sentences competent but lacking emphasis and variety; diction generally correct and idiomatic; tone acceptable for the subject.	Sentences lack necessary emphasis, subordination, and purpose; diction vague or unidiomatic; tone inconsistent with or inappropriate to the subject.	Incoherent, rudimentary, or redundant sentences thwart the meaning of the essay; diction nonstandard or unidiomatic; tone indiscernible or inappropriate to the subject.
U S A G E	Grammar, syntax, punctuation, and spelling adhere to the conventions of "edited American English."	Grammar, syntax, punctuation, and spelling contain no serious deviations from the conventions of "edited American English."	Content undercut by some deviations from the conventions of "edited American English."	Frequent mistakes in grammar, syntax, punctuation, and spelling obscure content.	Frequent and serious mistakes in grammar, syntax, punctuation, and spelling make the content unintelligible.

Avoiding Bias

In early editions of *The Elements of Style*, their classic guide to effective writing, William Strunk and E.B. White argued for the appropriateness of using "*he* as pronoun for nouns embracing both genders," writing that "*he* has lost all suggestion of maleness in these circumstances" (60).

More recent research by linguists and psychologists, however, suggests that readers do tend to envision male characters when reading *he* or *man*, even if the rest of the passage contains no references to gender, and that these assumptions affect the readers' understanding of and appreciation for what they are reading. Today, then, almost all handbooks and style manuals recommend that writers rely on gender-neutral word choice and on constructions that carry no specific designation of femininity or masculinity when no specific references are intended. These handbooks contain extensive practical and stylistically graceful suggestions for ways to avoid gender-biased language.

Bias-free writing extends beyond gender. As a writer, you want to consider both if and how you should refer to someone's age, ethnicity, appearance, physical abilities, religion, or sexual preference. Include this information if it is relevant to your context and point, and be consistent. For example, if you wouldn't refer to one person as a "heterosexual," why would you describe another as a "lesbian"? If you haven't described one character as "someone's husband," why would you describe another as "someone's wife"? If you haven't mentioned your European-American history professor's ethnicity, why would you mention the ethnicity of your African-American economics professor? When such references are appropriate, be sure that your descriptions are neither stereotypical nor degrading. For example, avoid references to "inscrutable" Asians, and refer to someone as "using" a wheelchair, rather than as "confined" to it.

Some may be concerned that avoiding biased language is merely a form of political correctness, an attempt to change beliefs or limit free exchange of ideas. Others may denigrate the issue by making jokes about "personhole covers." But in fact, all good writers should use bias-free language because it is actually more concise, more accurate, and more persuasive since it eliminates distracting and irrelevant observations and assumptions. All language is persuasive: Through language, we do not describe the world, but rather we create the human experience of the world, both for ourselves and for our listeners and readers, who are affected in one way or another by our words. As a writer, you want neither to reveal your own unacknowledged or unintended biases nor to trigger unintended biases in your readers.

Work Cited

Strunk, William and E.B. White. *The Elements of Style*. 3rd ed. New York: McMillan Publishing Company, 1979. Print.

On Plagiarism

Plagiarism is literary burglary. At its worst, it involves an outright intent to deceive, to pass off another's work as one's own. More often, it is the result of carelessness or ignorance. But whether intentional or unintentional (the distinction is often hard to draw), plagiarism is always an error, and a serious one. (Stone and Bell 214)

Copyright laws exist to protect authors' rights to their own ideas as well as their actual words. In addition, scholarly ethics demand that writers make accessible to their readers the research materials they have used to develop their written argument or presentation. Student writers are expected to observe at all times both the limits of the copyright laws and the ethics of scholarly research. To this end, all written work submitted in any course should be organized according to an original plan. Words taken from anyone else's work—spoken or written, in print or online—must be quoted and cited; and ideas taken from someone else's work, whether paraphrased or summarized, must be cited as well.

While the purpose of any argument should be to express an original idea and point of view, it is often desirable for students to draw information or ideas from responsible sources and to use those ideas to support or enhance their own observations and conclusions. All quotations and borrowed material must be properly credited to their sources.

Copying published material or borrowing the words of another person without acknowledging indebtedness constitutes plagiarism. SMU students who plagiarize may be subject to failure in the course and to any other disciplinary actions the Honor Council may impose.

Work Cited

Stone, Wilfred and J. G. Bell. *Prose Style: A Handbook for Writers*. New York: McGraw-Hill, 1968. Print.

Statement on Academic Honesty

Southern Methodist University has an Honor Code; students are expected to pledge that any work that they turn in is the product of their own minds and efforts. When you sign your name to the Honor Pledge—"On my honor, I have neither given nor received any unauthorized aid on this work"—you offer your own character as evidence that you have abided by SMU's Honor Code.

Each time you submit written work in your DISC class (or in any class), you automatically subscribe to the following:

1. You have not taken any words from any other piece of writing—published, unpublished, or online—without putting quotation marks around such words and indicating their source. This pledge pertains to phrases as well as whole sentences, and even to significant single words, such as those that express opinion or judgment.

2. You have not taken ideas from any source—including an online source—even if you express them in your own words in summary or in paraphrase, without giving credit to that source.

3. You have organized your material according to a plan of your own creation, based upon your own thorough exploration of the assignment.

4. While you may have asked someone for an opinion about your paper, you have received only suggestions. You have neither asked nor allowed someone else to write, revise, edit, proofread, or otherwise modify your work in any way.

SMU students understand that a violation of the Honor Code results in severe penalties. One minimum penalty given by the Honor Council is a notation of "Honor Violation" for the course, which will remain on a student's official transcript for three years after graduation. Other penalties recommended by the Honor Council can include deferred suspension for one calendar year, indefinite suspension, or even expulsion from the University.

The Revising and Editing Process

Rewriting encompasses a wide spectrum of activities, from extensive modifications in content and structure to minor changes in form. As you move from a loosely constructed first draft to the final polished essay, rewriting forces you to backtrack constantly, changing your meaning and refining your intention. **Revising** refers to substantive textual alteration-significant rhetorical changes in content, focus, organization, and meaning. Revising, then, implies that you discover your subject by writing about it. **Editing** refers to refinements in diction and sentence structure that make a text not only more correct but also more readable, more stylistically engaging and rhetorically appropriate. **Proofreading** refers to manuscript preparation; you eliminate distracting minor errors from the final copy of the text.

In DISC, we want you to revise your drafts substantially; only by examining your writing with a critical and careful eye can you know what further writing you need to do. Although we can't outline a specific procedure that applies to all writers or all projects, the following model does suggest ways in which practiced writers evaluate their prose.

I. After the first draft:
   a. ask yourself if you have followed the assignment directions closely;
   b. select a provisional title that will help you identify your subject's limits and develop a point of view towards it;
   c. emphasize cutting; keep writing until you have enough material to cut;
   d. mark your good passages with a check;
   e. figure out your main point; reformulate the thesis statement if necessary;
   f. add pieces that are missing and cut pieces that present unnecessary or unrelated matters;
   g. put the good passages in some kind of order reflecting a provisional pattern of organization: chronological, logical, cause/effect, etc.;
   h. write out the next draft.

II. During the intermediate drafts:
   a. continue to clarify through cutting; try reading your draft aloud to experience the writing from a reader's point of view;
   b. ask yourself if you are saying what you mean; do your words mean what you think? If not, keep writing and cutting until you achieve clarity and precision;
   c. consider your paragraphs; do they build confidence in your thesis? Are they fully developed? Have you made transitions between paragraphs?
   d. ask yourself if you have used too many words to make a point: circle prepositions and revise sentences that pile on too many prepositional

phrases; circle "to be" forms and substitute precise verbs; circle passive constructions and shift to the active voice; circle expletive constructions and revise to emphasize agency and action; combine and subordinate choppy sentences;

e. correct grammar, punctuation, and spelling errors.

Priorities in Evaluating an Essay

Whether you are revising your own draft, discussing a draft with your instructor, or responding to a classmate's draft, the following priorities should help you evaluate work in progress.

- Clear and concrete articulation of a thesis (a central idea, proposition, or assertion)
- Analysis or defense of that thesis in a series of points; careful development of those points into a series of paragraphs (logical and purposeful organization)
- Selection of relevant supporting evidence (concrete details)
- Clear transitions within and between paragraphs
- Style appropriate to the subject, purpose, and audience
- Effective sentences (logical relationships emphasized through combining, subordinating, and condensing)
- Effective diction (precision and purpose; special attention paid to nouns and verbs)
- *Mechanical accuracy (conventional grammar and punctuation; correct spelling, typography, and format)

---

*Mastery of the conventions of the language must be assumed in college work; that is, you must clear the static before a reader can begin to receive your message.

Revision Worksheet

Revision is the process of looking over what you have written and making substantial changes in such areas as organization, development, voice, argument, thesis, or evidence. Revision involves a careful rethinking of purpose and a reconsideration of audience. Think about the following questions as you revise or help another revise.

1. Is the **purpose** of the writing clear in its first paragraph? (If not, why not?)
2. Can you identify the **audience** for whom this is written? (Look for cues in the writing: tone, style, and word-choice)
3. How is the paper **organized**? (Look for a pattern here: chronological, topical, logical, compare/contrast, cause/effect, general to specific, specific to general, most important/least important or vice versa)
4. Is each body paragraph focused and unified by a topic sentence that supports the paper's thesis? (If not, why not?)
5. Is **evidence** used to support generalizations? (Look for examples, specific details, and concrete descriptions)
6. Do the ideas in the paper move smoothly one from another, both within and between paragraphs? (Look for appropriate transitions, for movement out of the familiar into the unfamiliar.)
7. Can you summarize the **main point** of the paper in a sentence or two? (Does the introduction or conclusion do this? Should it?)

Editing Worksheet

Editing is the process of fine-tuning your prose. In editing, you turn your attention to sentence-level matters of diction, tone, economy, emphasis, and precision. Think about the following questions as you edit or help another edit.

1. Do you use **active verbs** wherever you can? (Do you "decide" rather than "make a decision"?)

2. Do you have good reasons for using **passive constructions**? If not, make them active. ("The liquid was poured into the test tube by the chemist.")

3. Have you cut all the **dead wood** from your sentences? ("It is interesting to note that editing is easy.")

4. Have you avoided wordy, vague "there+be verb" and "it+be verb" constructions? ("There are many interstate highways in need of repair.")

5. Can you use a **smaller or precise word** where you have used a big one? ("Can you utilize this worksheet?" "In today's society, the economic situation is often an important factor.")

6. Do you find any **clichés** in your sentences? ("Can you cut through the red tape and get on the ball?")

7. Can you **combine** any sentences to avoid repetition? ("The water is brown . It is flowing fast. It is polluted.")

8. Do you express parallel ideas in parallel forms? ("I love walking and to swim and go sailing.")

9. Do you have any one-sentence **paragraphs**? Should you?

10. Are your **references, documentation,** and **calculations** complete and precise?

11. Have you proofread the paper to correct **punctuation, spelling,** and **grammar**?

Basics
Some Conventions of Correct Writing

Because observing the conventions of grammar, syntax, and punctuation helps a writer achieve clarity and precision, every writer needs to learn and to follow these conventions.

While the following ten principles, or "Basics," are by no means inclusive, most experienced writers consider them essential to achieving and communicating clear thinking in almost any writing, but particularly in professional, business, and academic writing.

1. **Learn to recognize and construct sentences.**
   The simple English sentence contains a subject and a predicate. Compound and complex sentences combine clauses and must contain appropriate conjunctions and punctuation.

   A. **Avoid sentence fragments.**

   Faulty: The woman who works hard and therefore will triumph in the end.

   Correct: The woman works hard and therefore will triumph in the end.
   The woman who works hard will triumph in the end.

   Faulty: When I go to New York, I want to visit the Museum of Natural History. Because I have always been interested in dinosaurs.

   Correct: When I go to New York, I want to visit the Museum of Natural History because I have always been interested in dinosaurs .

   B. **Avoid fused sentences and comma splices.**

   Faulty: The topic is difficult to write on it doesn't interest me.
   The topic is difficult to write on, it doesn't interest me.

   Correct: The topic is difficult to write on, and it doesn't interest me.
   Because the topic doesn't interest me, it is difficult to write on.

2. **Use the correct form of the verb.**
   Many English verbs change form to indicate person, number, tense, voice, and mood.

   A. **Subject and predicate must agree in person and number.**

   Faulty: Neither she nor her partner have left a message.

   Correct: Neither she nor her partner has left a message.

   Faulty: The truth about his many accomplishments are going to be revealed at this afternoon's meeting.

   Correct: The truth about his many accomplishments is going to be revealed at this afternoon's meeting.

B. **Use the tense that best expresses your idea or logically completes a sequence.**

Faulty: Last night my roommate and I reviewed our homework, took a practice test, and plan to get plenty of sleep.

Correct: Last night my roommate and I reviewed our homework, took a practice test, and planned to get plenty of sleep.

3. **Avoid misplaced or dangling modifiers.**

Any word, phrase, or clause used as a modifier should be so placed that it cannot appear to modify the wrong word or element in the sentence.

Faulty: While still warm, roll the cookies in powdered sugar.

Correct: While the cookies are still warm, roll them in powdered sugar.

Faulty: The girl who looks bored with red hair is my date.

Correct: The redhead who looks bored is my date.

4. **Avoid faulty parallelism.**

Use the same grammatical construction for parts of a sentence that are similar in function.

Faulty: He prides himself on his originality, looking chic, and acting macho.

Correct: He prides himself on being original, looking chic, and acting macho.

He prides himself on his originality, his stylishness, and his machismo.

5. **Avoid vague or faulty pronoun reference.**

A. **A pronoun should agree with its antecedent in person, number, and gender.**

Faulty: Everyone should turn in their essay on Friday.

Correct: Everyone should turn in his essay on Friday.
Everyone should turn in her essay on Friday.
Everyone should turn in his or her essay on Friday.
Students should turn in their essays on Friday.

B. **The antecedent of a pronoun should be apparent.**

Faulty: If you can't identify phrases and clauses, this will be a handicap to you.

If you can't identify phrases and clauses, it will be a handicap to you.

Correct: The inability to identify phrases and clauses will be a handicap to you.

If you can't identify phrases and clauses, you will be at a disadvantage.

6. **Use commas correctly.**
   Commas should be used intentionally, to clarify or to emphasize the meaning of a sentence.
   A. **Use a comma before a coordinate conjunction to join independent clauses of a compound sentence.**
      Faulty: Right now we consider the situation tragic but in time we'll be able to laugh about it.
      Correct: Right now we consider the situation tragic, but in time we'll be able to laugh about it.
   B. **Use a comma between all terms in a series.**
      Faulty: We had our choice of sandwiches: chicken salad, salami, ham and cheese.
      Correct: We had our choice of sandwiches: chicken salad, salami, ham, and cheese.
      We had our choice of sandwiches: chicken salad, salami, or ham and cheese.
   C. **Use a comma to set off introductory words, phrases, and clauses.**
      Faulty: Frightened he dialed the emergency number.
      Correct: Frightened, he dialed the emergency number.
      Faulty: After a long evening of study in the library my roommate and I went out for a hamburger.
      Correct: After a long evening of study in the library, my roommate and I went out for a hamburger.
      Faulty: Because I forgot to set my alarm I was late to class.
      Correct: Because I forgot to set my alarm, I was late to class.
   D. **Use a comma, or a pair of commas, to set off parenthetical expressions and non-restrictive words, phrases, and clauses.**
      Faulty: I had taken some aspirin. My headache, however was getting worse.
      Correct: I had taken some aspirin. My headache, however, was getting worse.
      Faulty: My teacher who was beginning to lose his patience repeated the instructions.
      Correct: My teacher, who was beginning to lose his patience, repeated the instructions.
7. **Use the semicolon correctly.**
   A. **The semicolon joins closely related independent clauses.**
      Faulty: Good intentions are not enough, intelligence is also required.

Correct: Good intentions are not enough; intelligence is also required.
Faulty: I had taken some aspirin, however, my headache was getting worse.
Correct: I had taken some aspirin; however, my headache was getting worse.

B. A semicolon sometimes replaces a comma when the stronger mark of punctuation is needed for clarity.

Example: I looked at my mother hopefully, trying to find some sign of encouragement; but before I could utter a word, Ms. Taylor's secretary appeared from nowhere and asked us to follow him.

Example: Attending the conference were Ms. Adams, the president; Mr. Byers, the secretary; and Mrs. Whelan, the treasurer.

8. Learn the correct use and formation of the possessive.

The possessive is usually formed by adding an apostrophe plus **s** to the singular form of a noun or by adding an apostrophe only to a plural noun ending in *s*. The possessive form of personal pronouns does not contain an apostrophe.

Faulty: The childrens uniforms were furnished by the Parents Club.
Correct: The children's uniforms were furnished by the Parents' Club.
Faulty: Its time you got the plant it's fertilizer.
Correct: It's time you got the plant its fertilizer.

9. Be sure that pronouns appear in the correct case.

A. Use the NOMINATIVE CASE for subjects and predicate nominatives.

Personal Pronouns:

Person	Singular	Plural
1st	I	we
2nd	you	you
3rd	he, she, it	they

Faulty: It was me who asked the question.
Correct: It was I who asked the question.
Faulty: No one is a more reliable friend than her.
Correct: No one is a more reliable friend than she.

B. Use the OBJECTIVE CASE for objects of prepositions, indirect objects, and direct objects.

Personal Pronouns:

Person	Singular	Plural
1st	me	us
2nd	you	you
3rd	him, her, it	them

Faulty: The duchess invited my friend and I to tea.
Correct: The duchess invited my friend and me to tea.

Faulty: Virginia Woolf is a writer who I admire.
Correct: Virginia Woolf is a writer whom I admire.

10. **Combine words logically.**

    In every clause, the subject and the predicate must combine to make a logical statement.

    A. **Be sure the subject, verb, and direct object make sense together.**

    Faulty: The ball, stolen from an SMU player, allowed an Aggie to score two points.

    Correct: Stealing the ball from an SMU player allowed an Aggie to score two points.
    Having stolen the ball from an SMU player, an Aggie scored two points.

    B. **When you use "to be" to assert the identity of two terms, make certain those terms are logically and grammatically equivalent.**

    Faulty: Waiting in line is when I get impatient.

    Correct: Waiting in line makes me impatient.
    When I have to wait in line, I get impatient.

SMU will not discriminate in any employment practice, education program or educational activity on the basis of race, color, religion, national origin, sex, age, disability or veteran status. SMU's commitment to equal opportunity includes nondiscrimination on the basis of sexual orientation. The Director of Institutional Access and Equity has been designated to handle inquiries regarding the nondiscrimination policies.